TEACHINGS OF PRESIDENTS OF THE CHURCH

LORENZO SNOW

Published by
The Church of Jesus Christ of Latter-day Saints
Salt Lake City, Utah

Books in the *Teachings of Presidents of the Church* Series

Teachings of Presidents of the Church: Joseph Smith (item number 36481)
Teachings of Presidents of the Church: Brigham Young (35554)
Teachings of Presidents of the Church: John Taylor (35969)
Teachings of Presidents of the Church: Wilford Woodruff (36315)
Teachings of Presidents of the Church: Lorenzo Snow (36787)
Teachings of Presidents of the Church: Joseph F. Smith (35744)
Teachings of Presidents of the Church: Heber J. Grant (35970)
Teachings of Presidents of the Church: George Albert Smith (36786)
Teachings of Presidents of the Church: David O. McKay (36492)
Teachings of Presidents of the Church: Harold B. Lee (35892)
Teachings of Presidents of the Church: Spencer W. Kimball (36500)

To obtain copies of these books, go to your local distribution center or visit store.lds.org. The books are also available electronically at LDS.org.

Your comments and suggestions about this book would be appreciated. Please submit them to Curriculum Development, 50 East North Temple Street, Room 2404, Salt Lake City, UT 84150-0024 USA.

E-mail: cur-development@ldschurch.org

Please list your name, address, ward, and stake. Be sure to give the title of the book. Then offer your comments and suggestions about the book's strengths and areas of potential improvement.

Printed in the United States of America
English approval: 8/02

Contents

Lorenzo Snow

Introduction

The First Presidency and the Quorum of the Twelve Apostles have established the *Teachings of Presidents of the Church* series to help you deepen your understanding of the restored gospel and draw closer to the Lord through the teachings of latter-day prophets. As the Church adds volumes to this series, you will build a collection of gospel reference books for your home. The volumes in this series are designed to be used for personal study and for Sunday instruction. They can also help you prepare other lessons or talks and answer questions about Church doctrine.

This book features the teachings of President Lorenzo Snow, who served as President of The Church of Jesus Christ of Latter-day Saints from September 13, 1898, to October 10, 1901.

Personal Study

As you study the teachings of President Lorenzo Snow, prayerfully seek the inspiration of the Holy Ghost. The questions at the end of each chapter will help you understand President Snow's teachings and apply them in your life. As you study these teachings, you may want to think about ways to share them with family members and friends. This will strengthen your understanding of what you read.

Teaching from This Book

This book has been designed for use at home and at church. The following guidelines may help you teach from the book.

Prepare to Teach

Seek the guidance of the Holy Ghost as you prepare to teach. Prayerfully study the assigned chapter to become confident in your understanding of President Snow's teachings. You will teach with greater sincerity and power when his words have influenced you personally (see D&C 11:21).

If you are teaching a Melchizedek Priesthood or Relief Society lesson, you should not set this book aside or prepare a lesson from other materials. Prayerfully select from the chapter those teachings that you feel will be most helpful to those you teach. Some chapters contain more material than you will be able to discuss during class time.

Encourage participants to study the chapter before the lesson and to bring the book with them. When they do so, they will be better prepared to participate in a discussion and edify one another.

Introduce the Chapter

As you introduce the chapter, and throughout the lesson, try to create an atmosphere in which the Spirit can touch the hearts and minds of those you teach. To start the lesson, help those you teach focus on the teachings of the chapter. Consider the following ideas:

- Read and discuss the section titled "From the Life of Lorenzo Snow" at the beginning of the chapter.
- Discuss a picture or scripture from the chapter.
- Sing a related hymn together.
- Briefly share a personal experience about the topic.

Lead a Discussion about President Snow's Teachings

As you teach from this book, invite others to share their thoughts, ask questions, and teach one another. When they actively participate, they will be more prepared to learn and to receive personal revelation. Allow good discussions to continue rather than trying to cover all the teachings. To encourage discussion, use the questions in each chapter. Notes throughout each chapter refer to those questions. You may also develop your own questions especially for those you are teaching.

The following options may give you additional ideas:

- Ask participants to share what they have learned from their personal study of the chapter. It may be helpful to contact a few participants during the week and ask them to come prepared to share what they have learned.

- Assign participants to read selected questions from the end of the chapter (either individually or in small groups). Ask them to look for teachings in the chapter that relate to the questions. Then invite them to share their thoughts and insights with the rest of the group.
- Read together a selection of President Snow's statements from the chapter. Ask participants to share examples from the scriptures and from their own experience that illustrate what President Snow taught.
- Ask participants to choose one section and read it silently. Invite them to gather in groups of two or three people who chose the same section and discuss what they have learned.

Encourage Sharing and Application

President Snow's teachings will be most meaningful for participants who share them with others and apply them in their lives. Consider the following ideas:

- Ask participants how they can apply President Snow's teachings in their responsibilities as parents or as home teachers or visiting teachers.
- Encourage participants to share some of President Snow's teachings with family members and friends.
- Invite participants to apply what they have learned and share their experiences at the beginning of the next class.

Conclude the Discussion

Briefly summarize the lesson or ask one or two participants to do so. Testify of the teachings you have discussed. You may also want to invite others to share their testimonies.

Information about the Sources Quoted in This Book

The teachings in this book are direct quotations from President Lorenzo Snow's sermons, published writings, letters, and journals.

In all quotations from his letters and journals, the punctuation, spelling, capitalization, and paragraphing have been standardized. Quotations from published sources have retained the punctuation, spelling, capitalization, and paragraphing of the original sources unless editorial or typographic changes have been necessary to improve readability. For this reason, you may notice minor inconsistencies in the text. For example, the word *gospel* is lowercased in some quotations and capitalized in others.

Also, President Snow often used terms such as *men, man,* or *mankind* to refer to all people, both male and female. He frequently used the pronouns *he, his,* and *him* to refer to both genders. This was common in the language of his era. Despite the differences between these language conventions and current usage, President Snow's teachings apply to both women and men.

Historical Summary

The following chronology provides a brief historical framework for the teachings of President Lorenzo Snow in this book.

April 3, 1814	Born in Mantua, Ohio, to Rosetta Leonora Pettibone Snow and Oliver Snow.
1832	Hears the Prophet Joseph Smith preach in Hiram, Ohio.
1835	Leaves home to study at Oberlin College in Oberlin, Ohio. Meets Elder David W. Patten of the Quorum of the Twelve Apostles on the way.
1836	Leaves Oberlin College and moves to Kirtland, Ohio, to study Hebrew. Embraces the restored gospel and is baptized and confirmed in June. Later is ordained an elder. Receives a patriarchal blessing from Joseph Smith Sr. in December.
1837	Preaches the gospel in Ohio.
October 1838 to May 1840	Serves another mission, preaching the gospel in Ohio, Missouri, Kentucky, and Illinois and working as a schoolteacher during the winter of 1839–40.
May 1840	Leaves Nauvoo, Illinois, to serve a mission in England. Under the direction of the Quorum of the Twelve Apostles, presides over the Church in London, England, and the surrounding area. Publishes a pamphlet titled *The Only Way to Be Saved*.

April 12, 1843	Arrives in Nauvoo, Illinois, with 250 Latter-day Saint converts from England.
Late 1843 and early 1844	Teaches school in Lima, Illinois.
1844	Supervises a campaign in Ohio to elect Joseph Smith as president of the United States. Returns to Nauvoo after learning of the martyrdom of Joseph and Hyrum Smith, which occurred on June 27.
January 1845	Appointed by President Brigham Young to travel through Ohio and collect donations for the construction of the Nauvoo Temple.
1845	Enters into plural marriage, as then practiced in the Church, by marrying Charlotte Squires and Mary Adaline Goddard.
February 1846	Leaves Nauvoo with family members and other Latter-day Saints after receiving endowments and sealings in the Nauvoo Temple.
1846 to 1848	Lives with his family at a settlement called Mount Pisgah in the state of Iowa. Presides over the settlement for a time. In the spring of 1848, leads a group of Saints to Salt Lake City.
February 12, 1849	Ordained an Apostle in Salt Lake City.
1849	Gathers donations for the Perpetual Emigrating Fund.
1849 to 1852	Serves a mission in Italy. Also serves in England, where he supervises the publication of the Book of Mormon in Italian, and in Switzerland and Malta. Publishes a pamphlet titled *The Voice of Joseph*.

1852	Elected to the Utah State Legislature.
1853	Called by President Brigham Young to preside over a settlement of Latter-day Saints in Box Elder County, located in northern Utah. Names the principal city Brigham City. Serves for many years as a leader in the Church and the community.
March 1864 to May 1864	With a group led by Elder Ezra T. Benson of the Quorum of the Twelve, serves a short mission in the Hawaiian Islands.
October 1872 to July 1873	With a group led by President George A. Smith, First Counselor in the First Presidency, tours parts of Europe and the Middle East, including the Holy Land. The trip is taken at the request of President Brigham Young.
1882	The United States Congress passes the Edmunds Act, making plural marriage a felony and prohibiting polygamists from voting, holding public office, or performing jury duty.
August 1885 to October 1885	Serves missions among American Indians in the northwestern United States and the state of Wyoming.
March 12, 1886, to February 8, 1887	Imprisoned for practicing plural marriage.
1887	The United States Congress passes the Edmunds-Tucker Act, another antipolygamy law, allowing the federal government to confiscate much of the Church's real estate. The act becomes law on March 3, 1887.

May 21–23, 1888	Reads the dedicatory prayer at sessions of the dedication of the Manti Utah Temple. President Wilford Woodruff had dedicated the temple on May 17.
April 7, 1889	Sustained as President of the Quorum of the Twelve Apostles.
May 19, 1893, to September 1898	Serves as the first president of the Salt Lake Temple.
September 2, 1898	Becomes the senior Apostle and presiding leader of the Church at the death of President Wilford Woodruff. Receives a divine manifestation in the Salt Lake Temple, in which the Lord instructs him to move forward with the reorganization of the First Presidency.
September 13, 1898	Sustained by the Quorum of the Twelve Apostles as President of the Church. Begins serving as President.
October 9, 1898	Sustained as President of the Church during general conference.
October 10, 1898	Set apart as President of The Church of Jesus Christ of Latter-day Saints.
May 1899	Travels to St. George, Utah, where he receives a revelation to preach the law of tithing to the Saints. Begins sharing this message in St. George and leads an effort to share it throughout the Church.
January 1, 1901	Publishes a declaration titled "Greeting to the World" to welcome the 20th century.
October 10, 1901	Dies in Salt Lake City, Utah, at age 87.

The Life and Ministry of Lorenzo Snow

When 21-year-old Lorenzo Snow rode his horse away from his parents' home one day in 1835, he set his course for Oberlin College in Oberlin, Ohio. He did not know that on this short trip, he would have an experience that would change the course of his life.

Riding down the road in his hometown of Mantua, Ohio, he met a man who was also on horseback. This man, named David W. Patten, had recently been ordained an Apostle of the Lord Jesus Christ. He was returning to the Latter-day Saints in Kirtland, Ohio, after having served a mission. The two men traveled together for about 30 miles (50 kilometers). Lorenzo Snow later recounted:

"Our conversation fell upon religion and philosophy, and being young and having enjoyed some scholastic advantages, I was at first disposed to treat his opinions lightly, especially so as they were not always clothed in grammatical language; but as he proceeded in his earnest and humble way to open up before my mind the plan of salvation, I seemed unable to resist the knowledge that he was a man of God and that his testimony was true."[1]

Lorenzo Snow was not a member of The Church of Jesus Christ of Latter-day Saints when he met Elder Patten, but he was familiar with some of the Church's teachings. In fact, the Prophet Joseph Smith had visited the home of the Snow family, and Lorenzo's mother and sisters Leonora and Eliza had been baptized and confirmed members of the Church. However, Lorenzo had been, as he said, "busy in other directions" at the time, and such things had "passed measurably out of [his] mind."[2] That began to change when he talked with Elder Patten. Referring to the experience, he said, "This was the turning point in my life."[3] He described how he felt during the conversation:

Lorenzo Snow's father, Oliver Snow

"I felt pricked in my heart. This he evidently perceived, for almost the last thing he said to me after bearing his testimony, was that I should go to the Lord before retiring at night and ask him for myself. This I did with the result that from the day I met this great Apostle, all my aspirations have been enlarged and heightened immeasurably."

Elder Patten's "absolute sincerity, his earnestness and his spiritual power"[4] had a lasting influence on a young man who would one day serve as an Apostle himself. And that quiet conversation led to other experiences that would prepare Lorenzo Snow to become President of The Church of Jesus Christ of Latter-day Saints, God's mouthpiece on the earth.

Growing Up in a Home of Faith and Hard Work

Two strong families, rich in faith and religious tradition, came together when Oliver Snow married Rosetta Leonora Pettibone on May 6, 1800. The groom and the bride were descendants of some of the earliest European settlers in the United States—English pilgrims who had crossed the Atlantic Ocean in the 1600s to escape religious persecution. Oliver and Rosetta spent the first few years of their married life in the state of Massachusetts, where their daughters Leonora Abigail and Eliza Roxcy were born. Then they moved to Mantua, Ohio, which was then one of the westernmost settlements in the United States. They were the eleventh family to move into the area. In Mantua, two more daughters, Amanda Percy and Melissa, were born into the family. Lorenzo, the fifth child and first son of Oliver and Rosetta, was born in Mantua on April 3, 1814. He was later joined by two younger brothers: Lucius Augustus and Samuel Pearce.[5]

Drawing on their families' traditions, Oliver and Rosetta taught their children the importance of faith, hard work, and education. As they shared stories of the difficulties they had endured to establish their home, their children learned to overcome discouragement and appreciate the blessings of God in their lives. Eliza wrote: "We can truly say of our parents, their integrity was unimpeachable, and they were trustworthy in all the social relations and business transactions of life; and carefully trained their children to habits of industry, economy, and strict morality."[6] Lorenzo expressed gratitude that they had always treated him with "care and tenderness."[7]

As Lorenzo grew up, he worked diligently in temporal and intellectual pursuits. His father was often away from home, serving the community "on public business." In Oliver's absence, Lorenzo, as the oldest son, was left in charge of the farm—a responsibility he took seriously and carried out successfully. When Lorenzo was not working, he was usually reading. "His book," Eliza said, "was his constant companion."[8]

Looking back on Lorenzo's developing personality, Eliza observed, "From early childhood [he] exhibited the energy and decision of character which have marked his progress in subsequent life."[9]

Rising above Youthful Ambitions

Oliver and Rosetta Snow encouraged honest inquiry about religion. They allowed their children to learn about different churches, opening their home to "the good and intelligent of all denominations." Even with this encouragement, Lorenzo "devoted little or no attention to the subject of religion, at least not sufficiently to decide in preference of any particular sect."[10] His dream was to be a military commander, and this dream overpowered other influences in his life, "not because he loved strife," wrote historian Orson F. Whitney, but because he "was charmed with the romance and chivalry of a military career."[11] But he soon replaced this ambition with another. He left home and enrolled at the nearby Oberlin College so he could pursue a "collegiate education."[12]

As Lorenzo studied at Oberlin, he developed a new interest in religion. Still influenced by his conversation with Elder Patten, he not only pondered the doctrines of the restored gospel but shared them with others at Oberlin—even with those who were studying to become ministers. In a letter to his sister Eliza, who had gathered with the Saints in Kirtland, he wrote: "Among the ministers and intended ministers I have had quite good success, I'll assure you, in advocating Mormonism. It is true I have not made many converts, as

I am not one myself, yet I have made some of them almost confess they perceived some [wisdom] in your doctrines. To remove the strong prejudice against Mormonism from the mind of an Oberlin student is a thing not easily accomplished."

In this same letter, Lorenzo responded to an invitation he had received from Eliza. She had arranged for him to stay with her in Kirtland and study Hebrew in a class that included the Prophet Joseph Smith and some members of the Quorum of the Twelve Apostles. He said: "I am delighted in learning that you enjoy so much happiness in Kirtland; though at present I am not disposed to exchange my location for yours; yet if the advantages of learning there were the same, I think I should be almost inclined to try an exchange. For, if nothing more, it would prove quite interesting to me and perhaps not unprofitable to hear those doctrines preached which I have so long endeavored to defend and support here in Oberlin."

Lorenzo Snow was baptized and confirmed in Kirtland, Ohio, in June 1836, two months after the Kirtland Temple, pictured here, was dedicated.

Although Lorenzo was impressed with the doctrines of The Church of Jesus Christ of Latter-day Saints, he hesitated to join the Church. But he was interested. In his letter to Eliza, he asked several questions about the Church. He said that the students at Oberlin who were preparing to become ministers were required to "devote seven years or upwards to arduous study before they are allowed to tell to the heathen that there is a God in Heaven, like a lawyer who must possess certain qualifications before he can procure permission to speak." In contrast, he said to his sister, "Your people I suppose depend more on divine assistance than on that which collegiate learning affords, when preaching your doctrines." He expressed a desire to understand the workings of the Spirit, asking if the Holy Ghost could be conferred on people "in this age of the world." If people could receive the Holy Ghost, he asked, "does God always confer it through the medium of a second person?"[13] In other words, he wanted to know if priesthood authority was necessary in order to receive the Holy Ghost.

Lorenzo appreciated the friendships and the education he had gained at Oberlin College, but he became increasingly dissatisfied with the religious teachings there. Eventually he left the college and accepted his sister's invitation to study Hebrew in Kirtland. He said that he attended the Hebrew class only so he could prepare to attend a college in the eastern United States.[14] Still, Eliza noted that in addition to learning Hebrew, "his mind also drank in, and his heart became imbued with the living faith of the everlasting Gospel."[15] Soon he found the answers to the questions he had asked at Oberlin College, and in June 1836 he was baptized by Elder John Boynton, one of the original members of the Quorum of the Twelve Apostles in this dispensation. He was also confirmed a member of The Church of Jesus Christ of Latter-day Saints.

About two weeks later a friend asked him, "Brother Snow, have you received the Holy Ghost since you were baptized?" He recalled, "That question struck me almost with consternation. The fact was, while I had received all I needed perhaps, I had not received that which I had anticipated"—meaning that although he had been confirmed, he had not received a special manifestation of the Holy

Ghost. "I felt dissatisfied," he said, "not with what I had done, but with myself. With that feeling I retired in the evening to a place where I had been accustomed to offer my devotions to the Lord." He knelt to pray and immediately received an answer to his prayers. "That will never be erased from my memory as long as memory endures," he later declared. ". . . I received a perfect knowledge that there was a God, that Jesus, who died upon Calvary, was His Son, and that Joseph the Prophet had received the authority which he professed to have. The satisfaction and the glory of that manifestation no language can express! I returned to my lodgings. I could now testify to the whole world that I knew, by positive knowledge, that the Gospel of the Son of God had been restored, and that Joseph was a Prophet of God, authorized to speak in His name."[16]

Strengthened by this experience, Lorenzo prepared himself to be a missionary. As his sister Eliza said, his conversion led to a change in his ambitions and "opened up a new world before him." She observed, "Instead of earthly military renown, he now enter[ed] the arena for championship with the armies of heaven."[17]

Meeting Challenges as a Full-Time Missionary

Lorenzo Snow began his missionary service in the state of Ohio in the spring of 1837. Like his decision to join the Church, his decision to serve as a full-time missionary required him to change his views and his plans. He wrote in his journal, "In the year 1837 [I] totally relinquished all my favorite ideas."[18] He gave up his plan to pursue a "classical education" at a college in the eastern United States.[19] He also agreed to travel without purse or scrip—in other words, to go without money, relying on the goodness of others to provide food and shelter. This was especially difficult for him because in his youth he had always felt it was important to pay his own way, using money he had helped his father earn on the family farm. He said: "I had not been accustomed to depend upon anybody for food or shelter. If I were going off any distance, my father would make sure that I started out with plenty of money for my expenses. And now, to go out and ask for something to eat and for a place to lay my head, was very trying to me, it being so different

Elder Lorenzo Snow

to my training."[20] He "determined to do it," but only because he received "a positive knowledge that God required it."[21]

Some of Elder Snow's uncles, aunts, cousins, and friends attended the first meetings he conducted as a missionary. Remembering the first time he preached, he said: "I was quite bashful then, and . . . it was a very difficult thing for me to get up there and preach to my kindred and the neighbors who were called in. I remember that I prayed nearly all day preceding the night I was to speak. I went out by myself and asked the Lord to give me something to say. My aunt told me afterwards that she almost trembled when she saw me getting up to speak, but I opened my mouth, and what I said I never did know, but my aunt said I spoke fine for about three-quarters of an hour."[22] With gratitude he recalled: "I believed and felt an assurance that a Spirit of inspiration would prompt and give me utterance. I had sought by prayer and fasting—I had humbled myself before the Lord, calling on Him in mighty prayer to impart the power and inspiration of the holy Priesthood; and when I stood before that congregation, although I knew not one word I could say, as soon as I opened my mouth to speak, the Holy Ghost rested mightily upon me, filling my mind with light and communicating ideas and proper language by which to impart them."[23] By the time he left the area, he had baptized and confirmed an uncle, an aunt, several cousins, and a few friends.[24]

Having shared the gospel with his family and friends, Elder Snow continued his missionary labors in other cities and towns, serving for about one year. He reported, "While on this mission, I traveled in various parts of the State of Ohio, and during the time baptized many persons who have remained faithful to the truth."[25]

Lorenzo Snow had not been home from this first mission long before he felt a desire to preach the gospel again. "The spirit of my missionary calling pressed so heavily upon my mind," he said, "that I longed to engage in its labors."[26] This time he preached the restored gospel in the states of Missouri, Kentucky, and Illinois and again in Ohio.

Some people were hostile toward Elder Snow and the message he shared. For example, he told of an experience he had in Kentucky when a group of people gathered in someone's house to hear him preach. After he preached, he learned that some of the people planned to mob him as soon as he left. He recalled that "amid the jostling of the crowd" in the house, one of the men "accidentally brought his hand in contact with one of the pockets in the skirt of my coat, which struck him with sudden alarm." Having felt something hard in Elder Snow's pocket, he immediately warned his friends that the missionary was armed with a pistol. Elder Snow later wrote, "That was sufficient—the would-be outlaws abandoned their evil designs." With some amusement, Elder Snow added, "The supposed pistol which caused their alarm and my protection, was my pocket Bible, a precious gift to me from the dearly beloved Patriarch, Father Joseph Smith [Sr.]"[27]

Other people welcomed Elder Snow and embraced the message he shared. In one Missouri settlement he taught five people who were baptized in the middle of winter. Elder Snow and others had to cut ice from a river so he could perform the ordinance. Despite the cold, some of the converts "came forth from the water, clapping their hands, and shouting praises to God."[28]

Elder Snow's first two missions spanned a period from the spring of 1837 to May 1840. Excerpts from his letters characterize this time in the Lord's service: "I spent the remainder of the winter [of 1838–39] in travel and preaching, . . . with varied success, and treatment—sometimes received in the most courteous manner and listened to with intense interest, and, at other times, abusively and impudently insulted; but in no instance treated worse than was Jesus, whom I profess to follow."[29] "When I now look back upon the scenes through which I passed, . . . I am astonished and caused to marvel."[30] "The Lord was with me, and I was greatly blessed in performing my arduous labors."[31]

Mission in England

In early May 1840, Lorenzo Snow joined the Saints in Nauvoo, Illinois, but he did not stay there long. He was called to cross the Atlantic Ocean and serve a mission in England, and he left Nauvoo that same month. Before he left, he took time to visit the families of some of the nine Apostles who were already serving in England.

When he visited the family of Brigham Young, he saw that their log hut did not have chinking to seal the gaps between the logs, leaving them "exposed to wind and storms." Sister Young was tired because she had just returned from a fruitless search for the family's milk cow. Despite her difficult circumstances, she said to Elder Snow, "You see my situation, but tell him [my husband] not to trouble, or worry in the least about me—I wish him to remain in his field of labor until honorably released." Stirred by Sister Young's "poverty-stricken, destitute condition," Elder Snow wanted to help: "I had but little money—not sufficient to take me one-tenth the distance to my field of labor, with no prospect for obtaining the balance, and was then on the eve of starting. I drew from my pocket a portion of my small pittance, . . . but she refused to accept it; while I strenuously insisted on her taking, and she persisting to refuse—partly purposely, and partly accidentally, the money was dropped on the floor, and rattled through the openings between the loose boards, which settled the dispute, and bidding her good bye, I left her to pick it up at her leisure."[32]

From Illinois, Elder Snow traveled to New York, where he boarded a ship to sail across the Atlantic Ocean. On the 42-day sea voyage, three fierce storms pounded the ship. Surrounded by fearful, weeping fellow passengers, Elder Snow remained calm, trusting that God would protect him. When the ship docked at Liverpool, England, Elder Snow's heart was "full of the highest gratitude to Him who preserves and sustains those whom He calls and sends forth as ministers of salvation to the nations of the earth."[33]

After serving as a missionary in England for about four months, Elder Snow received an additional responsibility. He was appointed to serve as president of the London Conference, a calling similar to district president today. He continued preaching the gospel, and he also supervised the work of priesthood leaders, such as branch presidents, in the area. As he served in this leadership position, he often reported to Elder Parley P. Pratt, a member of the Quorum of the Twelve and the president of the mission. He wrote of many people who were "inquiring the way of salvation," of a room "crowded to overflowing" for a Sunday meeting, and of "the pleasure of baptizing [converts] into the fold of our Lord and Savior Jesus Christ." Enthusiastic and optimistic about the work, he said, "Though surrounded with high-handed wickedness of every description, Zion begins to break forth, and, I trust, ere long will become a shining lamp in this city."[34]

The London Conference enjoyed significant growth with Elder Snow as president. While Elder Snow rejoiced in this success, he also wrestled with the responsibilities of leadership. In a letter to Elder Heber C. Kimball of the Quorum of the Twelve, he acknowledged that these challenges had led him to "take a different course in management than any other I had ever before taken."[35] He told Elder Kimball: "You and Elder [Wilford] Woodruff said it should prove a school of experience, which already has been the fact. . . . Ever since I came here something new has been continually coming up among the Saints. No sooner was one thing over than another would arise." He shared a truth that he had learned quickly in his new responsibilities: "I could not encounter the difficulties, [unless] God should assist me in a very great degree."[36] He expressed a similar feeling in a letter to Elder George A. Smith of the Quorum of the Twelve: "The little I have done was not of myself but of God. One thing I have full learned in my experience while endeavouring to magnify my office as a teacher in Israel, that is, of myself I know nothing nor can I do anything: I also see clearly that no Saint can prosper except he be obedient to the instructions and counsel of such as are placed to preside in the Church. I am confident that so long as I keep his laws, the Lord God will uphold and support me in my office. . . . While I walk in humility before him, he will give me power to counsel in righteousness and the spirit of revelation."[37]

In addition to preaching the gospel and serving as president of the London Conference, Elder Snow wrote a religious tract, or pamphlet, to help missionaries explain the restored gospel. This tract, called *The Only Way to Be Saved,* was later translated into several languages and used throughout the second half of the 19th century.

Elder Snow served in England until January 1843. Before he left, he fulfilled an assignment he had received from President Brigham Young. In the margin of a page in his journal, he wrote his only mention of this assignment: "Delivered two Books of Mormon to Queen Victoria and Prince Albert by request of Prest. B. Young."[38]

When Elder Snow left England, he led a group of British Latter-day Saints emigrating to Nauvoo. He wrote in his journal: "I had charge of a company of two hundred and fifty, many of whom were my intimate friends who had come into the covenant under my administrations. The situation I now occupied in recrossing the ocean surrounded by friends was a very enviable one in comparison to the lonely one I stood in two years and a half before."[39] Elder Snow's experiences on the ship *Swanton* showed his leadership skills and his faith in God. The following account is taken from his journal:

"I called [the Saints] together and by mutual consent formed them into divisions and subdivisions, appointing proper officers to each, and established regulations for the government of the company. I found there were several High Priests, and some thirty Elders among us, and knowing the natural itching that many Elders have to do even a little something by which they may be a little

Many early Saints emigrated from Europe to join the Saints in the United States of America.

distinguished, and if that cannot be done in one way it must in another, therefore I concluded it safer to fix their way of acting myself; accordingly I appointed as many as I possibly could to some one office of business or another and made them all responsible. The whole company assembled each evening in the week [for] prayers. We had preaching twice a week; meetings on Sundays and partaking of the sacrament.

"Our captain, with whom I wished to cultivate a friendly acquaintance, appeared very distant and reserved. . . . I could easily perceive that his mind had been prejudiced against us.—We had been out to sea about two weeks, during which nothing very material occurred more than what usually happens at sea, when the following occurrence transpired.

"The captain's steward, a young German, met with an accident which threatened his life. Being a very moral, sober and steady young man, having been with the captain [on] several voyages, he had succeeded greatly in winning the affections of the captain, officers and crew; the Saints also had become much attached to him. Hence the prospect of his death . . . created a great sensation of sorrow and grief throughout the whole ship.

"He would bleed at his mouth, attended with severe cramping and fits. At last, after having tried various remedies to no purpose, all hopes of his life were given up. The sailors, before retiring to their beds, were requested by the captain to go into the cabin one by one to bid him farewell; which accordingly was done without the least expectation of seeing him alive the next morning. Many eyes were wet with tears as they returned from the cabin.

"Sister Martin [one of the Latter-day Saints on the ship] while sitting alone by his bedside expressed to him her wish that I might be called on and administer to him and perhaps he might yet be restored. To this he gave a cheerful consent. I was asleep in my berth when the message came, it being about twelve o'clock of the night. I arose immediately and proceeded to the cabin, [and] on the way met the first mate, who had just been to see him. As soon as he passed me, he met a Brother Staines and observed to him that Mr. Snow was going in to lay hands on the steward. 'But,' said he (in a sorrowful strain), 'it is all of no use; it is all over with the poor fellow now.' 'Oh,' said Elder Staines, 'the Lord can restore him through the laying on of hands.' '. . . Do you think so?' returned the sailor in the simplicity of his heart.

"As I passed along I met the captain at the cabin door, who appeared to have been weeping. 'I am glad you have come, Mr. Snow,' said he, 'though it is of no use, for it must soon be over with the steward.' I stepped into his room and sat down by his bed. His breathing was very short and seemed as one dying. He could not speak loud, but signified his wish [that] I should administer to him. It appeared he had a wife and two children in Hamburg, Germany, who were dependent upon him for their support. He seemed much troubled about them.

"I laid my hands upon his head, and had no sooner got through the administration than he arose up into a sitting posture, spatted [slapped] his hands together, shouting praises to the Lord for being

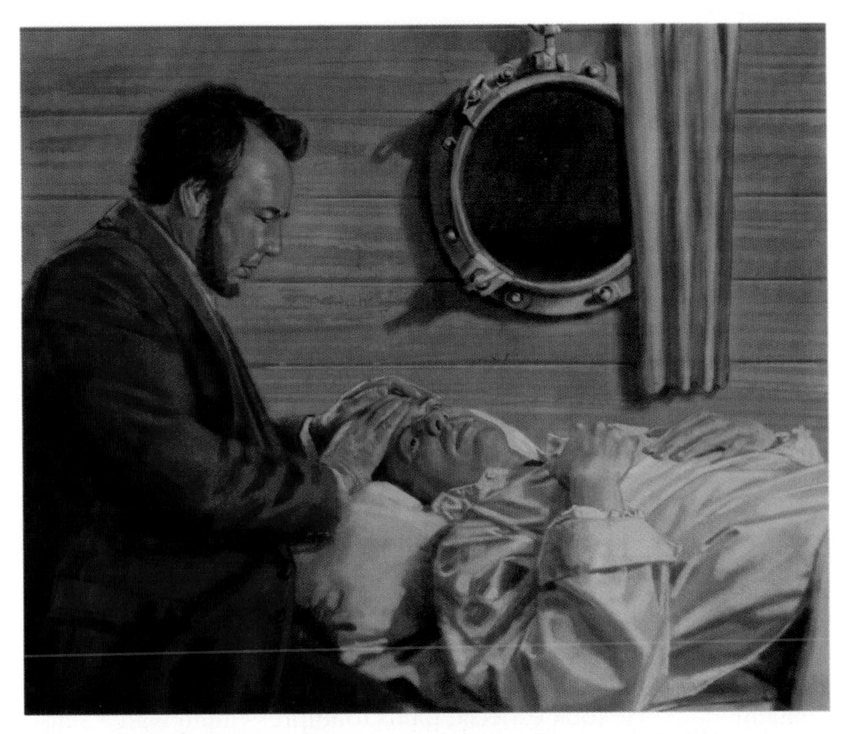

On the ship Swanton, *a severely injured man was healed immediately after an administration by Elder Lorenzo Snow.*

healed; very soon after, he arose from his bed [and] went out of the cabin and walked the deck.

"The next morning everybody was astonished to see the steward alive, and amazed to see him able to go about his business as usual. The sailors one and all swore that that was a miracle; the Saints knew it to be so, rejoiced and praised the Lord; the captain believed it firmly and felt deeply grateful, and his heart became knit with ours from that time forward. He granted us every favor and indulgence that was in his power to bestow, and constantly studied our convenience; attended all of our meetings, bought and read our books. The mates also did the same, and when I left them at New Orleans [Louisiana,] made me a promise that they would be baptized. I received a letter about a year afterwards from the chief mate, who informed me they had . . . fulfilled their promise. The captain also declared his intention of receiving the gospel at some future time and liv[ing] with the Saints. The steward was baptized when we reached New Orleans; and on parting with him made me a present of a Bible, which I now keep."[40]

Elder Snow wrote: "Several of the sailors wept when we took final leave of the *Swanton*. In fact, all of us had very solemn feelings."[41] From New Orleans, Elder Snow and his fellow Saints boarded a ferry boat and traveled up the Mississippi River. They arrived in Nauvoo on April 12, 1843.

Continued Devotion to the Lord's Work

After serving as a full-time missionary for the better part of seven years, Lorenzo Snow saw his opportunities for service change for a time. In the winter of 1843–44, the trustees of a local school offered him a job as a teacher. He accepted the offer, even though he knew many of the students "prided themselves on whipping teachers and breaking up schools." He decided that the way to win the students' respect was to show respect for them. His sister Eliza recounted: "He addressed those boys as though they were most respectable gentlemen. . . . He took especial pains to impress them with a sense of the interest he felt in their behalf" and his desire to "assist them forward in their studies. . . . In this way, by kindness and persuasion, their feelings relaxed—their confidence was won, and with patient and continued exertions, the unscrupulous roughs were transformed into respectful students; and long before the expiration of the term, with surprising progress, they had become habitually studious."[42]

In 1844 he received a new Church assignment. He was appointed to travel to Ohio and supervise a campaign to elect Joseph Smith as president of the United States. The Prophet had been disappointed with the way the Latter-day Saints had been treated by the United States government, and he had written the current candidates for president to determine their attitude toward the Church. Unsatisfied with their answers, he had decided to run for the presidency himself.

The Quorum of the Twelve appointed Lorenzo Snow and others to "form a political organization throughout the state of Ohio for the promotion of Joseph for the Presidency."[43] In doing so, they raised awareness of the ways in which the Saints' constitutional rights had been violated. Lorenzo said that he had "a very interesting time."[44] Some people vehemently opposed the Prophet's candidacy, while others felt that Joseph Smith could lead the nation to success and prosperity.

"In the midst of these extremes," recalled Lorenzo Snow, "my progress was suddenly brought to a close, by a well confirmed report of the massacre of the Prophet and his brother Hyrum."[45] He returned to Nauvoo "with saddened heart."[46]

Even during this time of tragedy, the Saints worked diligently to build up the kingdom of God. As Lorenzo later observed, "Under the guidance of the Almighty, the kingdom moved forward."[47] They continued to preach the gospel and strengthen one another, and they worked together to finish building a temple in their city.

When Lorenzo Snow gathered with the Saints in Nauvoo, he had determined that he would never get married, choosing instead to dedicate his life to preaching the gospel. His sister Eliza later observed, "To devote his time, his talents, his all to the ministry was his all-absorbing desire." He felt that family life would somehow "lessen his usefulness" in the Lord's work.[48]

Lorenzo's views on marriage and family began to change in 1843 when he spoke alone with the Prophet Joseph Smith on the banks of the Mississippi River. The Prophet testified of the revelation he had received regarding plural marriage. He told Lorenzo, "The Lord will open your way to receive and obey the law of Celestial Marriage."[49] With this counsel, Lorenzo began to understand that marriage was a commandment from the Lord and an essential part of Heavenly Father's plan of happiness.

In 1845, Lorenzo Snow entered into plural marriage, as then practiced in the Church, by marrying Charlotte Squires and Mary Adaline Goddard. He was later sealed to additional women. His devotion to his wives and children became part of his devotion to the work of the Lord.

The Saints continued to build up the kingdom of God in Nauvoo, but persecution continued as well. In February 1846, in the cold of

Lorenzo Snow served as a captain over pioneer companies that arrived in the Salt Lake Valley in 1848.

winter, mobs forced them to abandon their homes and their temple. They began a long westward trek toward a new home.

Helping the Saints Gather in the Salt Lake Valley

Although Lorenzo Snow and his family left Nauvoo with the rest of the Saints, they did not arrive in the Salt Lake Valley until more than a year after the first company of pioneers. Like most of the early Latter-day Saint pioneers, they stayed in temporary settlements along the way. Lorenzo and his family stayed for a short time at an Iowa settlement named Garden Grove, where they built log huts for the Saints who would follow them. From there they moved to a settlement called Mount Pisgah, also in Iowa.

In Mount Pisgah, Lorenzo worked with his family and the other Saints, again providing for their needs and for the needs of those who would follow them on the way to the Salt Lake Valley. They built log homes and even planted and cultivated crops, knowing that others would likely reap the harvest. During a portion of their time in Mount Pisgah, Lorenzo was called to preside over the settlement. As sorrow, sickness, and death plagued the people, including his own family, he worked diligently to help the people find hope, strengthen one another, and remain obedient to the commandments of the Lord.[50]

In the spring of 1848, President Brigham Young instructed Lorenzo Snow to leave Mount Pisgah and travel to the Salt Lake Valley. Lorenzo was again given a leadership position, this time as a captain over pioneer companies. The companies arrived in the Salt Lake Valley in September 1848.

Service as a Member of the Quorum of the Twelve

On February 12, 1849, Lorenzo Snow received a message that he was to attend a meeting of the Quorum of the Twelve Apostles. He immediately stopped what he was doing and went to the meeting, which was already in session. On the way, he wondered why he had been called before the Quorum of the Twelve. He was puzzled—had he been accused of wrongdoing? Knowing that he had been faithful in doing his duty, he dismissed that worry. But he could not imagine what was in store for him. When he arrived, he was surprised to learn that he had been called to serve as a member of the quorum. In that same meeting, he and three others—Elder Charles C. Rich, Elder Franklin D. Richards, and Elder Erastus Snow, a distant cousin—were ordained Apostles.[51]

Lorenzo Snow's ordination to the apostleship defined the rest of his life. His calling as one of the "special witnesses of the name of Christ" (D&C 107:23) influenced everything he did. He later expressed his feelings about the individual responsibilities of an Apostle:

"First, an Apostle must possess a Divine knowledge, by revelation from God, that Jesus lives—that He is the Son of the living God.

"Secondly, he must be divinely authorized to promise the Holy Ghost; a Divine principle that reveals the things of God, making known His will and purposes, leading into all truth, and showing things to come, as declared by the Savior.

"Thirdly, he is commissioned by the power of God to administer the sacred ordinances of the Gospel, which are confirmed to each individual by a Divine testimony. Thousands of people now dwelling in these mountain vales, who received these ordinances through my administrations, are living witnesses of the truth of this statement."[52]

In addition to the individual responsibility of his calling, Elder Snow had a conviction of what it meant to be a member of the Quorum of the Twelve: "We, the Twelve, are resolved to lay down everything that would draw our attention from the path of duty, that we may be one as the [First] Presidency are one, and be bound together by the principle of love that binds the Son of God with the Father."[53]

With this understanding of his personal calling and the mission of the Quorum of the Twelve, Elder Lorenzo Snow dedicated his life to help build up the kingdom of God on the earth. He answered the call to serve in many different ways and in many different places.

The Italian Mission

During the October 1849 general conference, Elder Snow was called to establish a mission in Italy. Although he was unfamiliar with the land and its cultures and languages, he did not hesitate to accept the calling. Less than two weeks after the conference, he was ready to go, having done his best to arrange help for his wives and children during his absence.

As he and other missionaries traveled to the eastern United States, where they would board a ship to cross the Atlantic Ocean, his thoughts turned both to his family and to the people he would soon serve. In a letter to his sister Eliza, he wrote: "Many conflicting feelings occupied my bosom. . . . We were hastening further and still further from the mighty magnet—HOME! but we knew that the work in which we were engaged was to carry light to those who sat in darkness, and in the Valley of the Shadow of Death, and our bosoms glowed with love, and our tears were wiped away."[54]

Elder Snow and his companions reached Genoa, Italy, in July 1850. They could see that the Lord's work would progress slowly. Elder Snow wrote: "I am alone and a stranger in this vast city, eight thousand miles from my beloved family, surrounded by a people [with] whose manners and peculiarities I am unacquainted. I am come to enlighten their minds, and instruct them in principles of righteousness; but I see no possible means of accomplishing this object. All is darkness in the prospect." Concerned about the "follies, . . . wickedness, gross darkness, and superstition" of the people he had been called to serve, he wrote: "I ask my Heavenly Father to look upon this people in mercy. O Lord, let them become the objects of Thy compassion, that they may not all perish. Forgive their sins, and let me be known among them, that they may know Thee, and know that Thou hast sent me to establish Thy Kingdom. . . . Hast Thou not some chosen ones among this people to whom I have been sent? Lead me unto such, and Thy name shall have the glory through Jesus Thy Son."[55]

Elder Snow found these "chosen ones" among a group of people called the Waldenses. The Waldenses lived in a mountain valley in the Piedmont region, just south of the Italy-Switzerland border and east of the Italy-France border. Their ancestors had been persecuted and driven from place to place because they believed in the authority of the ancient Apostles and wanted to follow the Apostles' teachings rather than join the religions of the day.

In a letter to President Brigham Young, Elder Snow wrote that the Waldenses had suffered through ages of "darkness and cruelty" and "had stood immovable, almost, as the wave-beaten rock in the stormy ocean." But just before the Latter-day Saint missionaries arrived in Italy, the Waldenses began to enjoy "a period of deep calm," and they seemed to have more religious freedom than others in Italy. "Thus," he observed, "the way was opened only a short period before the appointment of the mission, and no other portion of Italy is governed by such favourable laws."

Wanting to learn more about this people, Elder Snow went to a library to find a book about them. He recounted: "The librarian to whom I applied informed me he had a work of the description I required, but it had just been taken. He had scarcely finished the sentence when a lady entered with the book. 'Oh,' said he, 'this is a remarkable circumstance, this gentleman has just called for that book.' I was soon convinced that this people were worthy to receive the first proclamation of the Gospel in Italy."[56]

Elder Snow and his companions were eager to preach the gospel in the Piedmont region, but they felt they should proceed cautiously, cultivating friendships and showing the people they could be trusted. When they felt they had established good relationships with the people, they climbed a nearby mountain, sang "praises to the God of heaven," and offered a prayer, dedicating the land of Italy for missionary work. They also expressed their individual dedication to the work, and Elder Snow administered priesthood blessings to his companions to help them in their responsibilities. Inspired by their experience on the mountain, Elder Snow called the spot Mount Brigham.[57]

Even after this experience, almost two months passed before someone expressed a desire to join the Church. On October 27, 1850, the missionaries rejoiced to finally see the first baptism and confirmation in Italy.[58] Elder Snow later reported: "The work here is slow and tedious. . . . Nevertheless, the Church has been established. The tree has been planted and is spreading its roots."[59]

One night Elder Snow had a dream that helped him understand the nature of his mission in Italy. In the dream, he was fishing with his friends. "We were delighted to behold large and beautiful fish on the surface of the water, all around, to a vast distance," he said. "We beheld many persons spreading their nets and lines; but they seemed to be all stationary; whereas, we were in continual motion. While passing one of them, I discovered a fish had got upon my hook, and I thought it might, perhaps, disturb this man's feelings to have it caught, as it were, out of his hands; nevertheless, we moved along, and came to the shore. I then drew in my line, and was not a little surprised and mortified at the smallness of my prize. I thought it very strange that, among such a vast multitude of noble, superior-looking fish, I should have made so small a haul. But all my disappointments vanished when I came to discover that its qualities were of a very extraordinary character."[60]

Elder Snow's dream was prophetic. He did not see a great number of converts in Italy, and, as another missionary later observed, those who did accept the gospel were "not the rich and noble."[61] However, Elder Snow and his companions were instruments in the Lord's hands in bringing good, faithful people into the kingdom of God—people who expressed gratitude that they had "begun to walk in the pathway of a new and endless life."[62] And as a result of Elder Snow's leadership, the Book of Mormon was translated into Italian.

Almost a century and a half later, another Apostle, Elder James E. Faust, spoke about the men and women who joined the Church because of the work of Elder Snow and his companions: "Some were in the first handcart companies to come to the Salt Lake Valley. . . . Many of their descendants tended the vineyards of the newly restored church and today are making singular contributions to the worldwide church, believing, as did their forebears, that Apostles hold the keys that never rust."[63]

Building Up the Church

Elder Snow later served other missions, magnifying his calling as a member of the Quorum of the Twelve to work "under the direction of the [First] Presidency of the Church . . . to build up the church, and regulate all the affairs of the same in all nations" (D&C 107:33).

In 1853 President Brigham Young called Lorenzo Snow to lead a group of families to a settlement in the northern Utah county of Box Elder. The existing settlement was small, unorganized, and faltering. Elder Snow promptly went to work, organizing the people according to principles of the law of consecration as taught by the Prophet Joseph Smith. The people established a thriving city, which Elder Snow named Brigham City in honor of President Young. Working together and supporting one another, the citizens built up a school system, factories, an irrigation system, a mercantile organization, and even a theatrical society. Although they did not live the fulness of the law of consecration, they were guided by its principles, and they showed what a community can accomplish with cooperation and hard work. "There were no idlers in Brigham City," wrote President Snow's daughter Leslie. "A period of activity and prosperity existed that was probably never equalled in the history of any other settlement in the state."[64]

Elder Snow and his family lived in Brigham City for many years. He presided over the Saints there, leaving from time to time to serve short missions elsewhere. In 1864, he was gone for about three months, serving a short mission in the Hawaiian Islands. He went with Elder Ezra T. Benson, who was also a member of the Quorum of the Twelve, and Elders Joseph F. Smith, Alma Smith, and William W. Cluff.[65] In 1872–73, Elder Snow and others accompanied President George A. Smith, First Counselor in the First Presidency, on a nine-month tour through parts of Europe and the Middle East, including a visit to the Holy Land. They went by request of President Brigham Young, who hoped that their righteous influence would help prepare other nations to receive the restored gospel.[66] In 1885, Elder Snow was called to visit several groups of American Indians in the northwest United States and the state of Wyoming. Beginning in August and ending in October, he established missions there and organized Church leaders to help those who had been baptized and confirmed.

Temple Work

President Heber J. Grant, the seventh President of the Church, observed that President Lorenzo Snow "devot[ed] his life for years to laboring in the Temple."[67] This love for temple work began in the early days of President Snow's conversion and deepened during his service as an Apostle. He attended meetings in the Kirtland Temple soon after he was baptized and confirmed. Later he enthusiastically accepted a call to collect donations to build the temple in Nauvoo. Once the Nauvoo Temple was built, he served as an officiator there, helping Latter-day Saints receive the endowment and sealing ordinances before their exodus to the West. His responsibilities in the temple continued and expanded when he was called to serve as

Boots, shoes, harnesses, and hats were made in this building in Brigham City, Utah.

an Apostle. He spoke at the dedicatory services in the Logan Utah Temple. After President Wilford Woodruff dedicated the Manti Utah Temple, President Snow read the dedicatory prayer in sessions on subsequent days. When the capstone was placed on the highest spire of the Salt Lake Temple, he led a large congregation in the Hosanna Shout. After the Salt Lake Temple was dedicated, he served as the first temple president there.

On President Snow's 80th birthday, a local newspaper included this tribute: "In the evening of his days, [he is] still busy and earnest in the great cause to which he has given his earlier years, he is continuing within the sacred precincts of the Temple the glorious labors to which he and his associates have consecrated themselves—labors of such profound importance to this sin and death-afflicted world."[68]

Ministering to Individuals

As President Snow traveled from place to place, teaching large groups of people, he took time to minister to individuals and families. For example, in March 1891, when he was serving as President of the Quorum of the Twelve, he was speaking at a conference in Brigham City. In the middle of his discourse, a note was placed on the pulpit. An eyewitness said that he "stopped his talking, read the note and then explained to the Saints that it was a call to visit some people who were in deep sorrow." He asked to be excused and stepped away from the pulpit.

The note was from a Brigham City resident named Jacob Jensen. It said that Jacob's daughter Ella had died that day after a weeks-long bout with scarlet fever. Brother Jensen had written the note simply to inform President Snow of the death and to ask him to arrange for the funeral. But President Snow wanted to visit the family immediately, even though that required him to cut his talk short and leave a meeting where he presided. Before President Snow left the meeting, he called for Rudger Clawson, who was then president of the Box Elder Stake, to accompany him.

Jacob Jensen recounted what happened when President Snow and President Clawson arrived at his home:

"After standing at Ella's bedside for a minute or two, President Snow asked if we had any consecrated oil in the house. I was greatly surprised, but told him yes and got it for him. He handed the bottle of oil to Brother Clawson and asked him to anoint Ella. [President Snow] was then mouth in confirming the anointing.

"During the administration I was particularly impressed with some of the words which he used and can well remember them now. He said: 'Dear Ella, I command you, in the name of the Lord, Jesus Christ, to come back and live, your mission is not ended. You shall yet live to perform a great mission.'

"He said she should yet live to rear a large family and be a comfort to her parents and friends. I well remember these words. . . .

". . . After President Snow had finished the blessing, he turned to my wife and me and said: 'Now do not mourn or grieve any more. It will be all right. Brother Clawson and I are busy and must go, we cannot stay, but you just be patient and wait, and do not mourn, because it will be all right.' . . .

"Ella remained in this condition for more than an hour after President Snow administered to her, or more than three hours in all after she died. We were sitting there watching by the bedside, her mother and myself, when all at once she opened her eyes. She looked about the room, saw us sitting there, but still looked for someone else, and the first thing she said was: 'Where is he? Where is he?' We asked, 'Who? Where is who?' 'Why, Brother Snow,' she replied. 'He called me back.'"[69]

When Ella had been in the spirit world, she had felt such peace and happiness that she had not wanted to return. But she obeyed the voice of President Snow. From that very day, she comforted family members and friends, helping them understand that they did not need to mourn for their loved ones who had died.[70] Later she married, had eight children, and served faithfully in her Church callings.[71]

Leading the Church as the Lord's Prophet, Seer, and Revelator

On September 2, 1898, President Wilford Woodruff died after serving as President of the Church for more than nine years. President Lorenzo Snow, who was then serving as President of the Quorum of the Twelve Apostles, was in Brigham City when he heard the news. He boarded a train to Salt Lake City as soon as he could, knowing that the responsibility of Church leadership now rested on the Quorum of the Twelve.

Feeling inadequate but ready to follow the Lord's will, President Snow went to the Salt Lake Temple and prayed. In answer to his prayer, he was visited by the Lord Himself. President Snow later testified that he "actually saw the Savior . . . in the Temple, and talked with Him face to face." The Lord told him to proceed immediately with the reorganization of the First Presidency, not to wait as had been done when previous Presidents of the Church had died.[72] President Snow was sustained by the Quorum of the Twelve as President of the Church on September 13, 1898, after which he began serving as President. He was sustained by the general Church membership on October 9 and set apart as the fifth President of the Church on October 10.

The First Presidency and Quorum of the Twelve Apostles in 1898. Top row, left to right: Anthon H. Lund, John W. Taylor, John Henry Smith, Heber J. Grant, Brigham Young Jr., George Teasdale, Rudger Clawson, Marriner W. Merrill. Middle row: Francis M. Lyman, George Q. Cannon, Lorenzo Snow, Joseph F. Smith, Franklin D. Richards. Bottom row: Matthias F. Cowley, Abraham O. Woodruff.

Through President Snow's example and through the revelations he received, Latter-day Saints came to know him as their prophet. Those of other faiths also came to respect him as a true man of God.

Interactions with Latter-day Saints

President Snow often presided at stake conferences when he was President of the Church. As he met with the Saints, he expressed his love and respect for them. His words and actions showed that while he acknowledged the sacredness of his calling, he did not place himself above the people he served.

In one stake conference, President Snow attended a special session for the children of the stake. The children were invited to form an orderly line so they could approach the prophet one at a time and shake his hand. Before they did so, he stood and said: "When I shake hands with you I want you to look up into my face, that you may always remember me. Now I am not any better than many other men, but the Lord has placed great responsibilities upon me. Ever since the Lord made Himself known unto me, most perfectly as He did, I have endeavored to perform every duty resting on me. It is because of the high position that I occupy that I wish you to remember me, remember that you have shaken hands with the President of the Church of Jesus Christ. I hope you will not forget to pray for me and for my counselors, Presidents Cannon and Smith, and for the Apostles."[73]

President Snow's son LeRoi shared the following account from a stake conference in Richfield, Utah: "President Lorenzo Snow and Francis M. Lyman [of the Quorum of the Twelve] were present at a stake conference at Richfield. After the opening song the stake president asked Brother Lyman whom he should call upon to offer the opening prayer. Brother Lyman said: 'Ask President Snow,' meaning to ask President Snow who should offer the prayer. Instead, however, the stake president asked President Snow to offer the prayer. President Snow graciously responded and before beginning the prayer expressed his pleasure in being called upon and said it had been a long time since he had been given this pleasure. It is said that he offered a wonderful invocation."[74]

Interactions with Those of Other Faiths

President Snow's influence extended beyond his fellow Latter-day Saints. When people of other faiths met him, they came to respect him and the Church he represented. Reverend W. D. Cornell, a minister in another church, visited Salt Lake City and had the opportunity to spend time with President Snow. He wrote:

"I was taken into his august presence by his courteous and experienced secretary, and found myself shaking hands with one of the most congenial and lovable men I ever met—a man who has the peculiar ability to dispossess one at once of all uneasiness in his presence—a master in the art of conversation, with a rare genius, enabling him to make you feel a restful welcome in his society.

"President Snow is a cultured man, in mind and soul and body. His language is choice, diplomatic, friendly, scholarly. His mannerisms show the studied grace of schools. The tenor of his spirit is as gentle as a child. You are introduced to him. You are pleased with him. You converse with him, you like him. You visit with him long, you love him." Addressing his readers, who apparently had prejudiced ideas about the Church, Reverend Cornell commented: "And yet, he is a 'Mormon!' Well, if 'Mormonism' ever succeeds in making a coarse, brutal man of President Snow, it has much indeed to do. If 'Mormonism' has been the moulding force which has given to the world a man quiet in spirit, so possessed as he is, and accomplished in intellect, there must certainly be something in 'Mormonism' good after all."[75]

Another minister, a Reverend Prentis, also wrote of a meeting with President Snow: "The face which speaks of a soul where reigns the Prince of Peace is his best witness. Now and then in a life spent in the study of men, I have found such a witness. Such was a face I saw today. . . . I had expected to find intellectuality, benevolence, dignity, composure and strength depicted upon the face of the President of the Church of Jesus Christ of Latter-day Saints; but when I was introduced to President Lorenzo Snow, for a second I was startled. . . . His face was a power of peace; his presence a benediction of peace. In the tranquil depths of his eyes were not only the 'home of silent prayer,' but the abode of spiritual strength. As he talked of the 'more sure word of prophecy' and the certainty of the hope which was his, and the abiding faith which had conquered the trials and difficulties of tragic life, I watched the play of emotions and studied with fascinated attention the subtle shades of expression which spoke so plainly the workings of his soul; and the strangest feeling stole over me, that I 'stood on holy ground:' that this man did not act from the commonplace motives of policy, interest, or expediency, but he 'acted from a far-off center.' . . . If the Mormon Church can produce such witnesses, it will need but little the pen of the ready writer or the eloquence of the great preacher."[76]

Revelation on Tithing

President Lorenzo Snow is perhaps best known for a revelation he received on the law of tithing. In May 1899 he felt prompted to travel to St. George, Utah, with other Church leaders. Although he did not know why they needed to go, he and his brethren responded to the prompting quickly, and within about two weeks they were in St. George. On May 17, after arriving in St. George, President Snow received a revelation that he should preach the law of tithing. The next day he made the following declaration to the Saints: "The word of the Lord to you is not anything new; it is simply this: THE TIME HAS NOW COME FOR EVERY LATTER-DAY SAINT, WHO CALCULATES TO BE PREPARED FOR THE FUTURE AND TO HOLD HIS FEET STRONG UPON A PROPER FOUNDATION, TO DO THE WILL OF THE LORD AND TO PAY HIS TITHING IN FULL. That is the word of the Lord to you, and it will be the word of the Lord to every settlement throughout the land of Zion."[77]

After delivering this message in St. George, President Snow and his traveling companions shared the same message in southern Utah towns and in other communities between St. George and Salt Lake City. By the time they returned on May 27, they had held 24 meetings in which President Snow had delivered 26 discourses and shaken hands with 4,417 children. They had traveled 420 miles by train and 307 miles by horse and carriage.[78] President Snow was energized by the experience and was anxious to continue preaching the law of tithing throughout the Church. "I am so pleased with the result of this visit," he said, "that I contemplate traveling through all the stakes in Zion, in the near future."[79] He presided at many stake conferences, where he promised the Saints that obedience to this law would prepare Church members to receive temporal and spiritual blessings.[80] He also promised that obedience to the law of tithing would enable the Church to break free from indebtedness.[81]

Throughout the Church, members responded to President Snow's counsel with renewed dedication. In 1904, historian Orson F. Whitney, who would later serve as a member of the Quorum of the Twelve, wrote: "The effect of the movement was instantaneous. Tithes and offerings came pouring in with a promptness and plenitude unknown for years, and in many ways the Church's condition improved and its prospects brightened. President Snow had previously possessed the love and confidence of his people, and now these good feelings were increased and intensified."[82] President Heber J. Grant, who was a member of the Quorum of the Twelve when President Snow received the revelation on tithing, later declared: "Lorenzo Snow came to the presidency of the Church when he was eighty-five years of age, and what he accomplished during the next three years of his life is simply marvelous to contemplate. . . . In three short years this man, beyond the age of ability in the estimation of the world, this man who had not been engaged in financial affairs, who had been devoting his life for years to laboring in the Temple, took hold of the finances of the Church of Christ, under the inspiration of the living God, and in those three years changed everything, financially, from darkness to light."[83]

Bearing Testimony in the Final Days of His Ministry

On January 1, 1901, President Snow attended a special meeting in the Salt Lake Tabernacle to welcome the 20th century. People of all religions were invited to attend. President Snow had prepared a message for the event, but he was not able to read it himself because he had a severe cold. After an opening hymn, an opening prayer, and an anthem sung by the Tabernacle Choir, President Snow's son LeRoi stood and read the message, titled "Greeting to the World by President Lorenzo Snow."[84] The closing words of the message exemplified President Snow's feelings about the work of the Lord:

"In the eighty-seventh year of my age on earth, I feel full of earnest desire for the benefit of humanity. . . . I lift my hands and invoke the blessing of heaven upon the inhabitants of the earth. May the sunshine from above smile upon you. May the treasures of the ground and the fruits of the soil be brought forth freely for your good. May the light of truth chase darkness from your souls. May righteousness increase and iniquity diminish. . . . May justice triumph and corruption be stamped out. And may virtue and chastity and honor prevail, until evil shall be overcome and the earth shall be cleansed from wickedness. Let these sentiments, as the voice of the 'Mormons' in the mountains of Utah, go forth to the whole world, and let all people know that our wish and our mission are for the blessing and salvation of the entire human race. . . . May God be glorified in the victory that is coming over sin and sorrow and misery and death. Peace be unto you all!"[85]

On October 6, 1901, President Lorenzo Snow stood to speak to his fellow Saints in the closing session of general conference. He had been quite sick for several days, and when he reached the pulpit, he said, "My dear brethren and sisters, it is rather a marvel to me that I venture to talk to you this afternoon." He shared a brief message about leadership in the Church. Then he said the final words the general membership of the Church would hear from him: "God bless you. Amen."[86]

Four days later, President Snow died of pneumonia. After a funeral in the Salt Lake Tabernacle, his body was buried in a cemetery in his beloved Brigham City.

Notes

1. Lorenzo Snow, in Lycurgus A. Wilson, *Life of David W. Patten, the First Apostolic Martyr* (1900), v.
2. Lorenzo Snow, "The Grand Destiny of Man," *Deseret Evening News,* July 20, 1901, 22.
3. Lorenzo Snow, in *Life of David W. Patten, the First Apostolic Martyr,* v.
4. Lorenzo Snow, in *Life of David W. Patten, the First Apostolic Martyr,* v.
5. See Eliza R. Snow Smith, *Biography and Family Record of Lorenzo Snow* (1884), 1–2.
6. Eliza R. Snow Smith, *Biography and Family Record of Lorenzo Snow,* 2.
7. Lorenzo Snow, Journal and Letterbook, 1836–1845, Church History Library, 18.
8. Eliza R. Snow Smith, *Biography and Family Record of Lorenzo Snow,* 2–3.
9. Eliza R. Snow Smith, *Biography and Family Record of Lorenzo Snow,* 3.
10. Eliza R. Snow Smith, *Biography and Family Record of Lorenzo Snow,* 2, 3.
11. Orson F. Whitney, *History of Utah,* 4 vols. (1892–1904), 4:223.
12. See *Biography and Family Record of Lorenzo Snow,* 4.
13. Lorenzo Snow, Journal and Letterbook, 1836–1845, 57–62.
14. See Lorenzo Snow, Journal and Letterbook, 1836–1845, 32.
15. Eliza R. Snow Smith, *Biography and Family Record of Lorenzo Snow,* 6.
16. Lorenzo Snow, "The Grand Destiny of Man," 22. For more about Lorenzo Snow's conversion, see chapter 3.
17. Eliza R. Snow Smith, *Biography and Family Record of Lorenzo Snow,* 6.
18. Lorenzo Snow, Journal and Letterbook, 1836–1845, 33.
19. Lorenzo Snow, Journal and Letterbook, 1836–1845, 33; see also "The Grand Destiny of Man," 22.
20. Lorenzo Snow, "The Grand Destiny of Man," 22.
21. Lorenzo Snow, in *Biography and Family Record of Lorenzo Snow,* 15.
22. Lorenzo Snow, "The Grand Destiny of Man," 22.
23. Lorenzo Snow, in *Biography and Family Record of Lorenzo Snow,* 16.
24. See *Biography and Family Record of Lorenzo Snow,* 16, 19.
25. Lorenzo Snow, in *Biography and Family Record of Lorenzo Snow,* 19.
26. Lorenzo Snow, in *Biography and Family Record of Lorenzo Snow,* 30.
27. Lorenzo Snow, in *Biography and Family Record of Lorenzo Snow,* 37–38.
28. Letter from Lorenzo Snow to Oliver Snow, quoted in a letter from Eliza R. Snow to Isaac Streator, Feb. 22, 1839, Church History Library.
29. Lorenzo Snow, in *Biography and Family Record of Lorenzo Snow,* 37.
30. Letter from Lorenzo Snow to Oliver Snow, quoted in a letter from Eliza R. Snow to Isaac Streator, Feb. 22, 1839.
31. Lorenzo Snow, in *Biography and Family Record of Lorenzo Snow,* 19.
32. Lorenzo Snow, in *Biography and Family Record of Lorenzo Snow,* 47.
33. Lorenzo Snow, in *Biography and Family Record of Lorenzo Snow,* 50–51. For more about the voyage to England, see chapter 14.

34. Lorenzo Snow, in *Biography and Family Record of Lorenzo Snow,* 58–59.
35. Letter from Lorenzo Snow to Heber C. Kimball, Oct. 22, 1841, in Lorenzo Snow, Letterbook, 1839–1846, Church History Library.
36. Letter from Lorenzo Snow to Heber C. Kimball, Oct. 22, 1841, in Lorenzo Snow, Letterbook, 1839–1846.
37. Letter from Lorenzo Snow to George A. Smith, Jan. 20, 1842, in Lorenzo Snow, Letterbook, 1839–1846.
38. Lorenzo Snow, Journal and Letterbook, 1836–1845, 45.
39. Lorenzo Snow, Journal and Letterbook, 1836–1845, 65–66.
40. Lorenzo Snow, Journal and Letterbook, 1836–1845, 72–83.
41. Lorenzo Snow, Journal and Letterbook, 1836–1845, 91.
42. Eliza R. Snow Smith, *Biography and Family Record of Lorenzo Snow,* 74–75; see also page 73.
43. Lorenzo Snow, Journal and Letterbook, 1836–1845, 49.
44. Lorenzo Snow, in *Biography and Family Record of Lorenzo Snow,* 79.
45. Lorenzo Snow, in *Biography and Family Record of Lorenzo Snow,* 79.
46. Lorenzo Snow, in *Biography and Family Record of Lorenzo Snow,* 79, 82.
47. Lorenzo Snow, in "Laid to Rest: The Remains of President John Taylor Consigned to the Grave," *Millennial Star,* Aug. 29, 1887, 549. For more of Lorenzo Snow's comments about the martyrdom of Joseph Smith, see chapter 23.
48. See Eliza R. Snow Smith, *Biography and Family Record of Lorenzo Snow,* 84.
49. Joseph Smith, quoted by Lorenzo Snow in *Biography and Family Record of Lorenzo Snow,* 70.
50. For more on the experience at Mount Pisgah, see chapter 7.
51. See *Biography and Family Record of Lorenzo Snow,* 94–95.
52. Lorenzo Snow, "Address of Apostle Lorenzo Snow," *Millennial Star,* Feb. 15, 1886, 110.
53. Lorenzo Snow, *Deseret News,* Jan. 14, 1857, 355.
54. Letter from Lorenzo Snow to Eliza R. Snow, in *The Italian Mission* (1851), 5.
55. Letter from Lorenzo Snow to Franklin D. Richards, in *The Italian Mission,* 8–10.
56. Letter from Lorenzo Snow to Brigham Young, in *The Italian Mission,* 10–11.
57. See letter from Lorenzo Snow to Brigham Young, in *The Italian Mission,* 15–17.
58. See letter from Lorenzo Snow to Brigham Young, in *The Italian Mission,* 17.
59. Letter from Lorenzo Snow to Franklin D. Richards, in *The Italian Mission,* 20.
60. Letter from Lorenzo Snow to Orson Hyde, in *The Italian Mission,* 23.
61. Letter from Jabez Woodard to Lorenzo Snow, in *The Italian Mission,* 26.
62. Quoted in a letter from Jabez Woodard to Lorenzo Snow, in *The Italian Mission,* 26.
63. In Conference Report, Oct. 1994, 97; or *Ensign,* Nov. 1994, 74.
64. Leslie Woodruff Snow, "President Lorenzo Snow, as the Silver Grays of Today Remember Him," *Young Woman's Journal,* Sept. 1903, 391.
65. For more on Elder Snow's experience in the Hawaiian Islands, see chapter 4.
66. For more on Elder Snow's experience in the Holy Land, see chapter 24.
67. Heber J. Grant, in Conference Report, June 1919, 10.
68. *Deseret Evening News,* Apr. 3, 1894, 4.
69. Jacob Jensen, quoted in LeRoi C. Snow, "Raised from the Dead," *Improvement Era,* Sept. 1929, 884–86.
70. See LeRoi C. Snow, "Raised from the Dead," 886; LeRoi C. Snow, "Raised from the Dead (Conclusion)," *Improvement Era,* Oct. 1929, 975–79.
71. See LeRoi C. Snow, "Raised from the Dead (Conclusion)," 980.
72. See LeRoi C. Snow, "An Experience of My Father's," *Improvement Era,* Sept. 1933, 677; see also correspondence between Elder John A. Widtsoe and Noah S. Pond, husband of Alice Armeda Snow Young Pond, Oct. 30, 1945, and Nov. 12, 1946, Church History Library. President Brigham Young waited more than three years after the martyrdom of the Prophet Joseph Smith before he reorganized the First Presidency; President John Taylor waited more than three years after

the death of President Young; President Woodruff waited almost two years after the death of President Taylor. For more on the divine manifestation President Snow received in the temple, see chapter 20.

73. Lorenzo Snow, in "President Snow in Cache Valley," *Deseret Evening News,* Aug. 7, 1899, 1.
74. Biographical Notes on Lorenzo Snow, comp. LeRoi C. Snow, Church History Library, 2.
75. W. D. Cornell, quoted in "Mormonism in Salt Lake," *Millennial Star,* Sept. 14, 1899, 579.
76. Reverend Prentis, quoted in Nephi Anderson, "Life and Character Sketch of Lorenzo Snow," *Improvement Era,* June 1899, 569–70.
77. Lorenzo Snow, *Millennial Star,* Aug. 24, 1899, 533; see also *Deseret Evening News,* May 17, 1899, 2; *Deseret Evening News,* May 18, 1899, 2. The *Millennial Star* says that President Snow delivered this discourse on May 8, but other contemporary sources show that he delivered it on May 18. President Snow also spoke about tithing on May 17. For a more complete account of the revelation on tithing, see chapter 12.
78. See "Pres. Snow Is Home Again," *Deseret Evening News,* May 27, 1899, 1.
79. Lorenzo Snow, in "Pres. Snow Is Home Again," 1.
80. See, for example, *Deseret Evening News,* June 24, 1899, 3.
81. See, for example, *Improvement Era,* Aug. 1899, 793.
82. Orson F. Whitney, *History of Utah,* 4:226.
83. Heber J. Grant, in Conference Report, June 1919, 10.
84. See "Special New Century Services," *Deseret Evening News,* Jan. 1, 1901, 5.
85. Lorenzo Snow, "Greeting to the World by President Lorenzo Snow," *Deseret Evening News,* Jan. 1, 1901, 5.
86. Lorenzo Snow, in Conference Report, Oct. 1901, 60, 62.

Throughout his life, President Lorenzo Snow sought learning "by study and also by faith" (D&C 88:118).

CHAPTER 1

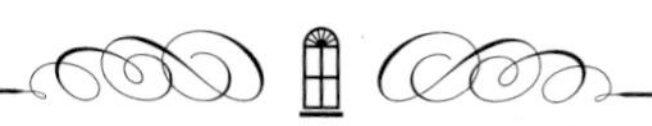

Learning by Faith

"Let us continue, brethren and sisters, to work in the name of the Lord our God; gathering wisdom and intelligence day by day, that every circumstance which transpires may minister to our good."

From the Life of Lorenzo Snow

When young Lorenzo Snow was not doing his chores on the family farm, he was usually reading—"hid up with his book," as his family members would say. According to his sister Eliza, he was "ever a student, at home as well as in school."[1] His love of learning increased as he grew up. In fact, he said that education was "the leading star" of his youth.[2] After attending public schools, he studied at Oberlin College, a private school in the state of Ohio, in 1835. In 1836, before he joined the Church, he accepted Eliza's invitation to move to Kirtland, Ohio, where he studied Hebrew in a class that included the Prophet Joseph Smith and many of the Apostles.

After he was baptized and confirmed, he eventually turned his interest more to "the education of the Spirit"[3] than to "book studies."[4] In this pursuit, he never lost his thirst for learning. For example, when he was 80 years old and serving as President of the Quorum of the Twelve Apostles, he stood before the Saints at the October 1894 general conference. Reflecting on the discourses his less experienced brethren had delivered earlier that day, he said, "Some ideas were advanced that I never thought of before, and they were very profitable."[5] Six years later, when he was President of the Church, he attended a conference conducted by the Sunday School organization. After hearing others speak, he finally stood at the pulpit. He began his address by saying: "I have been perfectly delighted and surprised at what I have seen and heard. . . . Indeed I may say, that I have been instructed; and if I, a man of eighty-six years, can be instructed, I see no reason why adults generally cannot derive profit as well as pleasure from attending your meetings."[6] [See suggestion 1 on page 44.]

Teachings of Lorenzo Snow

Learning requires faith, exertion, and perseverance.

In this system of religion that you and I have received there is something grand and glorious, and something new to learn every day, that is of great value. And it is not only our privilege but it is necessary that we receive these things and gather these new ideas.[7]

The whole idea of Mormonism is improvement—mentally, physically, morally and spiritually. No half-way education suffices for the Latter-day Saint.[8]

It is profitable to live long upon the earth and to gain the experience and knowledge incident thereto: for the Lord has told us that whatever intelligence we attain to in this life will rise with us in the resurrection, and the more knowledge and intelligence a person gains in this life the greater advantage he will have in the world to come [see D&C 130:18–19].[9]

There are some who do not learn, and who do not improve as fast as they might, because their eyes and their hearts are not upon God; they do not reflect, neither do they have that knowledge which they might have; they miss a good deal which they might receive. We have got to obtain knowledge before we obtain permanent happiness; we have got to be wide awake in the things of God.

Though we may now neglect to improve our time, to brighten up our intellectual faculties, we shall be obliged to improve them sometime. We have got so much ground to walk over, and if we fail to travel to-day, we shall have so much more to travel to-morrow.[10]

There must be a labor of mind, an exertion of those talents that God has given us; they must be put into exercise. Then, being enlightened by the gift and power of the Holy Ghost, we may get those ideas and that intelligence and those blessings that are necessary to prepare us for the future, for sceneries that are to come.

"The education of the spirit" is worthy of our "best attention."

The same principle will apply in all our actions in relation to the things of God. We have to exert ourselves. . . . This remaining idle without putting ourselves into action is of no use; if we remain perfectly neutral, nothing is accomplished. Every principle that is revealed from the heavens is for our benefit, for our life, for our salvation and for our happiness.[11]

We think, perhaps, that it is not necessary to exert ourselves to find out what God requires at our hands; or in other words, to search out the principles which God has revealed, upon which we can receive very important blessings. There are revealed, plainly and clearly, principles which are calculated to exalt the Latter-day Saints and preserve them from much trouble and vexation, yet, through lack of perseverance on our part to learn and conform to them, we fail to receive the blessings that are connected with obedience to them.[12]

Let us continue, brethren and sisters, to work in the name of the Lord our God; gathering wisdom and intelligence day by day, that every circumstance which transpires may minister to our good and increase our faith and intelligence.[13] [See suggestion 2 on page 44.]

The education of the Spirit is worthy of our best attention.

There is a kind of education worthy [of] the best attention of all, and in which all ought to engage—that is the education of the Spirit.[14]

A little spiritual knowledge is a great deal better than mere opinions and notions and ideas, or even very elaborate arguments; a little spiritual knowledge is very important and of the highest consideration.[15]

We must not neglect our spiritual improvements while we seek for worldly wealth. It is our duty to make every effort for the purpose of advancing ourselves in the principles of light and knowledge, as well as of increasing around us the temporal blessings and comforts of this life.[16]

If our minds are too one-sided, paying too much attention to the acquiring of earthly goods, to the neglect of spiritual wealth, we are not wise stewards.[17] [See suggestion 3 on page 44.]

We benefit from hearing gospel principles over and over again.

You have heard [some principles] perhaps hundreds of times, and yet it seems to be necessary that these things should be taught us over and over again. Again, it is something like I find in reading the Book of Doctrine and Covenants. Every time I read a revelation in that book I get some new idea, although I may have read that same revelation many and many a time. I presume this is your experience, too; if it is not, it is very different to mine.[18]

It is with us as with the child learning the alphabet. The teacher says to the child, "Here is the letter *a;* will you try and remember it?" The child replies, "Yes, I will try to remember it." The teacher goes to the next letter, and says, "This letter is *b;* will you look upon it and try to remember it?" "Oh, yes," says the child. Then the teacher turns back to the letter *a*. "What letter is this?" The child has forgotten it. The teacher once more tells the child that it is *a,* and turns to the letter *b,* and discovers that the child has forgotten that also, and again has to be instructed on the letter *b*. This is in the morning. In the afternoon the child is again called up and questioned, and the teacher once more finds that the child has forgotten the letters and has to be taught over again. And so the lesson has to be repeated over and over again, so much so that if the teacher had not had experience, and knew what to expect, he certainly would be discouraged. So it is with the Latter-day Saints. Though we may get tired of hearing things repeated, they have to be in order that we may learn them thoroughly. We must learn them. I know that the Latter-day Saints will eventually learn all the laws and commandments of God, and will learn to observe them strictly. But we have not arrived at that point yet.[19] [See suggestion 4 on page 44.]

When we gather to learn the gospel, both the teacher and the learner need the guidance of the Spirit.

When [a teacher] stands before the people he should do so realizing that he stands before them for the purpose of communicating knowledge, that they may receive truth in their souls and be built up in righteousness by receiving further light, progressing in their education in the principles of holiness.

This cannot be done, except by a labor of mind, by an energy of faith and by seeking with all one's heart the Spirit of the Lord our God. It is just so on the part of the hearers; unless particular attention is paid to that which is required of them from time to time by those who address the people from this stand, and unless individuals labor in their minds with all their mights and with all their strength in their prayers before the Lord, they will not receive that good and benefit to themselves which they ought to receive.[20]

What I want of the Latter-day Saints is that during this conference, as the Elders shall arise to address us, our faith and our prayers may be exercised for each one who speaks, that he may say such things, and that we may have the spirit to receive such things as shall be beneficial to all. This is our privilege and our duty. We have not come here accidentally; we have come in this conference expecting to receive something that will be advantageous to us.[21]

You should ask the Lord to let [the speakers] say something that you want to know, that they may suggest something to you that will

We should "prepare our hearts to receive and profit by" the messages shared in general conference and other meetings.

be of some advantage. If you have any desire to know certain matters that you do not understand, pray that [they] may say something that shall enlighten your mind in reference to that which troubles you, and we will have a grand and glorious Conference, a better one than we have ever had before. Strange as it may appear, our last Conference always seems the best, and may this be the case; and you brethren and sisters, let your hearts rise up to the Lord and exercise faith while our brethren are talking to you. We will not be disappointed, and you will not go home, you will not retire from this Conference, without feeling you have been greatly and abundantly blessed.[22]

I suppose that many of the audience now before me have come from a long distance to meet with us in this general conference; and that all have been moved to gather here by pure motives—by a desire to improve and perfect themselves in matters that pertain to their usefulness in the kingdom of God. In order that we may not be disappointed in this, it becomes necessary that we prepare our hearts to receive and profit by the suggestions that may be made by the speakers during the progress of the Conference, which may be prompted by the Spirit of the Lord. I have thought, and still think, that our being edified does not so much depend upon the speaker as upon ourselves.[23]

When we come together . . . , it becomes our privilege to receive instruction from those persons that address us, and if we do not, the fault, generally, is in ourselves.[24]

I have noticed on the part of the people what I have attributed to weakness. They come together, some of them, more for the purpose of being pleased with the oratory of their speaker, for the purpose of admiring the style in which he may address them, or they come together more for the purpose of seeing the speaker or speculating in regard to his character . . . than for the purpose of receiving instructions that will do them good and build them up in righteousness. . . .

. . . If we do not exercise those faculties given us and get the Spirit of the Lord, but little information will be received from speakers, even though ideas may be communicated of great value and worth. Notwithstanding ideas may be communicated in a very broken style, if the people will exert themselves, . . . they will soon learn that they will never return from meeting without their minds being benefited by the speakers.[25]

It is not always the lengthy discourse that affords to the Latter-day Saints that which is the most profitable; but in the various discourses delivered we may gather some idea, or some principle may flash upon our understanding which will prove valuable to us afterwards.[26]

We have gathered for the purpose of worshiping God and transacting business necessary for the furtherance of the cause of truth on the earth. The character of the instructions will depend largely upon the condition of our minds. We should dismiss therefrom our secular business and devote our attention to the purpose of this Conference.[27]

For our information and spiritual knowledge we are entirely dependent—we feel so dependent—upon the Lord. And in proportion to the exercise of our faith do we receive information, communicated through the Lord's servants. . . . He addresses us, through his servants, who address us on occasions of this character when we assemble together to worship our God.[28] [See suggestion 5 on page 44.]

Suggestions for Study and Teaching

Consider these ideas as you study the chapter or as you prepare to teach. For additional help, see pages v–vii.

1. Review pages 37–38, which describe some of President Snow's lifelong efforts to learn. What leads a person to continue learning throughout his or her life? Think about your own approach to learning, and ponder ways you can continue learning throughout your life.
2. Study President Snow's counsel about exertion and perseverance in gospel learning (pages 38–39). In what ways does your personal learning change when you truly exert yourself? How can we help children and youth exert themselves to learn?
3. President Snow encouraged the Saints to pursue "the education of the Spirit" (page 40). What does this mean to you? What can result when our education focuses too much on worldly wealth?
4. How does the example of a child learning the alphabet (pages 40–41) relate to our efforts to learn the gospel? As you have studied the words of ancient and latter-day prophets, what principles have you seen repeated?
5. In what ways can we prepare our hearts to learn in Church classes and meetings? How can we exert ourselves to learn, even when we are simply listening to a talk in a sacrament meeting or a conference? (For some examples, see pages 41–43.)

Related Scriptures: 2 Nephi 9:28–29; 28:30; Mosiah 2:9; D&C 50:13–22; 88:118, 122; 136:32–33

Teaching Help: "To help us teach from the scriptures and the words of latter-day prophets, the Church has produced lesson manuals and other materials. There is little need for commentaries or other reference material" (*Teaching, No Greater Call: A Resource Guide for Gospel Teaching* [1999], 52).

Notes

1. Eliza R. Snow Smith, *Biography and Family Record of Lorenzo Snow* (1884), 3.
2. In *Biography and Family Record of Lorenzo Snow,* 28.
3. *Deseret News: Semi-Weekly,* Mar. 31, 1868, 2.
4. In *Biography and Family Record of Lorenzo Snow,* 28.
5. "Glory Awaiting the Saints," *Deseret Semi-Weekly News,* Oct. 30, 1894, 1.
6. "Tithing," *Juvenile Instructor,* Apr. 1901, 214–15.
7. In Conference Report, Apr. 1898, 13.
8. "'Mormonism' by Its Head," *The Land of Sunshine,* Oct. 1901, 257.
9. In "Old Folks Are at Saltair Today," *Deseret Evening News,* July 2, 1901, 1; message prepared by Lorenzo Snow and read by his son LeRoi.
10. *Deseret News,* Oct. 21, 1857, 259.
11. *Deseret News,* Jan. 28, 1857, 371.
12. *Deseret News: Semi-Weekly,* July 16, 1878, 1.
13. *Deseret News: Semi-Weekly,* Dec. 7, 1869, 7.
14. *Deseret News: Semi-Weekly,* Mar. 31, 1868, 2.
15. *Deseret News,* Nov. 22, 1882, 690.
16. *Deseret News,* July 19, 1865, 330.
17. *Deseret News,* July 19, 1865, 330.
18. *Deseret Semi-Weekly News,* Mar. 30, 1897, 1.
19. *Deseret Semi-Weekly News,* July 28, 1899, 10; italics added.
20. *Deseret News,* Jan. 28, 1857, 371.
21. In Conference Report, Oct. 1899, 2.
22. In Conference Report, Oct. 1900, 5.
23. In Conference Report, Oct. 1898, 1.
24. In Conference Report, Apr. 1898, 61.
25. *Deseret News,* Jan. 28, 1857, 371.
26. In Conference Report, Apr. 1899, 2.
27. *Deseret News,* Apr. 11, 1888, 200; from a detailed paraphrase of a discourse Lorenzo Snow delivered in the April 1888 general conference.
28. *Salt Lake Daily Herald,* Oct. 11, 1887, 2.

Jesus Christ set an example for us when He was baptized by immersion.

CHAPTER 2

Baptism and the Gift of the Holy Ghost

"This . . . was the Gospel order in the days of the apostles, belief on Jesus Christ, repentance, baptism by immersion for the remission of sins, and the laying on of hands for the reception of the Holy Ghost. When this order was understood and properly attended to, power, gifts, blessings, and glorious privileges followed immediately."

From the Life of Lorenzo Snow

Even after receiving a witness that Joseph Smith was a prophet, Lorenzo Snow wrestled with the decision to join The Church of Jesus Christ of Latter-day Saints. He knew that if he became a member of the Church, he would have to abandon some of his worldly aspirations. But following an experience that he called his "fiercest struggle of heart and soul," he agreed to be baptized. He recounted: "Through the help of the Lord—for I feel certain He must have helped me—I laid my pride, worldly ambition and aspirations upon the altar, and, humble as a child, went to the waters of baptism, and received the ordinances of the gospel. . . . I received baptism and the ordinance of laying on of hands by one who professed to have divine authority."[1]

Having received this blessing himself, he was anxious to share it with others. In a letter he wrote as a missionary in Italy, he said: "In most countries the opening of the door of the kingdom of God has been attended with much trouble and anxiety. Not a little of this has fallen to our share. It was, therefore, with no small degree of pleasure, I went down into the water with the first candidate for eternal life. Never to us did sound so sweet the Italian language as at this interesting time, when I administered this sacred ordinance, and opened a door which *no man can shut.*"[2] [See suggestion 1 on page 57.]

Teachings of Lorenzo Snow

We receive blessings from God when we follow the principles He has established.

There are certain principles established of God, which being understood and observed, will put men in possession of spiritual knowledge, gifts, and blessings. In early ages of the world, also in the days of the apostles, people came into possession of spiritual powers and various privileges by obtaining an understanding of and faithfully attending to certain rules which the Lord established. As for instance, Abel, one of the sons of Adam, obtaining information that offering up sacrifices was an order instituted of God, through which men might receive blessings, he set himself to work, observed the order, performed the sacrifice, whereby he obtained glorious manifestations of the Most High [see Genesis 4:4; Hebrews 11:4].

Again, when the Antediluvians [the people before the great flood] had corrupted themselves, and the time arriving at which destruction was coming upon them, the Lord revealed a course whereby the righteous might escape; accordingly, all who understood and observed the course were sure to realize the blessing promised [see Genesis 6–8].

Joshua, before obtaining possession of Jericho, had to observe certain steps appointed of God. The steps having been properly taken, according to commandment, the object immediately fell into his possession. [See Joshua 6.]

Another instance: the case of Naaman, captain of the Assyrian host;—it appears, being afflicted with the leprosy and hearing of Elisha, the prophet, he made application to him for the removal of that affliction. The prophet, having the Holy Ghost upon him, which [communicates] the Mind of God, informed him that by washing in Jordan's waters seven times, he might be restored. At first, Naaman thought this most too simple and was displeased and disposed not to conform—not to make use of means so simple. After more due consideration, however, humbling himself, he went forth complying with the rules; when lo! the blessing directly followed. [See 2 Kings 5:1–14.] . . .

When the Gospel dispensation was introduced, gifts and blessings were obtained upon similar principles; that is, upon obedience to certain established rules. The Lord still marked out certain acts, promising to all those who would do them, certain peculiar privileges; and when those acts were performed—observed in every particular—then those blessings promised were sure to be realized.[3]

The outward ordinances of baptism and confirmation are inseparably connected with the inward works of faith and repentance.

Some vainly imagine that under the Gospel dispensation, gifts and blessings were obtained not by external observances, or external works, but merely through faith and repentance, through mental operations, independent of physical. But, laying aside the traditions, superstitions, and creeds of men, we will look to the word of God, where we shall discover that external works, or outward ordinances, under the Gospel dispensation, were inseparably connected with inward works, with faith and repentance. In proof of this, I introduce the following observation:—

The Saviour said, "Why call ye me Lord, Lord, and do not the things which I say?" [Luke 6:46.] Again; he says, "He that heareth my words, and doeth them, shall be likened unto a man that built his house upon a rock." [See Matthew 7:24.] And, "He that believeth and is baptized, shall be saved." [Mark 16:16.] Likewise, he says, "Except a man be born of water and of the Spirit, he cannot enter into the kingdom of God." [John 3:5.] These sayings of our Saviour require men to perform external works in order to receive their salvation.

On the day of Pentecost, Peter says, to the surrounding multitude, "Repent and be baptized for the remission of sins, and you shall receive the gift of the Holy Ghost." [See Acts 2:38.] In this prophetic statement, we learn that people were to perform an external work, baptism in water, in order that they might receive the remission of sins, and afterwards the gift of the Holy Ghost. But, before attending

On the day of Pentecost, about 3,000 people were baptized.

to the outward work, the inward work must be performed—faith and repentance. Faith and repentance go before baptism; and baptism before the remission of sins and the reception of the Holy Ghost. . . .

Some deem it wrong to number baptism among the essential principles ordained of God, to be attended to in obtaining remission of sins. In reply, we say that the Saviour and apostles have done so before us; therefore, we feel obligated to follow their example. . . . Baptism . . . doth now remove our souls from sins and pollutions, through faith on the great atonement. . . .

It is plainly manifest that external works must be attended to, as well as faith and repentance, in order to receive Gospel privileges.[4] [See suggestion 2 on page 57.]

Baptism is administered by immersion, and the gift of the Holy Ghost is bestowed by the laying on of hands.

Baptism in water, forming a part of the Gospel of Christ, we notice therefore that the servants of God in early ages were very particular in attending to its administration. . . .

We will now occupy a moment in endeavouring to obtain a proper view of the mode in which baptism was administered. It is quite evident that there was but one way or mode in which this ordinance was to be administered, and that mode was explained to the apostles and strictly adhered to in all their administrations. In order that we may obtain a proper notion of this subject, it will be necessary to refer to the circumstances under which baptism was administered.

It says of John [the Baptist] that he baptized at Aenon, because there was much water [see John 3:23]; then if sprinkling had been the mode, we can hardly suppose he would have gone to Aenon, because there was much water at that place, for a very little water, indeed, would have sprinkled all Judea, which he could have obtained without having performed a journey to Aenon. We are told, also, that he baptized in Jordan, and that after the ordinance was administered to our Saviour, he came up out of the water, expressly signifying that he had been down into the water, in order that the ordinance might be administered in a proper manner [see Matthew 3:16]. Again; it speaks of the Eunuch, that he went down into the water with Philip, and then came up out of the water [see Acts 8:26–38]; now it must be acknowledged by every one who makes any pretensions to reason and consistency that had sprinkling a little water on the forehead answered the purpose, then those persons never would have gone into the water to have received the ordinance. Paul, in writing to the saints, gives us a plain testimony in favour of immersion. . . . That apostle states there that the saints had been buried with Christ by baptism [see Romans 6:4; Colossians 2:12].

It is plainly evident they could not have been buried by baptism without having been entirely overwhelmed or covered in water. An object cannot be said to be buried when any portion of it remains uncovered; so, also, a man is not buried in water by baptism unless his whole person is put into the watery element. This explanation of the apostle upon the mode of baptism very beautifully corresponds with that given by our Saviour, Except ye be born of water, etc. To be born of a thing signifies being placed in that thing; and emerging, or coming forth from it, to be born of water, must also signify being placed in the womb of waters and being brought forth again.

I trust sufficient has already been said to convince every reasonable and unprejudiced mind that immersion was the mode in which the ordinance of baptism was administered in the early days of Christianity, when the Gospel was proclaimed in its purity and fulness, therefore, I will close my observations upon this point.

We learn from the 6th [chapter] of Hebrews that the laying on of hands was enumerated among the principles of the Gospel. It is known by all that this ordinance, as well as baptism for the remission of sins, by immersion, is quite neglected at the present day in the Christian churches; a few remarks, therefore, upon this subject, I hope, will prove profitable. We have several instances where Christ laid his hands upon the sick and healed them; and in his commission to the apostles, last chapter of Mark, he says, These signs shall follow them that believe; they shall lay hands on the sick, and they shall recover, etc. Ananias laid his hands on Saul, who immediately received his sight after this ordinance was administered [see Acts 9:17–18]. Paul, when shipwrecked upon the island of Melita, laid his hands upon the father of Publius, the governor of the island, and healed him of a fever [see Acts 28:8]. These few remarks show clearly that laying on of hands has been appointed of God to be a [means] through which heavenly blessings may be obtained.

Although the healing of the sick was connected with the administration of this ordinance, yet, when we peruse the subject farther, we shall discover that a still greater blessing was connected with this ordinance. We are told, in the city of Samaria, men and women had been baptized by Philip, which caused great rejoicing in them baptized. They probably were rejoicing in consequence of having received remission of sins, through faith, repentance, and baptism, and of receiving some portion of the Holy Spirit of God, which naturally followed them, after having obtained the answer of a good conscience by the remission of their sins. Through this portion of the Holy Spirit, which they came in possession of, they began to see the kingdom of God. For it will be recollected that our Saviour has declared, That no man can see the kingdom of God, unless he

We receive the gift of the Holy Ghost by the laying on of hands.

is born again; and in [the] verse following, he says, He cannot enter into it, except he is born twice; first of water, then of the Spirit [see John 3:3–5].

Now those people at Samaria had been born of water—they had received the first birth, therefore, they were in a state of seeing the kingdom of God, of contemplating with the eye of faith its various blessings, privileges, and glories; but as they had not been born the second time, that is, of the Spirit, they had not entered into the kingdom of God—they had not entered into possession of Gospel privileges in their fulness. When the apostles at Jerusalem heard of the success of Philip, they sent Peter and John to Samaria, for the purpose of administering the laying on of hands. Accordingly, when they arrived at Samaria, they laid their hands upon those that had been baptized, and they received the Holy Ghost. [See Acts 8:5–8, 12, 14–17.][5] [See suggestion 3 on page 57.]

The blessings of baptism and confirmation come only when those ordinances are administered by the proper authority.

Unless [ordinances] are administered by one who is actually sent of God, the same blessings will not follow. The apostles and seventies were ordained by Jesus Christ to administer in the ordinances of the Gospel, through which the gifts and blessings of the eternal worlds were to be enjoyed. Hence, Christ says to the apostles, Whosesoever sins ye remit, they shall be remitted; and whosesoever sins ye retain, they shall be retained [see John 20:23]: that is, every man that would come in humility, sincerely repenting of his sins, and receive baptism from the apostles should have his sins forgiven through the atoning blood of Jesus Christ, and through the laying on of hands should receive the Holy Ghost; but those that would refuse receiving this order of things from the apostles would have their sins remain upon them. . . . This power and authority of administering the Gospel was conferred upon others by the apostles; so that the apostles were not the only ones who held this responsible office. . . . Now, until some one can be found that holds an office like this, some one having authority to baptize and lay hands on, no one is under any obligation to receive those ordinances, nor need he expect the blessings, unless they have been administered legally.

. . . The authority of administering in Gospel ordinances [was] lost for many centuries. . . . The church established by the apostles gradually fell away, wandered into the wilderness, and lost its authority, its priesthood, and departing from the order of God, it lost also its gifts and graces; it transgressed the laws and changed the ordinances of the Gospel; changed immersion into sprinkling, and quite neglected laying on of hands; despised prophecy and disbelieved in signs. . . .

John, in his Revelations, having seen and spoken of the wandering of the church into darkness, . . . speaks, in [chapter 14, verse 6], of the restoration of the Gospel. "I saw another angel flying in the midst of heaven, having the everlasting Gospel to preach unto them that dwell on the earth;" so it is evident that prophecy was to be fulfilled at some time previous to our Saviour's second advent.

. . . I now bear testimony, having the highest assurance by revelation from God, that this prophecy has already been fulfilled, that an Angel from God has visited man in these last days and restored that which has long been lost, even the priesthood,—the keys of the kingdom,—the fulness of the everlasting Gospel.[6] [See suggestion 4 on page 57.]

When we keep the baptismal covenant and seek the guidance of the Holy Ghost, the promised blessings are sure to follow.

This then was the Gospel order in the days of the apostles, belief on Jesus Christ, repentance, baptism by immersion for the remission of sins, and the laying on of hands for the reception of the Holy Ghost. When this order was understood and properly attended to, power, gifts, blessings, and glorious privileges followed immediately; and in every age and period, when these steps are properly attended [to] and observed in their proper place and order, the same blessings are sure to follow; but when neglected, either wholly or in part, there will be either an entire absence of those blessings, or a great diminishment of them.

Christ, in his commission to the apostles, speaks of some supernatural gifts that those receive[d] that yielded obedience to this order of things [see Mark 16:15–18]. Paul . . . gives a more full account of the various gifts that attended the fulness of the Gospel; he mentions nine of them and informs us that they are the effects or fruits of the Holy Ghost [see 1 Corinthians 12:8–10]. Now the Holy Ghost was promised unto all, even as many as the Lord should call [see Acts 2:37–39]. This gift, being unchangeable in its nature and operations, and being inseparably connected by promise with this scheme or order of things, it becomes reasonable, consistent, and Scriptural to anticipate the same gifts and blessings; and if Noah, after having built the Ark, could claim and obtain his temporal salvation according to promise [see Moses 7:42–43]; or Joshua, having compassed Jericho the number of times mentioned, could go up upon her prostrated walls and make captive her inhabitants [see

Joshua 6:12–20]; or the Israelites, having offered up the sacrifices commanded, could then, as promised, [have] their sins forgiven [see Leviticus 4:22–35]; or Naaman, after having complied with the injunction of Elisha, in washing seven times in Jordan's waters, could demand and obtain his recovery [see 2 Kings 5:1–14]; or lastly, the blind man, after having washed in the pool of Siloam, if he could then claim and realize the promised reward [see John 9:1–7], then, I say, with propriety and consistency, that whenever a man will lay aside his prejudice, and sectarian notions, and false traditions, and conform to the whole order of the Gospel of Jesus Christ, then there is nothing beneath the celestial worlds that will operate against claiming and receiving the gift of the Holy Ghost and all the blessings connected with the Gospel in the apostolic age.

To obtain religion that will save us in the presence of God, we must obtain the Holy Ghost, and in order to obtain the Holy Ghost, we must believe on the Lord Jesus, then repent of our sins, that is, forsake them, then go forward and be immersed in water for the remission of sins, then receive the laying on of hands.[7]

When we received this Gospel, we covenanted before God that we would be led, that we would be governed, and would follow the suggestions of the Holy Spirit, that we would follow the suggestions of the principle that gives life, that gives knowledge, that gives understanding of the things of God, that communicates the mind of God; and that we would labor for the accomplishment of the purposes of God in the salvation of the human family, adopting as a motto of life, "The Kingdom of God, or nothing." How far we have kept these covenants . . . and followed the dictates of the Holy Spirit, we ourselves must be the judges. So far as we have done this, so far have the blessings of the Almighty descended upon us, and our minds have been enlightened, our understandings enlarged, and we have moved forward in the path of holiness, in the path of perfection. . . . Just so far as we have failed in our faithfulness, . . . just so far have we been losers in this enterprise in which we have engaged to obtain eternal life, to obtain wisdom and knowledge and divine intelligence sufficiently to stem the tide of evils and temptations that surround us. And just so far as we have followed the suggestions of this divine Spirit, have we experienced peace and joy to our souls, we have discomfited the enemy, we have laid up unto ourselves treasures that moth and rust cannot destroy, so far have we forwarded ourselves in the path of the celestial kingdom.[8] [See suggestion 5 below.]

Suggestions for Study and Teaching

Consider these ideas as you study the chapter or as you prepare to teach. For additional help, see pages v–vii.

1. As you read the accounts on pages 47–48, reflect on your own baptism and confirmation or a time when you saw someone else receive these ordinances. What covenants did you make when you received these ordinances? How have these covenants influenced your life?
2. Why are faith and repentance not enough without ordinances? Why are ordinances not enough without faith and repentance? As you ponder or discuss these questions, review President Snow's teachings about inward works and outward ordinances (pages 49–50).
3. Study President Snow's teachings on pages 50–53, noting the scriptures he referred to. In what ways do these scriptures enhance your understanding of the need for immersion? Why do you think the laying on of hands for the gift of the Holy Ghost is a "greater blessing" than the laying on of hands for the blessing of the sick?
4. Read the section that begins on page 54. What "gifts and graces" do you have in your life because the priesthood has been restored?
5. Study the final two paragraphs of the chapter. What does it mean to you to be led and governed by "the suggestions of the Holy Spirit"?
6. How does Doctrine and Covenants 68:25–28 relate to the teachings in this chapter? What can parents do to help their children understand faith, repentance, baptism, and the gift of the Holy Ghost?

Related Scriptures: 2 Nephi 31:12, 17–20; Mosiah 18:8–10; Alma 5:14; D&C 20:37; 36:2; 39:6; 130:20–21

Teaching Help: "[Avoid] the temptation to cover too much material. . . . We are teaching people, not subject matter per se; and . . . every lesson outline that I have ever seen will inevitably have more in it than we can possibly cover in the allotted time" (Jeffrey R. Holland, "Teaching and Learning in the Church," *Ensign,* June 2007, 91).

Notes

1. "How He Became a 'Mormon,'" *Juvenile Instructor,* Jan. 15, 1887, 22.
2. "Organization of the Church in Italy," *Millennial Star,* Dec. 15, 1850, 373.
3. *The Only Way to Be Saved* (pamphlet, 1841), 2–3; italics in original have been removed; punctuation has been standardized. Lorenzo Snow wrote this pamphlet eight years before his call to serve as an Apostle. It was later translated into other languages, including Italian, French, Dutch, Danish, German, Swedish, Bengali, Turkish Armenian, and Turkish Greek. It was reprinted from time to time throughout the rest of the 1800s, during his ministry as an Apostle.
4. *The Only Way to Be Saved,* 3–4, 6; italics in original have been removed.
5. *The Only Way to Be Saved,* 6–9.
6. *The Only Way to Be Saved,* 10–12; italics in original have been removed.
7. *The Only Way to Be Saved,* 9–10.
8. In Conference Report, Apr. 1880, 79–80.

CHAPTER 3

Lifelong Conversion: Continuing to Advance in the Principles of Truth

"Our religion should be incorporated within ourselves, a part of our being that cannot be laid off."

From the Life of Lorenzo Snow

Lorenzo Snow was baptized and confirmed in June 1836. Recalling his developing testimony, he later said: "I believed they [the Latter-day Saints] had the true religion, and I joined the Church. So far my conversion was merely a matter of reason."[1] He remembered, "I was perfectly satisfied that I had done what was wisdom for me to do under the circumstances."[2] Although he was content for a time with this understanding, he soon yearned for a special manifestation of the Holy Ghost. He said, "I had had no manifestation, but I expected one."[3]

"This manifestation did not immediately follow my baptism, as I expected," he recalled. "But, although the time was deferred, when I did receive it, its realization was more perfect, tangible and miraculous than even my strongest hopes had led me to anticipate. One day while engaged in my studies, some two or three weeks after I was baptized, I began to reflect upon the fact that I had not obtained a *knowledge* of the truth of the work—that I had not realized the fulfillment of the promise: 'He that doeth my will shall know of the doctrine;' [see John 7:17] and I began to feel very uneasy.

"I laid aside my books, left the house and wandered around through the fields under the oppressive influence of a gloomy, disconsolate spirit, while an indescribable cloud of darkness seemed to envelop me. I had been accustomed, at the close of the day, to retire

"We ought to dig deep into the things of God, lay our foundation upon the rock, until we come to that water which shall be in us an everlasting fountain of eternal life."

for secret prayer to a grove, a short distance from my lodgings, but at this time I felt no inclination to do so.

"The spirit of prayer had departed, and the heavens seemed like brass over my head. At length, realizing that the usual time had come for secret prayer, I concluded I would not forego my evening service, and, as a matter of formality, knelt as I was in the habit of doing, and in my accustomed retired place, but not feeling as I was wont to feel.

"I had no sooner opened my lips in an effort to pray, than I heard a sound, just above my head, like the rustling of silken robes, and immediately the Spirit of God descended upon me, completely enveloping my whole person, filling me from the crown of my head to the soles of my feet, and O, the joy and happiness I felt! No language can describe the instantaneous transition from a dense cloud of mental and spiritual darkness into a refulgence of light and knowledge, as it was at that time imparted to my understanding. I then received a perfect knowledge that God lives, that Jesus Christ is the Son of God, and of the restoration of the Holy Priesthood, and the fulness of the gospel.

"It was a complete baptism—a tangible immersion in the heavenly principle or element, the Holy Ghost; and even more real and physical in its effects upon every part of my system than the immersion by water; dispelling forever, so long as reason and memory last, all possibility of doubt or fear in relation to the fact handed down to us historically, that the 'Babe of Bethlehem' is truly the Son of God; also the fact that He is now being revealed to the children of men, and communicating knowledge, the same as in the apostolic times. I was perfectly satisfied, as well I might be, for my expectations were more than realized, I think I may safely say, in an infinite degree.

"I cannot tell how long I remained in the full flow of this blissful enjoyment and divine enlightenment, but it was several minutes before the celestial element, which filled and surrounded me, began gradually to withdraw. On arising from my kneeling posture, with my heart swelling with gratitude to God beyond the power of expression, I felt—*I knew* that he had conferred on me what only

Soon after being baptized and confirmed, Lorenzo Snow received a quiet, life-changing manifestation of the Holy Ghost.

an Omnipotent Being can confer—that which is of greater value than all the wealth and honors worlds can bestow."[4]

Lorenzo Snow remained faithful to the witness he received that day, and he worked diligently to increase in his spiritual knowledge and help others do the same. "From that time on," he said, "I have tried to live in such a way as not to lose His Holy Spirit, but to be guided by it continually, trying to get rid of my selfishness and any wrongful ambition, and endeavoring to work in His interest."[5] He declared, "As long as memory continues and reason shall assert its throne, I never can permit the powerful testimony and knowledge that was communicated to me to remain silent."[6] [See suggestion 1 on page 68.]

Teachings of Lorenzo Snow

Gaining a testimony is a good starting point for Latter-day Saints.

The foundation upon which we have placed our faith is grand and glorious. I know this for myself. I had been in this Church but a short time when I succeeded in securing the most perfect knowledge that there was a God, that there was a Son, Jesus Christ, and that Joseph Smith was acknowledged of God as His prophet. It was a knowledge that no man could communicate. It came through a revelation from the Almighty. That is a very good starting point for a Latter-day Saint, and it is something that every person, who has any ambition at all to advance in this path, will need at some time or other. He will come into circumstances of such a nature that he will need strength, and that strength will come from a knowledge of the fact that the path in which he is traveling will lead him to the possession of his highest and best desires.[7]

Brethren and sisters, there are some things that you and I ought to think about. The time is come when it behooves every man and every woman to know for themselves in relation to the foundation on which they stand. We should all strive to get a little nearer to the Lord. It is necessary for us to advance a little and obtain a full knowledge of those things which we should more fully understand. It is the privilege of every Latter-day Saint.[8] [See suggestion 2 on page 69.]

We can increase in our faith and spiritual knowledge.

Men and women can increase their spiritual knowledge; they can grow better as years multiply upon them.[9]

I feel that the Latter-day Saints are advancing; that they are receiving an education. We are getting up higher and higher. We are advancing to a higher condition and sphere and to a higher plane, and we are receiving such an education that the wisdom of the world with all its attainments and false doctrines and principles, will have no effect upon the Latter-day Saints, for they are rising above the theories and hypothesis of human inventions and soaring

"Men and women can increase their spiritual knowledge; they can grow better as years multiply upon them."

in things of truth that raise the mind, exalt the understanding, and establishing them[selves] more and more fully in the true principles of life and glory. We are filled in our hearts with these truths and we cannot tell the day or the hour in which our faith has been increased, but we feel, when we look back over the last week, month or year, that we have increased in faith and in the knowledge of faith and power of God; we know that we have got nearer our God and we feel that we are in fellowship with God our Father.[10] [See suggestion 3 on page 69.]

If we desire to increase in our faith and spiritual knowledge, we must exert ourselves.

Every man has got to learn to stand upon his own knowledge; he cannot depend upon his neighbor; every man must be independent; he must depend upon his God for himself entirely. It depends upon himself to see if he will stem the tide of trouble and overcome the impediments that are strewn in the pathway of life to prevent his progress. A man can get information by the operations of the Holy Spirit, and he approaches to God and increases in his faith in proportion as he is diligent.[11]

It is impossible to advance in the principles of truth, to increase in heavenly knowledge, [unless] we exercise our reasoning faculties and exert ourselves in a proper manner. We have an instance recorded in the Doctrine and Covenants of a misunderstanding on the part of Oliver Cowdery, touching this principle. The Lord promised him the gift to translate ancient records. Like many of us to-day, he had misconceptions in regard to the exercise of the gift. He thought all that was necessary for him to do, inasmuch as this gift had been promised him of God, was to allow his mind to wait in idleness without effort, until it should operate spontaneously. But when those records were placed before him, there was no knowledge communicated, they still remained sealed, as it were, for no power to translate came upon him.

Although the gift to translate had been conferred, he could not prosecute the work, simply because he failed to exert himself before God with the view of developing the gift within him; and he became greatly disappointed, and the Lord, in his goodness and mercy, informed him of his mistake, using the following language—

"Behold, you have not understood; you have supposed that I would give it unto you when you took no thought, save it was to ask me; but, behold, I say unto you, that you must study it out in your mind; then you must ask me if it be right, and if it is right I will cause that your bosom shall burn within you," etc. [See D&C 9.]

So in regard to us, respecting the things which we are undertaking. If we expect to improve, to advance in the work immediately before us, and finally to obtain possession of those gifts and glories, coming up to that condition of exaltation we anticipate, we must take thought and reflect, we must exert ourselves, and that too to the utmost of our ability.[12]

We ought to . . . get the Spirit ourselves, and not be satisfied to walk in the light as it is shadowed forth by others; we should have it incorporated with our spiritual organizations. . . .

An individual undertaking to learn to play upon a flute at first finds a difficulty in making the notes, and in order to play a tune correctly there is a great deal of diligence and patience required. He has to go on, to pause, to turn back and commence afresh, but after a time he is enabled, through a great deal of exertions, to master that tune. When called upon to play that tune afterwards, there is no necessity for remembering where to place the fingers, but he plays it naturally. It was not natural at the first; there had to be a great deal of patience and labor, before it became natural to go through with the tune.

It is just so in regard to matters that pertain to the things of God. We have to exert ourselves and go from grace to grace, to get the law of action so incorporated in our systems, that it may be natural to do those things that are required of us.[13] [See suggestion 4 on page 69.]

As we dig deep into the things of God and remain faithful, our religion becomes a part of our being.

There is a danger of our being satisfied with a superficial advancement, with merely advancing on the surface. We talk of walking in the light of the Spirit and of feeling it upon us, but do we do these things? We ought to dig deep into the things of God, lay our foundation upon the rock, until we come to that water which shall be in us an everlasting fountain of eternal life.[14]

There are men among us upon whom the Spirit of the Almighty once rested mightily, whose intentions were once as good and pure as those of angels, and who made covenants with God that they would serve Him and keep His commandments under every and all circumstances. . . . But how is it now with some of those Elders? They do not feel so to-day. Their affections are set upon the things of this world which the Lord has enabled them to acquire, that they wait now until they are called, and in many instances when called, they obey more out of a desire to retain their standing and position, than a real heart-felt love of the labor to which they may have been called.

This is the condition of all men, no matter how well they start out, who allow their thoughts and affections to run after the world and its ways, and it is a plain and indisputable proof that when this is the case with men they love the world more than they love the Lord and His work upon the earth. Having received the light of the everlasting Gospel, and partaken of the good things of the kingdom, and being of the seed of Israel and heirs to great and glorious promises, we should labor with fidelity and diligence to accomplish what God has designed to do through us; we should be men and women of faith and power as well as good works, and when we discover ourselves careless or indifferent in the least, it should be sufficient for us to know it in order to mend our ways and return to the path of duty.[15]

Nothing can be more foolish than the idea of a man laying off his religion like a cloak or garment. There is no such thing as a man laying off his religion unless he lays off himself. Our religion should be incorporated within ourselves, a part of our being that cannot be laid off. If there can be such a thing as a man laying off his religion, the moment he does so he gets on to ground he knows nothing about, he gives himself over to the powers of darkness, he is not on his own ground, he has no business there. The idea of Elders in Israel swearing, lying and giving way to intoxication is far beneath them; they ought to be above such things. Let us put from us every evil and live by every word that proceeds from the mouth of God [see D&C 98:11]. Let us lay hold of every duty assigned to us with ambition and energy that we may have the spirit of our God, the light of truth and the revelations of Jesus Christ within us continually.[16]

Stick to the ship of Zion. If boats come to the side, showing beautiful colors and making wonderful promises, do not get off the ship to go to the shore on any other boat; but keep on the ship. If you are badly used by any of those that are on the ship, who have not got the proper spirit, remember the ship itself is allright. We should not allow our minds to become soured because of anything that the people on the ship may do to us; the ship is allright, and the officers are allright, and we will be right if we stick to the ship. I can assure you it will take you right into the land of glory.[17]

I will [present a] figure in regard to bringing about and getting this spirit in us, and digging deep that we in the time of storm, may not be driven off. Place a cucumber in a barrel of vinegar and there is but little effect produced upon it the first hour, nor in the first 12 hours. Examine it and you will find that the effect produced is merely upon the rind, for it requires a longer time to pickle it. A person's being baptized into this church has an effect upon him, but not the effect to pickle him immediately. It does not establish the law of right and of duty in him during the first 12 or 24 hours; he must remain in the church, like the cucumber in the vinegar, until he becomes saturated with the right spirit, until he becomes pickled in 'Mormonism,' in the law of God; we have got to have those things incorporated in our systems.

. . . Brethren and sisters, I . . . leave the subject to your close application, consideration and meditation, praying the Lord God of our fathers to pour out His Spirit upon His people. You are those whom the Lord has selected to glorify Him in His presence, and may the Lord bless you and fill you with His Spirit, and may your eyes be clear to discern the things that pertain to your salvation. And if there is any man or woman that is not fairly awake, may the time soon come that the Spirit and power of the Holy Ghost may be upon them, that it may teach them things past, present and to come, and by the assistance of the Lord, plant righteousness and the principle of truth in their systems, that they may be prepared for the storms that are coming.[18] [See suggestion 5 on page 69.]

Suggestions for Study and Teaching

Consider these ideas as you study the chapter or as you prepare to teach. For additional help, see pages v–vii.

1. Review Lorenzo Snow's experience recorded on pages 59, 61–62. How did your testimony become real for you? Consider sharing your experience with a family member or with a friend, such as someone you serve as a home teacher or visiting teacher.

2. President Snow said that gaining a testimony is "a very good starting point for a Latter-day Saint" (page 63). Why is a testimony only a starting point—not a final destination?
3. In the section that begins at the bottom of page 63, President Snow contrasts the world's education with the "higher" education the Lord offers. How can we pursue this "higher education"? What blessings have come to you as you have done so?
4. Read the section that begins on page 64. When have you needed to "stand upon [your] own knowledge"? What can parents and teachers do to help children and youth stand upon their own knowledge?
5. Review President Snow's counsel in the final section of the chapter (pages 66–68). What do you think it means to "dig deep into the things of God"? What do you think it means to have our religion "incorporated within ourselves"?

Related Scriptures: 2 Nephi 31:20; Mosiah 5:1–4, 15; Alma 12:9–10; 3 Nephi 9:20; Moroni 10:5; D&C 50:24

Teaching Help: "Quite a bit of teaching that is done in the Church is done so rigidly, it's lecture. We don't respond to lectures too well in classrooms. We do in sacrament meeting and at conferences, but teaching can be two-way so that you can ask questions. You can sponsor questions easily in a class" (Boyd K. Packer, "Principles of Teaching and Learning," *Ensign,* June 2007, 87).

Notes

1. In Frank G. Carpenter, "A Chat with President Snow," quoted in *Deseret Semi-Weekly News,* Jan. 5, 1900, 12.
2. "The Grand Destiny of Man," *Deseret Evening News,* July 20, 1901, 22.
3. In "A Chat with President Snow," 12.
4. *Juvenile Instructor,* Jan. 15, 1887, 22–23.
5. "The Object of This Probation," *Deseret Semi-Weekly News,* May 4, 1894, 7.
6. *Millennial Star,* Apr. 18, 1887, 242.
7. "Glory Awaiting the Saints," *Deseret Semi-Weekly News,* Oct. 30, 1894, 1.
8. *Millennial Star,* Apr. 18, 1887, 244.
9. *Deseret News: Semi-Weekly,* Mar. 31, 1868, 2.
10. *Salt Lake Daily Herald,* Oct. 11, 1887, 2.
11. *Deseret News,* Apr. 11, 1888, 200; from a detailed paraphrase of a discourse Lorenzo Snow delivered in the April 1888 general conference.
12. *Deseret News,* June 13, 1877, 290.
13. *Deseret News,* Jan. 28, 1857, 371.
14. *Deseret News,* Jan. 28, 1857, 371.
15. *Deseret News: Semi-Weekly,* Aug. 15, 1882, 1.
16. *Deseret News: Semi-Weekly,* Mar. 31, 1868, 2.
17. *Deseret Semi-Weekly News,* Mar. 30, 1897, 1.
18. *Deseret News,* Jan. 28, 1857, 371.

Early missionary work in the Hawaiian Islands

C H A P T E R 4

Strengthened by the Power of the Holy Ghost

"Make up your minds to live humbly and in such a way that you will always have the Spirit of the Lord to be your friend."

From the Life of Lorenzo Snow

In his first general conference address as President of the Church, Lorenzo Snow taught, "We are dependent upon the Spirit of the Lord to aid us and to manifest to us from time to time what is necessary for us to accomplish under the peculiar circumstances that may surround us."[1] President Snow might not have been alive to make that statement if two of his friends had not depended upon the Spirit of the Lord in a peculiar circumstance 34 years earlier.

In 1864, Elders Lorenzo Snow and Ezra T. Benson of the Quorum of the Twelve Apostles went on a mission to the Hawaiian Islands. They were accompanied by three other missionaries: Elders Joseph F. Smith, William Cluff, and Alma L. Smith. When their ship anchored off the coast of the island of Maui, all but Joseph F. Smith boarded a smaller boat to go ashore. As they approached the island, high waves struck, causing the steersman to lose control of the boat. The boat capsized, and all the occupants were thrown into the water. Soon everyone surfaced except Elder Snow. A group of islanders rushed to help, taking William Cluff and Alma L. Smith in a lifeboat to search for their friend. Elder Cluff related:

"The first I saw of Brother Snow was his hair floating upon the water around one end of the capsized boat. As soon as we got him into our boat, we told the boatmen to pull for the shore with all possible speed. His body was stiff, and life apparently extinct.

When Elder Lorenzo Snow served a mission in the Hawaiian Islands, his life was saved through the inspired administration of his companions.

"Brother A. L. Smith and I were sitting side by side. We laid Brother Snow across our laps, and, on the way to shore, we quietly administered to him and asked the Lord to spare his life, that he might return to his family and home.

"On reaching the shore, we carried him a little way to some large barrels that were lying on the sandy beach. We laid him face downwards on one of them, and rolled him back and forth until we succeeded in getting the water he had swallowed out of him. . . .

"After working over him for some time, without any indications of returning life, the by-standers said that nothing more could be done for him. But we did not feel like giving him up, and still prayed and worked over him, with an assurance that the Lord would hear and answer our prayers.

"Finally we were impressed to place our mouth over his and make an effort to inflate his lungs, alternately blowing in and drawing out the air, imitating, as far as possible, the natural process of breathing. This we persevered in until we succeeded in inflating his lungs. After a little, we perceived very faint indications of returning life. A slight wink of the eye, which, until then, had been open and death-like, and a very faint rattle in the throat, were the first symptoms of returning vitality. These grew more and more distinct, until consciousness was fully restored."

Looking back on this experience, Elder William Cluff knew why he and Elder Alma L. Smith were able to save Elder Snow's life. "We did not only what was customary in such cases," he said, "but also what the Spirit seemed to whisper to us."[2] [See suggestion 1 on page 80.]

Teachings of Lorenzo Snow

Through the gift of the Holy Ghost, we are led to all truth and strengthened in our faith.

There [is] a certain blessing connected only with obedience to the gospel, that [is] the gift of the Holy Ghost. . . . The Savior, who undoubtedly knew best about the nature and character of this gift, said it should lead those who received it into all truth and show them things to come [see John 16:13]. It should be more than that spirit which proceeds from God, filling the immensity of space and enlightening every man that comes into the world [see D&C 84:46]; the gift of the Holy Ghost should lead into all truth, and show them things to come.

Furthermore, in speaking of its effects, the Apostle [Paul] says: "The spirit is given to every man to profit withal. To one is given faith." [See 1 Corinthians 12:7, 9.] Not a common, ordinary faith, which some people pretend to at the present day; but a faith which enabled its possessors to be sawn asunder, to be cast into dens of lions, fiery furnaces, and to undergo tortures of every description. This was the kind of faith that the Holy Ghost conferred upon those who possessed it, enabling its possessor to stand in the midst of every difficulty, defy every opposition and lay down his life, if necessary, for the cause that he had espoused. There was an almighty inspiring power in this faith, given by the Lord through the Holy Ghost, which no other principle could communicate. To one was given faith, to another knowledge [see 1 Corinthians 12:8], not that which is gained by reading books merely, but knowledge from the Almighty. A self-inspiring principle was upon them, which was tangible, giving them a knowledge of the cause they had espoused. They knew by revelation from God that the cause they had obeyed was true, it was revealed to them in a manner they could not dispute, and they knew for themselves. They were then established . . . upon the rock of revelation.[3]

Peter in preaching to the people said, "Repent and be baptized every one of you in the name of Jesus Christ for the remission of sins, and ye shall receive the gift of the Holy Ghost. For this promise is unto you and to your children, and to all that are afar off, even as many as the Lord our God shall call." [Acts 2:38–39.] This gift of the Holy Ghost is a different principle from anything that we see manifested in the sectarian world. It is a principle of intelligence, and revelation. It is a principle that reveals things past, present and to come, and these gifts of the Holy Ghost were to be received through obedience to the requirements of the gospel as proclaimed in those days and as proclaimed by the Elders of the Church of Jesus Christ of Latter-day Saints in these days. It was upon this rock that their faith should be grounded; from this quarter they should receive a knowledge of the doctrine they had espoused, and we are told by the Savior "that the gates of hell should not prevail against them." [See 3 Nephi 11:39.] . . .

. . . The foundation upon which the Church of Jesus Christ of Latter-day Saints is built is the rock of revelation—upon the rock that Jesus said He would build His church, and the gates of hell should not prevail against it [see Matthew 16:17–18]. We have not received this knowledge through flesh and blood, we have not received this testimony from man, we have not received it through the reading of the Bible . . . or Book of Mormon, but we have received it through the operations of the Holy Ghost, that teaches of the things of God,

"It is our right to have the manifestations of the Spirit every day of our lives."

things past, present and to come, and that takes of the things of God, making them clearly manifest unto us. You cannot take this knowledge from us by imprisonment or any kind of persecution. We will stand by it unto death.[4] [See suggestion 2 on page 80.]

Every Latter-day Saint can have the Holy Ghost as a friend to give counsel.

There is a way by which persons can keep their consciences clear before God and man, and that is to preserve within them the Spirit of God, which is the spirit of revelation to every man and woman. It will reveal to them, even in the simplest of matters, what they shall do, by making suggestions to them. We should try to learn the nature of this Spirit, that we may understand its suggestions, and then we will always be able to do right. This is the grand privilege of every Latter-day Saint. We know that it is our right to have the manifestations of the Spirit every day of our lives.

Persons come to me very anxious to receive counsel upon some subject or other. They need not come to me always (under some circumstances, of course, it would be highly proper), for the Spirit is within them to bring about good and to accomplish the purposes of God. . . . It is not always necessary for them to come to the President of the Church, or to the Twelve, or to the Elders of Israel, to get counsel; they have it within them; there is a friend that knows just exactly what to say to them. From the time we receive the Gospel, go down into the waters of baptism and have hands laid upon us afterwards for the gift of the Holy Ghost, we have a friend, if we do not drive it from us by doing wrong. That friend is the Holy Spirit, the Holy Ghost, which partakes of the things of God and shows them unto us. This is a grand means that the Lord has provided for us, that we may know the light, and not be groveling continually in the dark.[5] [See suggestion 5 on page 80.]

The Holy Ghost can bring us happiness and peace of mind.

The Lord has established certain constitutional desires and feelings in our bosoms, and it is so with all mankind, with the whole human family. There are implanted and interwoven in their constitutions certain desires and capacities for enjoyment, desires for certain things that are in their nature calculated to promote our peace and well-being, that answer their feelings and promote their happiness, but how to obtain the gratification of those capacities and desires the world [does] not know nor understand, but the Lord has seen fit to put us in the channel and in the way of understanding those things by being faithful and walking in the light of the Holy Spirit and receiving truth.[6]

It is the privilege of the Latter-day Saints to live in the Gospel in such a way that they will feel approved of God. Of course, we do things sometimes that we are ashamed of when we come to consider them, but we repent of them in our hearts and determine to do them no more. That is all the Lord asks of us; and men and women who so live, live without condemnation. They have righteousness and joy in the Holy Ghost.[7]

If we keep the light of the Spirit within us, we can so walk in the gospel that we can measurably enjoy peace and happiness in this world; and while we are traveling onward, striving for peace and happiness that lies in our path, in the distance, we shall have a peace of mind that none can enjoy but those who are filled with the Holy Spirit.[8] [See suggestion 3 on page 80.]

We need the assistance of the Holy Ghost as we endure trials, fulfill our duties, and prepare for celestial glory.

There are many important things required at our hands, and many things which we can do, when assisted by the Spirit of the Lord, which may at times seem almost impossible to accomplish.[9]

I wish to remind my brethren and sisters . . . that we are dependent for our information and intelligence upon the Spirit of God, which may be in us, if properly cultivated, a spirit of inspiration, of revelation, to make manifest clearly to our understanding the mind and will of God, teaching our duties and obligations, and what is required at our hands. . . . We need assistance. We are liable to do that which will lead us into trouble and darkness, and those things which will not tend to our good, but with the assistance of that comforter which the Lord has promised his Saints, if we are careful to listen to its whisperings, and understand the nature of its language, we may avoid much trouble and serious difficulty.[10]

We are entirely dependent upon the spirit of inspiration, and if there ever was a time, since Adam occupied the Garden of Eden, when the Spirit of God was more needed than at the present time, I am not aware of it. The signs of the times, and the rapid approach of scenes that will try the hearts of the Latter-day Saints and their integrity, demand that we *now* seek earnestly the Spirit of God, and Divine assistance, for it will certainly be needed in the scenes now rapidly approaching. We know that we have needed it in the past. We can easily see that if we had not been in the possession of the

Spirit of God to direct us through many of the scenes through which we have passed, we should not have been in the enjoyment of our present prospects of exaltation and glory, and our circumstances would have been much less favorable. And if we have needed the Holy Spirit in the past, we may truly understand that it will be needed in the future.[11]

We ought to understand—and I presume that we do generally—that the work which we have come into this life to perform cannot be done to the glory of God or to the satisfaction of ourselves merely by our own natural intelligence. We are dependent upon the Spirit of the Lord to aid us and to manifest to us from time to time what is necessary for us to accomplish under the peculiar circumstances that may surround us.[12]

It would be simply foolish indeed to expect the Latter-day Saints in these days to comply with the celestial law, with the law that proceeds from God, and with his designs to elevate the people into his presence, except they were sustained by a supernatural [heavenly] power. The gospel promises this. It promises the gift of the Holy Ghost, which is divine in its character, and which is not enjoyed by any other class of people, and which we are told by the Saviour, should lead into all truth, and inspire those who possessed it, and give them a knowledge of Jesus, a knowledge of the Father, and of things pertaining to the celestial world; that it should inspire those who possessed it with a knowledge of things to come, and things that were past; and inspire them to an extent that they should enjoy supernatural gifts—the gift of tongues and prophecy, to lay hands upon the sick, by which they should be healed.

Those who received this gospel were promised these supernatural power[s] and gifts, and a knowledge for themselves, that they might not depend upon any man or set of men, in regard to the truth of the religion that they had received; but that they should receive a knowledge from the Father that the religion came from him, that the gospel came from him, and that his servant had the right and authority to administer those ordinances, so that no wind of doctrine should shake them or remove them from the path in which they were walking; so that they might be prepared for the glory that should be revealed, and be made participators therein;

so that they might endure any trial or affliction that it should be the will of God to be brought upon them, to prepare them more fully for celestial glory; so that they should walk not in darkness, but in the light and power of God, and be raised above the things of the world, and be superior to the things around them, so that they might walk independently beneath the celestial world, and in the sight of God and heaven, as free men, pursuing that course that should be marked out to them by the Holy Ghost, that course by which they could elevate themselves to knowledge and power, and thus prepare themselves to receive the glory that God proposed to confer upon them, and to occupy the exalted position to which God designed to raise them.[13]

We should so live that we shall know that our course of life is acceptable to God. We should understand the voice and whisperings of the Holy Spirit. In the day when the sky is not obscured by clouds, we discover surrounding objects, their beauty and purpose. So are we dependent on the Spirit of God for light upon the principles of truth and salvation. No professing Latter-day Saint can enjoy any great degree of happiness unless he thus lives, and thus places himself under divine guidance.[14] [See suggestion 4 on page 80.]

When we live humbly, the Holy Ghost helps us in our onward path.

Make up your minds to live humbly and in such a way that you will always have the Spirit of the Lord to be your friend, to make such suggestions to you from time to time as shall be needed under the peculiar circumstances in which you may be placed. . . .

. . . How much longer I may live, I know nothing about, and I do not worry about it. I do desire, and it is something that you should desire, to have that humility, and that meekness, and that simplicity to enjoy the spirit of revelation. It is your privilege, every one of you, to have enough of the spirit of revelation to know exactly what is proper for you to do. It is your privilege to have it just as much as it is my privilege to know what to do tomorrow, when tomorrow comes, for the best interests of the Church in general.[15]

We should endeavor, as far as possible, to forget all worldly matters which grieve and vex us, and fix our minds upon the Lord, having a sufficiency of His Holy Spirit that we may be enabled to receive such knowledge and suggestions as will help us in our onward path.[16] [See suggestion 5 below.]

Suggestions for Study and Teaching

Consider these ideas as you study the chapter or as you prepare to teach. For additional help, see pages v–vii.

1. As you review the account on pages 71–73, think about times when you have been blessed because someone else has followed the promptings of the Holy Ghost. Also think about times when you have followed a prompting to help someone else.
2. Read the section that begins on page 73. What do you think it means to be "established . . . upon the rock of revelation"? (For some examples, see pages 73–75.) How can personal revelation give us strength to "stand in the midst of every difficulty" and "defy every opposition"?
3. President Snow said that the Holy Ghost can help us "enjoy peace and happiness in this world" (page 77). When has the Holy Ghost helped you be happy and feel peace? What are some other ways the Holy Ghost can help us? (For some examples, see pages 77–80.)
4. As you study the section beginning on page 77, think about how you have learned to recognize promptings from the Holy Ghost. How might you help a family member or friend learn to recognize the Spirit's promptings?
5. This chapter includes two references to the Holy Ghost as a friend (pages 76 and 79). Why do you think we need humility and simplicity to have the Holy Ghost as our friend?

Related Scriptures: Luke 12:12; John 14:26–27; Romans 14:17; 1 Corinthians 12:4–11; Galatians 5:22–25; 1 Nephi 10:17–19; 2 Nephi 32:5

Teaching Help: "To encourage discussion, use the questions in each chapter. . . . You may also develop your own questions especially for those you are teaching" (from page vi in this book).

Notes

1. In Conference Report, Oct. 1898, 2.
2. See Eliza R. Snow Smith, *Biography and Family Record of Lorenzo Snow* (1884), 276–79.
3. *Deseret News,* Jan. 24, 1872, 597.
4. *Deseret News: Semi-Weekly,* Dec. 2, 1879, 1.
5. In Conference Report, Apr. 1899, 52.
6. *Deseret News,* Oct. 21, 1857, 259.
7. *Deseret Weekly,* Nov. 4, 1893, 609.
8. *Deseret News,* Oct. 21, 1857, 259.
9. In Conference Report, Apr. 1898, 12.
10. *Deseret News: Semi-Weekly,* July 16, 1878, 1.
11. *Deseret Semi-Weekly News,* June 4, 1889, 4.
12. In Conference Report, Oct. 1898, 2.
13. *Deseret News,* Jan. 14, 1880, 786.
14. *Millennial Star,* Oct. 31, 1895, 690–91; from a detailed paraphrase of a discourse Lorenzo Snow delivered in the October 1895 general conference.
15. In "Anniversary Exercises," *Deseret Evening News,* Apr. 7, 1899, 9.
16. *Millennial Star,* Nov. 25, 1889, 737; from a detailed paraphrase of a discourse Lorenzo Snow delivered in the October 1889 general conference.

"It is a wonderful pleasure to speak upon the great things that God proposes to bestow upon His sons and daughters."

CHAPTER 5

The Grand Destiny of the Faithful

"It is a wonderful pleasure to speak upon the great things that God proposes to bestow upon His sons and daughters, and that we shall attain to if we are faithful."

From the Life of Lorenzo Snow

In the spring of 1840, Lorenzo Snow was in Nauvoo, Illinois, preparing to leave for a mission in England. He visited the home of his friend Henry G. Sherwood, and he asked Brother Sherwood to explain a passage of scripture. "While attentively listening to his explanation," President Snow later recalled, "the Spirit of the Lord rested mightily upon me—the eyes of my understanding were opened, and I saw as clear as the sun at noonday, with wonder and astonishment, the pathway of God and man. I formed the following couplet which expresses the revelation, as it was shown me. . . .

"As man now is, God once was:
"As God now is, man may be."[1]

Feeling that he had received "a sacred communication" that he should guard carefully, Lorenzo Snow did not teach the doctrine publicly until he knew that the Prophet Joseph Smith had taught it.[2] Once he knew the doctrine was public knowledge, he testified of it frequently.

In addition to making this truth a theme for many of his sermons, he adopted it as the theme for his life. His son LeRoi said, "This revealed truth impressed Lorenzo Snow more than perhaps all else; it sank so deeply into his soul that it became the inspiration of his life and gave him his broad vision of his own great future and the mighty mission and work of the Church."[3] It was his "constant light and guide" and "a bright, illuminating star before him all the time—in his heart, in his soul, and all through him."[4]

In this chapter, President Snow teaches the doctrine that we can become like our Heavenly Father. In chapter 6, he gives practical counsel on how we can apply this doctrine in our lives.

Teachings of Lorenzo Snow

Because we have divinity within us, we can become like our Father in Heaven.

We were born in the image of God our Father; he begat us like unto himself. There is the nature of deity in the composition of our spiritual organization; in our spiritual birth our Father transmitted to us the capabilities, powers and faculties which he himself possessed, as much so as the child on its mother's bosom possesses, although in an undeveloped state, the faculties, powers and susceptibilities of its parent.[5]

I believe that we are the sons and daughters of God, and that He has bestowed upon us the capacity for infinite wisdom and knowledge, because He has given us a portion of Himself. We are told that we were made in His own image, and we find that there is a character of immortality in the soul of man. There is a spiritual organism within this tabernacle [the physical body], and that spiritual organism has a divinity in itself, though perhaps in an infantile state; but it has within itself the capability of improving and advancing, as the infant that receives sustenance from its mother. Though the infant may be very ignorant, yet there are possibilities in it that by passing through the various ordeals of childhood to maturity enable it to rise to a superiority that is perfectly marvellous, compared with its infantile ignorance.[6]

We have divinity within ourselves; we have immortality within ourselves; our spiritual organism is immortal; it cannot be destroyed; it cannot be annihilated. We will live from all eternity to all eternity.[7]

It is a wonderful pleasure to speak upon the great things that God proposes to bestow upon His sons and daughters, and that we shall attain to if we are faithful. . . . Our travel in this path of

As we study the scriptures, we learn of our divine nature.

exaltation will bring to us the fullness of our Lord Jesus Christ, to stand in the presence of our Father, to receive of His fullness, to have the pleasure of increasing in our posterity worlds without end, to enjoy those pleasant associations that we have had in this life, to have our sons and our daughters, our husbands and our wives, surrounded with all the enjoyment that heaven can bestow, our bodies glorified like unto the Savior's, free from disease and all the ills of life, and free from the disappointments and vexations and the unpleasant sacrifices that we are making here.[8]

Through a continual course of progression our Heavenly Father has received exaltation and glory and he points us out the same path and, inasmuch as he is clothed with power, authority and glory, he says, "walk ye up and come in possession of the same glory and happiness that I possess."[9]

The people of God are precious in His sight; His love for them will always endure, and in His might and strength and affection, they will triumph and be brought off more than conqueror. They are His children, made in His image and destined through obedience to His laws to become like unto Him. . . .

. . . This is the high destiny of the sons of God, they who overcome, who are obedient to His commandments, who purify themselves even as He is pure. They are to become like Him; they will see Him as He is; they will behold His face and reign with Him in His glory, becoming like unto Him in every particular.[10] [See suggestion 1 on page 91.]

The scriptures teach of our divine potential.

The Lord has placed before us incentives of the grandest character. In the revelations which God has given, we find what a person can reach who will travel this path of knowledge and be guided by the Spirit of God. I had not been in this Church [very long] when it was clearly shown to me what a man could reach through a continued obedience to the Gospel of the Son of God. That knowledge has been as a star continually before me, and has caused me to be particular in trying to do that which was right and acceptable to God. . . . It seems, after all the education that we had in things pertaining to the celestial worlds, that there are some Latter-day Saints who are so well satisfied with simply knowing that the work is true that when you come to talk to them of our great future they seem surprised, and think it has nothing to do particularly with them. John the Revelator, in the third chapter of his first epistle, says:

"Now are we the sons of God." [1 John 3:2.]

. . . And he goes on:

"And it doth not yet appear what we shall be: but we know that when He shall appear, we shall be like Him; for we shall see Him as He is.

"And every man that hath this hope in him purifieth himself, even as God is pure." [See 1 John 3:2–3.]

. . . The Spirit of God has conveyed to us that there are solid and solemn truths in expressions of this kind. Paul, in speaking to the Philippians, suggested that they cultivate an ambition which is quite strange to the people at the present time, though not so to the Latter-day Saints, especially those who are not satisfied to be but babes in the things of God. He says:

"Let this mind be in you, which was also in Christ Jesus:

"Who, being in the form of God, thought it not robbery to be equal with God." [Philippians 2:5–6.]

. . . This [is] what Paul taught, and he understood what he was talking about. He was caught up to the third heaven and heard things, he tells us, that were unlawful for man to utter [see 2 Corinthians 12:1–7]. . . . Would it be wrong for us to ask the people here to cultivate an ambition of this character? There are a number of sayings in the Bible, particularly in the New Testament, that seem strange to people not in possession of the Spirit of the Lord.

"He that overcometh shall inherit all things." [Revelation 21:7.]

What an expression is that? Who believes it? If a father were to say to his son, "My son, be faithful, and follow my counsels, and when you become of age you shall inherit all that I possess," it would mean something, would it not? If the father told the truth, that son would have something to encourage him to be faithful. Did Jesus want to deceive us when He made use of this expression? I will assure you that there is no deception in the language. He meant precisely what He said. Again, Jesus said:

"To him that overcometh will I grant to sit with me in my throne, even as I also overcame, and am set down with my Father in His throne." [Revelation 3:21.]

That is a wonderful saying. Is there any truth in it? It is all true. It is the Lord Almighty that said it. We are told in the Scriptures by the Apostle Paul:

"For we know that if our earthly house of this tabernacle were dissolved, we have a building of God, an house not made with hands, eternal in the heavens." [2 Corinthians 5:1.]

I believe that. And when he says that Jesus "shall change our vile body, that it may be fashioned like unto His glorious body" [Philippians 3:21] I believe that also. Do the Latter-day Saints believe these things that I am talking about? You must, of course, believe them. Again:

"For he that receiveth my servants receiveth me;

"And he that receiveth me receiveth my Father;

In his epistles, the Apostle Paul testified of our potential to become like Heavenly Father and Jesus Christ.

"And he that receiveth my Father, receiveth my Father's kingdom; therefore all that my Father hath shall be given unto him." [D&C 84:36–38.]

Could anyone think of anything more that could be given? . . . Paul comprehended these things very well, for he said he "pressed forward to the mark of the prize of the high calling of God in Christ Jesus." [See Philippians 3:14.]

In these remarks which I have made we may see something in regard to the nature of this high calling in Christ Jesus. . . .

. . . I do not know how many there are here that have got a real knowledge of these things in their hearts. If you have, I will tell you what its effects will be. As John said:

"Every man that hath this hope in him purifieth himself, even as God is pure." [See 1 John 3:3.]

. . . God has pointed out the results of traveling upon this road of glory and exaltation and the promises are sure. The Lord knew precisely what He could do. He knew what materials He had to operate with, and He knew just what He said. If we do the part that He has assigned unto us, and keep our second estate, we shall be sure to realize these promises in every particular, and more than you and I can possibly comprehend.[11] [See suggestion 2 on page 91.]

As we remember the blessings the Lord has prepared for us, we find joy amid the cares and vexations of life.

There is no Latter-day Saint within the sound of my voice but that certainly has this prospect of coming forth in the morning of the first resurrection and being glorified, exalted in the presence of God, having the privilege of talking with our Father as we talk with our earthly father.[12]

There could not be placed before men more glorious prospects than are placed before the Saints. No mortal man could wish anything greater or that will ultimately prove more satisfactory. Everything that pertains to perfect peace, happiness, glory and exaltation is before the Latter-day Saints. We should enjoy the spirit of this, and keep it actively before us. We should not let our prospects be darkened in the least by doing that which is not acceptable before the Lord.[13]

My hopes in reference to the future life are supremely grand and glorious, and I try to keep these prospects bright continually; and that is the privilege and the duty of every Latter-day Saint.[14]

We do not all of us fully comprehend the blessings and privileges that are prepared in the gospel for us to receive. We do not fully comprehend and we do not have before our view the things which await us in the eternal worlds, nor indeed the things which await us in this life and that are calculated to promote our peace and happiness and answer the desires of our hearts. . . .

We frequently, in the multitude of cares around us, get forgetful and these things are not before us, then we do not comprehend that the gospel is designed and calculated in its nature to bestow upon us those things that will bring glory, honor and exaltation, that will bring happiness, peace and glory. We are apt to forget these things in the midst of the cares and vexations of life, and we do not fully understand that it is our privilege, and that the Lord has placed it in our reach to pursue that gospel whereby we may have peace within us continually. . . .

Where is there cause to mourn? Where is there cause for the Saints to wear long faces? Where is there cause for weeping or repining? There is none; but it is life or death that is set before us; principalities and powers are ours if we continue faithful; sorrow and banishment if we disregard the gospel.

What can we wish for more than is comprehended in our religion? If we will stand firm upon the rock and will follow the Spirit that has been placed in our bosoms, we shall act right in the way of our duties, we shall act right to those who are placed over us, we shall act right whether in the light or in the dark.

Where is the man that will turn aside and throw away those prospects that are embraced in the gospel which we have received? In it there is satisfaction, there is a joy, there is stability, there is something upon which to rest our feet, there is a sure foundation to build upon and upon which to yield that which is required of us.[15]

Let us never allow our prospects to become dimmed; let them be fresh before us by day and by night, and I will assure you that if we will do this our growth from day to day and from year to year will be marvelous.[16]

We are all aiming for celestial glory, and the grandeur of the prospects before us cannot be expressed in human language. If you will continue faithful to the work in which you are engaged, you will attain unto this glory, and rejoice evermore in the presence of God and the Lamb. This is worth striving for; it is worth sacrificing for, and blessed is the man or the woman who is faithful unto the obtaining of it.[17] [See suggestion 3 on page 91.]

Suggestions for Study and Teaching

Consider these ideas as you study the chapter or as you prepare to teach. For additional help, see pages v–vii.

1. President Lorenzo Snow frequently taught that we are children of God (pages 84–86). How can this truth influence the way we feel about ourselves and others? How can we help children and youth remember that they are sons and daughters of God?
2. What are your thoughts about the scriptures President Snow quoted to teach about our divine potential? (See pages 86–89.)
3. Read the section starting on page 89. How can the "cares and vexations of life" lead us to forget the eternal blessings of the gospel? What can we do to keep our potential "fresh" and "actively before us"? In what ways might remembering our destiny affect the way we live?
4. As you have studied this chapter, what have you learned about your Heavenly Father? What have you learned about your destiny as a daughter or son of God?

Related Scriptures: Romans 8:16–17; 1 Corinthians 2:9–10; Alma 5:15–16; Moroni 7:48; D&C 58:3–4; 78:17–22; 132:19–24

Teaching Help: "Testify whenever the Spirit prompts you to do so, not just at the end of each lesson. Provide opportunities for those you teach to bear their testimonies" (*Teaching, No Greater Call,* 45).

Notes

1. In Eliza R. Snow Smith, *Biography and Family Record of Lorenzo Snow* (1884), 46; see also "The Grand Destiny of Man," *Deseret Evening News,* July 20, 1901, 22.
2. See *Biography and Family Record of Lorenzo Snow,* 46–47; "Glory Awaiting the Saints," *Deseret Semi-Weekly News,* Oct. 30, 1894, 1.
3. LeRoi C. Snow, "Devotion to a Divine Inspiration," *Improvement Era,* June 1919, 656.
4. LeRoi C. Snow, "Devotion to a Divine Inspiration," 661.
5. *Deseret News,* Jan. 24, 1872, 597.
6. In Conference Report, Apr. 1898, 63.
7. In "Anniversary Exercises," *Deseret Evening News,* Apr. 7, 1899, 10.
8. *Millennial Star,* Aug. 24, 1899, 530.
9. *Deseret News,* Oct. 21, 1857, 259.
10. *Deseret Semi-Weekly News,* Oct. 4, 1898, 1.
11. "Glory Awaiting the Saints," 1.
12. In Conference Report, Oct. 1900, 4.
13. In Conference Report, Oct. 1898, 3.
14. In Conference Report, Oct. 1900, 4.
15. *Deseret News,* Oct. 21, 1857, 259.
16. In Conference Report, Apr. 1899, 2.
17. In "Prest. Snow to Relief Societies," *Deseret Evening News,* July 9, 1901, 1.

In the Sermon on the Mount, the Savior said, "Be ye therefore perfect, even as your Father which is in heaven is perfect" (Matthew 5:48).

CHAPTER 6

Becoming Perfect before the Lord: "A Little Better Day by Day"

"Do not expect to become perfect at once. If you do, you will be disappointed. Be better today than you were yesterday, and be better tomorrow than you are today."

From the Life of Lorenzo Snow

President Lorenzo Snow once attended a priesthood meeting in which a representative of each elders quorum stood and reported on the work his quorum had done. As President Snow listened to these young men, he was reminded of himself many years earlier. When he stood to speak, he said:

"I want to say something, if possible, that you will never forget, and I think that I can perhaps do so.

"I see, as I see almost always when young Elders are together, and in fact when middle-aged Elders are together, a kind of reluctance to speak before an audience. I see this here this morning in the young men who have risen to express themselves and to give information regarding the particular work they have been doing.

"It would not be amiss, perhaps, if I should tell you a little of my experience, when I commenced to talk in public, even before I was an Elder. I remember the first time I was called upon to bear my testimony. . . . It was something I very much dreaded, yet at the same time I felt that it was my duty to get up, but I waited, and waited. One bore testimony, another gave his testimony, then another, and they were nearly through, but I still dreaded to get up. I had never spoken before an audience. . . . I [finally] concluded it was about time for me to get up. I did so. Well, how long do you suppose I talked? I judge about half a minute—it couldn't possibly have been more than a minute. That was my first effort; and the second, I think, was about the same. I was bashful, . . . but I made up my mind, solidly and firmly, that whenever I was called upon to perform a duty of this nature or of any other, I would do it no matter what might be the result. That is a part of the foundation of my success as an Elder in Israel."

President Snow told the young men that not long after this experience, he held his first meeting as a full-time missionary. "I never dreaded anything so much in my life as I did that meeting," he recalled. "I prayed all day, went off to myself and called upon the Lord. I had never spoken [in public] before except in those testimony meetings. I dreaded it. I don't suppose a person ever dreaded a condition of affairs more than I at that time. The meeting was called, and the room was pretty well filled. . . . I commenced to speak and I think I occupied about three-quarters of an hour."[1] In another account of the same meeting, he recorded: "When I stood before that congregation, although I knew not one word I could say, as soon as I opened my mouth to speak, the Holy Ghost rested mightily upon me, filling my mind with light and communicating ideas and proper language by which to impart them. The people were astonished and requested another meeting."[2]

President Snow shared the lesson he wanted the young men to learn from his experience: "My young friends, there is an opportunity for you to become great—just as great as you wish to be. In starting out in life you may set your hearts upon things very difficult to attain to, but possibly within your reach. In your first efforts to gratify your desires you may fail, and your continued efforts may not prove what may be termed a success. But inasmuch as your efforts were honest efforts, and inasmuch as your desires were founded in righteousness, the experience you obtain while pursuing your hearts' desires must necessarily be profitable to you, and even your mistakes, if mistakes you make, will be turned to your advantage."[3]

This was a favorite theme of President Snow. He often reminded the Saints of the Lord's command to be perfect, and he assured them that through their own diligence and with the Lord's help, they could obey that command. He taught, "We ought to feel in our hearts that God is our Father, and that while we make mistakes and are weak yet if we live as nearly perfect as we can all will be well with us."[4]

Teachings of Lorenzo Snow

With diligence, patience, and divine aid, we can obey the Lord's command to be perfect.

"And when Abram was ninety years old and nine, the Lord appeared to Abram and said unto him, I am the Almighty God; walk before me and be thou perfect." [Genesis 17:1.]

In connection with this I will quote part of the words of the Savior in his sermon on the Mount, as contained in the last verse of the 5th chapter of Matthew.

"Be ye therefore perfect, even as your Father which is in heaven is perfect." [Matthew 5:48.] . . .

We learn that the Lord appeared to Abraham and made him very great promises, and that before he was prepared to receive them a certain requirement was made of him, that he [Abraham] should become perfect before the Lord. And the same requirement was made by the Savior of his Disciples, that they should become perfect, even as He and His Father in Heaven were perfect. This I conceive to be a subject that concerns the Latter-day Saints; and I wish to offer a few remarks by way of suggestion, for the reflection of those whom it concerns.

The Lord proposes to confer the highest blessings upon the Latter-day Saints; but, like Abraham, we must prepare ourselves for them, and to do this the same law that was given to him of the Lord has been given to us for our observance. We also are required to arrive at a state of perfection before the Lord; and the Lord in this case, the same as in every other, has not made a requirement that cannot be complied with, but on the other hand, He has placed for the use of the Latter-day Saints the means by which they can conform to His holy order. When the Lord made this requirement of Abraham, He gave him the means by which he could become

The Lord commanded Abraham, "Walk before me, and be thou perfect" (Genesis 17:1).

qualified to obey that law and come up fully to the requirement. He had the privilege of the Holy Spirit, as we are told the gospel was preached to Abraham, and through that gospel he could obtain that divine aid which would enable him to understand the things of God, and without it no man could do so; without it no man could arrive at a state of perfection before the Lord.

So in reference to the Latter-day Saints; they could not possibly come up to such a moral and spiritual standard except through supernatural [heavenly] aid and assistance. Neither do we expect that the Latter-day Saints, at once will or can conform to this law under all circumstances. It requires time; it requires much patience and discipline of the mind and heart in order to obey this commandment. And although we may fail at first in our attempts, yet this should not discourage the Latter-day Saints from endeavoring to exercise a determination to comply with the great requirement. Abraham, although he might have had faith to walk before the Lord according to this divine law, yet there were times when his faith was sorely tried, but still he was not discouraged because he exercised a determination to comply with the will of God.

We may think that we cannot live up to the perfect law, that the work of perfecting ourselves is too difficult. This may be true in part, but the fact still remains that it is a command of the Almighty to us and we cannot ignore it. When we experience trying moments, then is the time for us to avail ourselves of that great privilege of calling upon the Lord for strength and understanding, intelligence and grace by which we can overcome the weakness of the flesh against which we have to make a continual warfare.[5] [See suggestions 1 and 2 on page 104.]

When we comply with a requirement from the Lord, we are perfect in that sphere.

Abraham was called to leave his kindred and country [see Abraham 2:1–6]. Had he not complied with this requirement, he would not have been approved of the Lord. But he did comply; and while he was leaving his home he no doubt was living in obedience to this divine law of perfection. Had he failed in this he certainly could not have obeyed the requirements of the Almighty. And while he was leaving his father's house, while he was subjecting himself to this trial he was doing that which his own conscience and the Spirit of God justified him in doing, and nobody could have done better, providing he was doing no wrong when he was performing this labor.

When the Latter-day Saints received the gospel in the nations afar, and when the voice of the Almighty to them was, to leave the lands of their fathers, to leave their kindred as Abraham did, so far as they complied with this requirement, so far they were walking in obedience to this law, and they were as perfect as men could be under the circumstances and in the sphere in which they were acting, not that they were perfect in knowledge or power, etc.; but in their feelings, in their integrity, motives and determination. And while they were crossing the great deep, providing they did not murmur nor complain, but obeyed the counsels which were given them and in every way comported themselves in a becoming manner, they were as perfect as God required them to be.

The Lord designs to bring us up into the celestial kingdom. He has made known through direct revelation that we are His offspring, begotten in the eternal worlds, that we have come to this earth for the special purpose of preparing ourselves to receive a fulness of our Father's glory when we shall return into His presence. Therefore, we must seek the ability to keep this law to sanctify our motives, desires, feelings and affections that they may be pure and holy and our will in all things be subservient to the will of God, and have no will of our own except to do the will of our Father. Such a man in his sphere is perfect, and commands the blessing of God in all that he does and wherever he goes.

But we are subject to folly, to the weakness of the flesh and we are more or less ignorant, thereby liable to err. Yes, but that is no reason why we should not feel desirous to comply with this command of God, especially seeing that he has placed within our reach the means of accomplishing this work. This I understand is the meaning of the word perfection, as expressed by our Saviour and by the Lord to Abraham.

A person may be perfect in regard to some things and not others. A person who obeys the word of wisdom faithfully is perfect as far as that law is concerned. When we repented of our sins and were baptized for the remission of them, we were perfect as far as that matter was concerned.[6] [See suggestion 3 on page 104.]

Rather than become discouraged when we fail, we can repent and ask God for strength to do better.

Now we are told by the Apostle John, that "we are the sons of God, but it does not appear what we shall be: but we know that when he shall appear, we shall be like him; for we shall see him as he is. And every man that hath this hope in him purifieth himself, even as he, Christ is pure." [See 1 John 3:2–3.] The Latter-day Saints expect to arrive at this state of perfection; we expect to become as our Father and God, fit and worthy children to dwell in his presence; we expect that when the Son of God shall appear, we shall receive our bodies renewed and glorified, and that "these vile bodies will be changed and become like unto his glorious body." [See Philippians 3:21.]

These are our expectations. Now let all present put this question to themselves: Are our expectations well founded? In other words, are we seeking to purify ourselves? How can a Latter-day Saint feel justified in himself unless he is seeking to purify himself even as God is pure, unless he is seeking to keep his conscience void of offence before God and man every day of his life? We doubtless, many of us, walk from day to day and from week to week, and from month to month, before God, feeling under no condemnation, comporting ourselves properly and seeking earnestly and in all meekness for the Spirit of God to dictate our daily course; and yet there may be a certain time or times in our life, when we are greatly tried and perhaps overcome; even if this be so, that is no reason why we should not try again, and that too with redoubled energy and determination to accomplish our object.[7]

The Lord wishes to show leniency towards His children on earth, but He requires of them true repentance when they transgress or fail in any duty. He expects their obedience and that they will endeavor to cast aside all sin, to purify themselves and become indeed His people, His Saints, so that they may be prepared to come into His presence, be made like unto Him in all things and reign with Him in His glory. To accomplish this they must walk in the strait and narrow way, making their lives brighter and better, being filled with faith and charity, which is the pure love of Christ, and attending faithfully to every duty in the Gospel.[8]

If we could read in detail the life of Abraham or the lives of other great and holy men we would doubtless find that their efforts to be righteous were not always crowned with success. Hence we should not be discouraged if we should be overcome in a weak moment; but, on the contrary, straightway repent of the error or the wrong we may have committed, and as far as possible repair it, and then seek to God for renewed strength to go on and do better.

Abraham could walk perfectly before God day after day when he was leaving his father's house, and he showed evidences of a superior and well disciplined mind in the course he suggested when his herdsmen quarrelled with the herdsmen of his nephew Lot [see Genesis 13:1–9]. There came a time in Abraham's life however, which must have been very trying; in fact anything more severe can

We should strive day by day to improve our relationships with family members.

scarcely be conceived of; that was when the Lord called upon him to offer as a sacrifice his beloved and only son, even him through whom he expected the fulfilment of the great promise made him by the Lord; but through manifesting a proper disposition he was enabled to surmount the trial, and prove his faith and integrity to God [see Genesis 22:1–14]. It can hardly be supposed that Abraham inherited such a state of mind from his idolatrous parents; but it is consistent to believe that under the blessing of God he was enabled to acquire it, after going through a similar warfare with the flesh as we are, and doubtless being overcome at times and then overcoming until he was enabled to stand so severe a test.

"Let this same mind be in you," says the Apostle Paul, "which was also in Christ Jesus: who being in the form of God, thought it not robbery to be equal with God." [See Philippians 2:5–6.] Now every man that has this object before him will purify himself as God is pure, and try to walk perfectly before him. We have our little follies and our weaknesses; we should try to overcome them as fast as possible, and we should inculcate this feeling in the hearts of our children, that the fear of God may grow up with them from their very youth, and that they may learn to comport themselves properly before Him under all circumstances.

If the husband can live with his wife one day without quarrelling or without treating anyone unkindly or without grieving the Spirit of God in any way, that is well so far; he is so far perfect. Then let him try to be the same the next day. But supposing he should fail in this his next day's attempt, that is no reason why he should not succeed in doing so the third day. . . .

The Latter-day Saints should cultivate this ambition constantly which was so clearly set forth by the apostles in former days. We should try to walk each day so that our conscience would be void of offence before everybody. And God has placed in the Church certain means by which we can be assisted, namely, Apostles and Prophets and Evangelists, etc., "for the perfecting of the Saints," etc. [See Ephesians 4:11–12.] And he has also conferred upon us his Holy Spirit which is an unerring guide, standing, as an angel of God, at our side, telling us what to do and affording us strength and succor when adverse circumstances arise in our way. We must not allow ourselves to be discouraged whenever we discover our weakness. We can scarcely find an instance in all the glorious examples set us by the prophets, ancient or modern, wherein they permitted the Evil One to discourage them; but on the other hand they constantly sought to overcome, to win the prize and thus prepare themselves for a fulness of glory.[9] [See suggestion 4 on page 104.]

With divine help, we can live above the follies and vanities of the world.

When we once get it into our minds that we really have the power within ourselves through the gospel we have received, to conquer our passions, our appetites and in all things submit our will to the will of our Heavenly Father, and, instead of being the means of generating unpleasant feeling in our family circle, and those with whom we are associated, but assisting greatly to create a little heaven upon earth, then the battle may be said to be half won. One of the chief difficulties that many suffer from is, that we are too apt to forget the great object of life, the motive of our Heavenly Father in sending us here to put on mortality, as well as the holy calling with which we have been called; and hence, instead of rising above the little transitory things of time, we too often allow ourselves to come down to the level of the world without availing ourselves of the divine help which God has instituted, which alone can enable us to overcome them. We are no better than the rest of the world if we do not cultivate the feeling to be perfect, even as our Father in heaven is perfect.

This was the exhortation of the Savior to the former-day saints, who were people of like passions and who were subject to the same temptations as ourselves, and He knew whether the people could conform to it or not; the Lord never has, nor will He require things of His children which it is impossible for them to perform. The Elders of Israel who expect to go forth to the world to preach the gospel of salvation in the midst of a crooked and perverse generation, among a people who are full of evil and corruption should cultivate this spirit especially. And not only they, but everybody, every young man and woman belonging to this Church who is worthy to be called a saint should cultivate this desire to live up to this requirement that their consciences may be clear before God. It is a beautiful thing either in young or old to have this object in view; it is especially delightful to see our young people take a course that the light and intelligence of God can beam in their countenances, that they may have a correct understanding of life and be able to live above the follies and vanities of the world and the errors and wickedness of man.[10]

There is no necessity for Latter-day Saints to worry over the things of this world. They will all pass away. Our hearts should be set on things above; to strive after that perfection which was in Christ Jesus, who was perfectly obedient in all things unto the Father, and so obtained His great exaltation and became a pattern unto His brethren. Why should we fret and worry over these temporal things when our destiny is so grand and glorious? If we will cleave unto the Lord, keep His commandments, pattern after His perfections and reach out unto the eternal realities of His heavenly kingdom, all will be well with us and we shall triumph and obtain the victory in the end.[11]

In all your acts and conduct ever have the consciousness that you are now preparing and making yourselves a life to be continued through eternities; act upon no principle that you would be ashamed or unwilling to act upon in heaven, employ no means in the attainment of an object that a celestial enlightened conscience would disapprove. Whilst feelings and passions excite you to action, let principles pure, honorable, holy, and virtuous, always rule and govern.[12]

We cannot become perfect at once, but we can be a little better day by day.

The child grows from childhood to boyhood, and from boyhood to manhood, with a constant and steady growth; but he cannot tell how or when the growth occurs. He does not realize that he is growing; but by observing the laws of health and being prudent in his course he eventually arrives at manhood. So in reference to ourselves as Latter-day Saints. We grow and increase. We are not aware of it at the moment; but after a year or so we discover that we are, so to speak, away up the hill, nearing the mountain top. We feel that we have faith in the Lord; that His providences are always beneficial; that we are connected with Him; that He is actually our Father, and that He leads us along in life.[13]

Do not expect to become perfect at once. If you do, you will be disappointed. Be better today than you were yesterday, and be better tomorrow than you are today. The temptations that perhaps partially overcome us today, let them not overcome us so far tomorrow. Thus continue to be a little better day by day; and do not let your life wear away without accomplishing good to others as well as to ourselves.[14]

Each last day or each last week should be the best that we have ever experienced, that is, we should advance ourselves a little every day, in knowledge and wisdom, and in the ability to accomplish good. As we grow older we should live nearer the Lord each following day.[15] [See suggestion 5 on page 104.]

Suggestions for Study and Teaching

Consider these ideas as you study the chapter or as you prepare to teach. For additional help, see pages v–vii.

1. President Snow acknowledged that the command to be perfect causes concern for some Latter-day Saints (pages 95–97). As you study this chapter, look for counsel that might comfort someone who is troubled by the command to be perfect.
2. In the section beginning on page 95, the phrase "supernatural aid" refers to help from the Lord. In what ways does the Lord help us become perfect?
3. On page 97, examine President Snow's comments about Abraham and the early Latter-day Saint pioneers. What do you think it means to be perfect "in the sphere in which [we are] acting"? Ponder what you can do to become more perfect in your "feelings, . . . integrity, motives and determination."
4. President Snow said, "We must not allow ourselves to be discouraged whenever we discover our weakness" (page 101). How can we rise above feelings of discouragement? (For some examples, see pages 98–101.)
5. How does it help you to know that you should not "expect to become perfect at once"? (See page 103.) Think about specific ways you can follow President Snow's counsel to "be a little better day by day."
6. Look for one or two statements in this chapter that are particularly inspiring to you. What do you like about these statements?

Related Scriptures: 1 Nephi 3:7; 3 Nephi 12:48; Ether 12:27; Moroni 10:32–33; D&C 64:32–34; 67:13; 76:69–70

Teaching Help: "Individuals are touched when their contributions are acknowledged. You might make a special effort to acknowledge each person's comments and, if possible, make the comments part of class discussions" (*Teaching, No Greater Call,* 35–36).

Notes

1. In "Anniversary Exercises," *Deseret Evening News,* Apr. 7, 1899, 9.
2. In Eliza R. Snow Smith, *Biography and Family Record of Lorenzo Snow* (1884), 16.
3. In "Anniversary Exercises," 9.
4. In "Impressive Funeral Services," *Woman's Exponent,* Oct. 1901, 36.
5. *Deseret News: Semi-Weekly,* June 3, 1879, 1.
6. *Deseret News: Semi-Weekly,* June 3, 1879, 1.
7. *Deseret News: Semi-Weekly,* June 3, 1879, 1.
8. *Deseret Semi-Weekly News,* Oct. 4, 1898, 1.
9. *Deseret News: Semi-Weekly,* June 3, 1879, 1.
10. *Deseret News: Semi-Weekly,* June 3, 1879, 1.
11. *Deseret Semi-Weekly News,* Oct. 4, 1898, 1.
12. *Millennial Star,* Dec. 1, 1851, 363.
13. In Conference Report, Apr. 1899, 2.
14. *Improvement Era,* July 1901, 714.
15. *Improvement Era,* July 1899, 709.

When the Latter-day Saints were driven from their homes in Nauvoo, Illinois, many found joy amid their suffering.

CHAPTER 7

Faithfulness in Times of Trial: "From the Shadows into the Glorious Sunshine"

"Every man and woman who serves the Lord, no matter how faithful they may be, have their dark hours; but if they have lived faithfully, light will burst upon them and relief will be furnished."

From the Life of Lorenzo Snow

In February 1846 the Latter-day Saints were forced to leave their homes in Nauvoo, Illinois. As they prepared to make the trek west to their new promised land, they followed President Brigham Young's counsel to establish settlements along the way. They lived in temporary shelters and planted crops for the Saints who would follow them. After spending a short time in the state of Iowa at a settlement called Garden Grove, Lorenzo Snow and his family moved to a place the Saints called Mount Pisgah, also in Iowa. This settlement was named after the mountain where the prophet Moses had seen his people's promised land.

Several months after arriving in Mount Pisgah, Lorenzo was called to preside over the settlement. "By this time," he later recorded, "the Saints in Pisgah were in a very destitute condition, not only for food and clothing, but also for teams and wagons to proceed on their journey. Several families were entirely out of provision, and dependent on the charity of their neighbors, who, in most cases, were illy prepared to exercise that virtue. But, above all this, a sweeping sickness had visited the settlement, when there were not sufficient well ones to nurse the sick; and death followed in the wake, and fathers, mothers, children, brothers, sisters and dearest friends fell victims to the destroyer, and were buried with little ceremony, and some destitute of proper burial clothes. Thus were sorrow and mourning added to destitution."

Lorenzo knew these trials firsthand. He and his family experienced sickness, disappointments, and heartache, including the death of his newborn daughter Leonora. He wrote, "Little Leonora was taken sick and died, and with deep sorrow we bore her remains to their silent resting place, to be left alone, far from her father and the mother who gave her birth."

Under these circumstances, Lorenzo helped the Saints face their trials with faith. His sister Eliza wrote, "With an indomitable energy—a mind fruitful in expedients, and a firmness of purpose that never yielded to discouragement, he proved himself equal to an emergency which would have terrified men of ordinary abilities." She recalled, "In the first place he moved to arouse and combine the energies of the people." He organized the men into work groups. Some went to nearby towns to earn money for provisions and clothing. Others stayed at the camp, where they looked after the families there, planted crops, and produced and repaired goods that could be used in neighboring settlements.

In addition to helping the Saints work together, Lorenzo encouraged them to nourish themselves spiritually and to enjoy wholesome entertainment. "During the long winter months," he said, "I sought to keep up the spirits and courage of the Saints in Pisgah, not only by inaugurating meetings for religious worship and exercises, in different parts of the settlement, but also by making provisions for, and encouraging proper amusements of various kinds. . . .

"As a sample, I will attempt a description of one, which I improvised for the entertainment of as many as I could reasonably crowd together in my humble family mansion, which was a one-story edifice, about fifteen by thirty [about four and one-half meters by nine meters], constructed of logs, with a dirt roof and ground floor, displaying at one end a chimney of modest height, made of turf cut from the bosom of Mother Earth. Expressly for the occasion we carpeted the floor with a thin coating of clean straw, and draped the walls with white sheets drawn from our featherless beds.

One of the Latter-day Saints who settled in Mount Pisgah drew this sketch in a journal.

"How to light our hall suitably for the coming event was a consideration of no small moment, and one which levied a generous contribution on our ingenuity. But we succeeded. From the pit where they were buried, we selected the largest and fairest turnips—scooped out the interior, and fixed short candles in them, placing them at intervals around the walls, suspending others to the ceiling above, which was formed of earth and cane. Those lights imparted a very peaceable, quiet . . . influence, and the light reflected through those turnip rinds imparted a very picturesque appearance.

"During the evening exercises, several of my friends, in the warmest expressions possible, complimented me and my family for the peculiar taste and ingenuity displayed in those unique and inexpensive arrangements."

Lorenzo recalled that "the hours were enlivened, and happily passed." He and his guests entertained one another with speeches, songs, and recitations. He said, "At the close, all seemed perfectly satisfied, and withdrew, feeling as happy as though they were not homeless."[1] [See suggestion 1 on page 115.]

Teachings of Lorenzo Snow

Trials and tribulations help us improve spiritually and prepare for celestial glory.

It is impossible for us to work out our salvation and accomplish the purposes of God without trials or without sacrifices.[2]

Trials and tribulations have been the experience of the Latter-day Saints. God so designed that it should be. I daresay that in the [premortal] spirit world, when it was proposed to us to come into this probation, and pass through the experience that we are now receiving, it was not altogether pleasant and agreeable; the prospects were not so delightful in all respects as might have been desired. Yet there is no doubt that we saw and understood clearly there that, in order to accomplish our exaltation and glory, this was a necessary experience; and however disagreeable it might have appeared to us, we were willing to conform to the will of God, and consequently we are here.[3]

The Lord has determined in His heart that He will try us until He knows what He can do with us. He tried His Son Jesus. . . . Before He [the Savior] came upon earth the Father had watched His course and knew that He could depend upon Him when the salvation of worlds should be at stake; and He was not disappointed. So in regard to ourselves. He will try us, and continue to try us, in order that He may place us in the highest positions in life and put upon us the most sacred responsibilities.[4]

If we succeed in passing through the approaching fiery ordeals with our fidelity and integrity unimpeached, we may expect at the close of our trials, a great and mighty outpouring of the Spirit and power of God—a great endowment upon all who shall have remained true to their covenants. . . .

Some of our brethren have queried whether hereafter, they could feel themselves worthy of full fellowship with Prophets and Saints of old, who endured trials and persecutions; and with Saints . . . who suffered in Kirtland, in Missouri and Illinois. The brethren referred to have expressed regrets that they had not been associated in those scenes of suffering. If any of these are present, I will say, for the consolation of such, you have to wait but a short time and you will have similar opportunities, to your heart's content. You and I cannot be made perfect except through suffering: Jesus could not [see Hebrews 2:10]. In His prayer and agony in the Garden of Gethsemane, He foreshadowed the purifying process necessary in the lives of those whose ambition prompts them to secure the glory of a celestial kingdom. None should try to escape by resorting to any compromising measures.[5]

There is no other way in which the Saints can make spiritual improvement and be prepared for an inheritance in the celestial kingdom than through tribulation. It is the process by which knowledge is increased and peace will ultimately be established universally. It [has] been said that if all our surroundings were peaceful and prosperous now, we would become indifferent. It would be a condition that would be all that would be desired by a good many natures; they would not stretch out after the things of eternity.[6]

Take it individually or take it collectively, we have suffered and we shall have to suffer again, and why? Because the Lord requires it at our hands for our sanctification.[7] [See suggestion 2 on page 115.]

In times of trial, we can turn to our Father in Heaven for comfort and strength.

When we remain faithful during trials and temptations, we show that we love God more than we love the world.

Among our trials are temptations, by which we are enabled to show how much we value our religion. You are familiar with the experience of Job in that respect. He was given a knowledge of the resurrection, and of the Redeemer, and he knew that although he should die yet should he, in the latter days, see his Redeemer on the earth [see Job 19:25–26]. The temptations to which he was subjected showed that he valued these heavenly considerations above everything else. . . .

. . . Because God is our Friend we do not fear. We may have to continue to be subjected to many conditions that are disagreeable. By them we are enabled to show the angels that we love the things of God better than the things of the world.[8] [See suggestion 3 on page 115.]

As we remain faithful, the Lord strengthens us to overcome temptations and endure trials.

Many of you may have severe trials, that your faith may become more perfect, your confidence be increased, your knowledge of the powers of heaven be augmented; and this before your redemption takes place. If a stormy cloud sweep over the horizon . . . ; if the cup of bitter suffering be offered, and you compelled to partake; Satan let loose to go among you, with all his seductive powers of deceivings and cunning craftiness; the strong relentless arm of persecution lifted against you;—then, in *that* hour, lift up your heads and rejoice that you are accounted worthy to suffer thus with Jesus, the Saints, and holy prophets; and know that the period of your redemption has approached.

I feel, my brethren and sisters, to exhort you with heartfelt expression. Be of good cheer—be not disheartened; for assuredly the day rapidly comes when your tears shall be dried, your hearts comforted, and you shall eat of the products of your labours. . . .

Be honest, be virtuous, be honourable, be meek and lowly, courageous and bold, cultivate simplicity, be like the Lord; hold to the truth though through fire or sword, torture or death.[9]

From the time of our receiving the Gospel to the present, the Lord has from time to time given us trials and afflictions, if we may so call them; and sometimes these trials have been of that nature that we have found it very difficult to receive them without murmur and complaint. Yet at such times the Lord blessed us and gave us sufficient of His Spirit to enable us to overcome the temptations and endure the trials.[10]

Every man and woman who serves the Lord, no matter how faithful they may be, have their dark hours; but if they have lived faithfully, light will burst upon them and relief will be furnished.[11]

All that is required of us to make us perfectly safe under all circumstances of trouble or persecution, is to do the will of God, to be honest, faithful and to keep ourselves devoted to the principles that we have received; do right one by another; trespass upon no man's rights; live by every word that proceedeth from the mouth of God and his Holy Spirit will aid and assist us under all circumstances, and we will come out of the midst of it all abundantly blessed in our houses, in our families, in our flocks, in our fields—and in every way God will bless us. He will give us knowledge upon knowledge, intelligence upon intelligence, wisdom upon wisdom.

May God add his blessing upon this people. May we be faithful to ourselves, faithful to all the principles we have received, seeking one another's interests with all our heart, and God will pour out his Spirit upon us, and we will come off victorious in the end.[12] [See suggestion 3 on page 115.]

Looking back on difficult times, we see that our trials have helped us draw nearer to God.

When we contemplate what the Lord has done for us in the past, our present surroundings, and our future prospects, what a blest people we are! I have thought sometimes that one of the greatest virtues the Latter-day Saints could possess is gratitude to our Heavenly Father for that which He has bestowed upon us and the path over which He has led us. It may be that walking along in that path has not always been of the most pleasant character; but we have afterwards discovered that those circumstances which have been very unpleasant have often proved of the highest advantage to us.[13]

Every trial a man goes through, if he is faithful in that trial and does honor to God and his religion he has espoused, at the end of that trial or affliction that individual is nearer to God, nearer in regard to the increase of faith, wisdom, knowledge and power, and hence is more confident in calling upon the Lord for those things he desires. I have known individuals who have trembled at the idea of passing through certain ordeals who after they were through the temptation have said they could approach the Lord in more confidence and ask for such blessings as they desired. . . .

We have every reason to rejoice and to be full of joy and satisfaction, notwithstanding the difficulties that surround us. And how far have we advanced, how much knowledge have we obtained and how much more are we able to bear now than one, two or five years ago, and are we able to stand more now than a few years ago?

The Lord has strengthened us and increased us in our growth. Like the infant, when it grows up it knows not how it received gradual strength and the manner in which it increased in stature. It is larger this year than last. So in regard to our spiritual advancement. We feel stronger today than we did a year ago.[14]

The sacrifices you have made, the hardships you have endured and the privations you have suffered will . . . sink into insignificance, and you will rejoice that you have obtained the experience which they have furnished. . . . Some things we have to learn by that which we suffer, and knowledge secured in that way, though the process may be painful, will be of great value to us in the other life. . . .

. . . I know that your lives have not been all sunshine; you have doubtless passed through many a trial, and perhaps have come up through much tribulation; but by continued integrity you will soon emerge from the shadows into the glorious sunshine of the celestial world.[15] [See suggestion 4 below.]

Suggestions for Study and Teaching

Consider these ideas as you study the chapter or as you prepare to teach. For additional help, see pages v–vii.

1. Ponder the account on pages 107–10. How were many of the Saints in this account able to be happy despite their suffering? What can we do to encourage people who are experiencing trials?
2. Study President Snow's teachings about why we must have trials (pages 110–11). What do you think it means to "stretch out after the things of eternity"? Why do you think many people would not "stretch out after the things of eternity" without trials?
3. In what ways should we respond to trials and temptations? (For some examples, see pages 112–14.) How does the Lord help us in times of trial?
4. Read the last section in this chapter. What have you gained from the challenges you have experienced?

5. Look for one or two statements in this chapter that give you hope. What do you appreciate about the statements you have chosen? Consider ways you might share these truths with a family member or friend who needs encouragement.

Related Scriptures: Deuteronomy 4:29–31; Psalm 46:1; John 16:33; Romans 8:35–39; 2 Corinthians 4:17–18; Mosiah 23:21–22; 24:9–16; D&C 58:2–4

Teaching Help: Consider contacting a few participants in advance, asking them to prepare to share experiences that relate to the chapter. For example, before teaching from this chapter, it may be helpful to ask a few people to prepare to talk about what they have learned from their trials.

Notes

1. See Eliza R. Snow Smith, *Biography and Family Record of Lorenzo Snow* (1884), 89–93.
2. *Millennial Star,* Apr. 18, 1887, 245.
3. *Deseret Weekly,* Nov. 4, 1893, 609.
4. *Millennial Star,* Aug. 24, 1899, 532.
5. *Deseret News: Semi-Weekly,* Feb. 9, 1886, 1.
6. *Deseret News,* Apr. 11, 1888, 200; from a detailed paraphrase of a discourse Lorenzo Snow delivered in the April 1888 general conference.
7. *Deseret News,* Oct. 28, 1857, 270.
8. *Deseret News,* Apr. 11, 1888, 200.
9. "Address to the Saints in Great Britain," *Millennial Star,* Dec. 1, 1851, 364.
10. *Deseret Weekly,* Nov. 4, 1893, 609.
11. *Millennial Star,* Aug. 24, 1899, 531.
12. *Deseret News: Semi-Weekly,* Dec. 2, 1879, 1.
13. In Conference Report, Apr. 1899, 2.
14. *Deseret News,* Apr. 11, 1888, 200.
15. In "Old Folks Are at Saltair Today," *Deseret Evening News,* July 2, 1901, 1; message to a group of elderly Church members; prepared by Lorenzo Snow at age 88 and read by his son LeRoi.

CHAPTER 8

"Search Me, O God, and Know My Heart"

Righteous Latter-day Saints strive to "establish a character before God that could be relied upon in the hour of trial."

From the Life of Lorenzo Snow

On December 15, 1899, President Lorenzo Snow, then President of the Church, spoke at the funeral of President Franklin D. Richards, who had served as President of the Quorum of the Twelve Apostles. Near the end of his sermon, President Snow said, "I ask the Lord of Israel to bless the Latter-day Saints and that we may be prepared for the events of the near future, with our hearts right before the Lord."

Illustrating the need to keep "our hearts right before the Lord," President Snow told of an experience he and President Richards shared in the 1850s, when they were new Apostles. At that time, President Brigham Young led a reformation in the Church, calling on Latter-day Saints everywhere to repent and renew their commitment to righteous living.

"When President Young was aroused to call upon the people to repent and reform," recalled President Snow, "he talked very strongly as to what ought to be done with some people—that their Priesthood ought to be taken from them, because of their failure to magnify it as they should have done. The brethren who lived in those days will remember how vigorously he spoke in this direction. Well, it touched Brother Franklin's heart, and it touched mine also; and we talked the matter over to ourselves. We concluded we would go to President Young and offer him our Priesthood. If he felt in the name of the Lord that we had not magnified our Priesthood,

President Franklin D. Richards

we would resign it. We went to him, saw him alone, and told him this. I guess there were tears in his eyes when he said, 'Brother Lorenzo, Brother Franklin, you have magnified your Priesthood satisfactorily to the Lord. God bless you.'"[1]

Throughout his life, President Snow wanted his heart to be right before the Lord, and he also encouraged the Saints to examine their own worthiness. He spoke with "a view of riveting more forcibly upon our understanding" the need to establish "a proper character, as Latter-day Saints, before God our Father."[2] [See suggestion 1 on page 125.]

Teachings of Lorenzo Snow

If we have established a proper character, we can confidently invite God to search our hearts.

I am under the strongest impression, that the most valuable consideration, and that which will be of the most service when we return to the spirit world, will be that of having established a proper and well defined character as faithful and consistent Latter-day Saints in this state of probation.

In cases where a stranger applies for employment, or an office of trust, it is often required that he produce papers attesting his worthiness, from reliable parties, letters of recommendation and of introduction which are exceedingly useful in their way, assisting in obtaining favors and privileges which otherwise would be difficult to secure. It is, however, comparatively easy to obtain a written character, as it is termed, a character that one can put in his pocket; and, indeed, according to my observation it is not infrequently the case that people are the bearers of written characters which their real and true character fails to attest.

There are those among us who are recognized as members of this Church who take a vast amount of pains to be favorably known by those around them, but whose real character, or the inwardness so to speak, of such people, is veiled or disguised. . . . Now this prayer that I [refer] to—"Search me, O God, and know my heart: try me, and know my thoughts; and see if there be any wicked way in me, and lead me in the way everlasting" [Psalm 139:23–24]—is very significant; it was a prayer that David in the principal course of his life could conscientiously and with a degree of confidence offer up to the Lord. But there were times when he would feel the faltering and quivering sensation of weakness in offering up a prayer of this kind.

I have reason to believe that many of the Latter-day Saints, during a great portion of their lives, could approach the Lord in all confidence and make this same prayer—"Search me, O God, and know my heart, and see if there be any wicked way in me;" but if we, as a people, could live so as to be able at all times to bow before the Lord and offer up a prayer like this, what a delightful thing it would be, what an attainment we should have acquired in righteousness and good works! . . . I would recommend that [every person] adopt this prayer of David, and see how near he can live according to the light that he has, so as to make it in all sincerity part of his devotions to God. Many fail in coming up to this standard of excellence because they do things in secret where mortal eye cannot penetrate, that have a direct tendency to alienate them from the Almighty and to grieve away the Spirit of God. Such persons cannot in their private closet use this prayer; they could not unless they had repented of their sins and repaired the wrong they may have committed, and determined to do better in the future than they had done in the past, and to establish a character before God that could be relied upon in the hour of trial, and that would fit them to associate with holy beings and with the Father himself when they shall have passed into the spirit world.

. . . We must be true men and true women; we must have faith largely developed, and we must be worthy of the companionship of the Holy Ghost to aid us in the work of righteousness all the day long, to enable us to sacrifice our own will to the will of the Father, to battle against our fallen nature, and to do right for the love of doing right, keeping our eye single to the honor and glory of God. To do this there must be an inward feeling of the mind that is conscious of the responsibility that we are under, that recognizes the fact that the eye of God is upon us and that our every act and the motives that prompt it must be accounted for; and we must be constantly *en rapport* [in harmony] with the Spirit of the Lord.[3] [See suggestion 2 on page 125.]

Examples in the scriptures teach us how to improve our character.

There are many things that I admire in the character of the prophets, and especially in that of Moses. I admire his determination to carry out the word and will of God with regard to Israel, and his readiness to do everything that was in the power of man, assisted by the Almighty; and above all I admire his integrity and fidelity to the Lord. . . .

God admires the men and women today who pursue a course of rectitude and who, notwithstanding the powers of Satan that are arrayed against them, can say, Get thee behind me Satan [see Luke 4:8], and who live a righteous, a Godly life, and such people have influence with God and their prayers avail much [see James 5:16]. Moses, for instance, had such power with the Almighty as to change His [God's] purpose on a certain occasion. It will be remembered that the Lord became angry with the Israelites and declared to Moses that He would destroy them, and He would take Moses and make of him a great people, and would bestow upon him and his posterity what He had promised to Israel. But this great leader and lawgiver, faithful to his trust, stood in the gap and there pled with the Lord on behalf of his people; by the power that he could exercise and did exercise, he was the means of saving the people from threatened destruction. [See Exodus 32:9–11; Joseph Smith Translation, Exodus 32:12.] How noble and glorious Moses must have appeared in the eyes of the Lord, and what a source of satisfaction it must have been to Him to know that His chosen people, in their obstinate and ignorant condition, had such a man at their head.

In Jonah again we find an interesting trait of character. When upon the raging water, and fears were expressed by the sailors as to their ability to save the ship, Jonah feeling conscience stricken at the course he had taken in not proceeding to Nineveh as commanded of the Lord, came forward and confessed himself as being the cause of the disaster that was about to befall them, and was willing to be sacrificed in the interest of those on board. [See Jonah

Although Jonah "exhibited weaknesses," we can learn from his "grand and admirable" characteristics.

1:4–12.] Also in other prophets and men of God, although they may have on certain occasions, like Jonah, exhibited weaknesses, there is something really grand and admirable shown in their character.[4] [See suggestion 3 on page 125.]

Righteous character traits develop within us gradually as we exercise faith and repent of our wrongdoings.

Such traits of character as we find evinced in the ancient worthies are not the products of accident or chance, neither are they acquired in a day, a week, a month, or a year, but are gradual developments, the results of continued faithfulness to God and to truth, independent of either the plaudits or criticisms of men.

. . . It is important that we, as Latter-day Saints, should understand and bear in mind that salvation comes through the grace of God and through the development in us of those principles that governed those righteous people before mentioned. The idea is not to do good because of the praise of men; but to do good because in doing good we develop godliness within us, and this being the case we shall become allied to godliness, which will in time become part and portion of our being. . . .

Do we not at times do things that we feel sorry for having done? It may be all very well provided we stop doing such things when we know them to be wrong; when we see the evil and then reform, that is all we can do, and all that can be asked of any man. But undoubtedly, it is too much the case with some that they consider and fear the publicity of the wrong they commit more than committing the wrong itself; they wonder what people will say when they hear of it, etc. And, on the other hand, some are induced to do certain things in order to receive the approbation of their friends, and if their acts fail to draw forth favorable comments or to be recognized, they feel as though their labor had been lost, and what good they may have done was a total failure.

Now, if we really desire to draw near to God; if we wish to place ourselves in accord with the good spirits of the eternal worlds; if we wish to establish within ourselves that faith which we read about and by which ancient Saints performed such wonderful works we must, after we obtain the Holy Spirit, hearken to its whisperings and conform to its suggestions, and by no act of our lives drive it from us: It is true that we are weak erring creatures liable at any time to grieve the Spirit of God; but so soon as we discover ourselves in a fault, we should repent of that wrongdoing and as far as possible repair or make good the wrong we may have committed. By taking this course we strengthen our character, we advance our own cause, and we fortify ourselves against temptation; and in time we shall have so far overcome as to really astonish ourselves at the progress we have made in self-government, and improvement.[5] [See suggestion 4 on page 125.]

As we preserve our righteous character, we draw nearer to the Lord.

We have received a Gospel that is marvelous in its operations: through obedience to its requirements we may receive the choicest blessings that have ever been promised to or bestowed upon mankind in any age of the world. But, like the child with the toy or the plaything, we too often satisfy ourselves with the perishable things of time, forgetting the opportunities we have of developing within us the great, the eternal principles of life and truth. The Lord wishes to establish a closer and more intimate relationship between Himself and us; He wishes to elevate us in the scale of being and intelligence, and this can only be done through the medium of the everlasting Gospel which is specially prepared for this purpose. Says the Apostle John: "Every man that has this hope in him purifieth himself, even as He (Christ) is pure." [1 John 3:3.] Are the Latter-day Saints applying the principles of the Gospel to their lives, and thus accomplishing the design of God?

. . . What can we do under the circumstances to elevate ourselves still higher in the righteousness of our God? What advantages, blessings and privileges does this system of salvation, which we have obeyed, afford, and what means shall be employed to realize them? If there should be a sacrifice demanded it will be very opportune for all those who wish to make their religion a study, and who are endeavoring to conform to its requirements, by living it in their everyday life, to show their willingness to bow to the will of Jehovah, acknowledging his hand in adversity as in prosperity.

. . . It would be well to examine ourselves, hold communion with ourselves in the secret closet, to ascertain how we stand . . . before the Lord, so that if need be we may renew our diligence and faithfulness, and increase our good works.

There is no doubt, speaking of the people as a whole, that we are greatly improving in the sight of God. But although this is undoubtedly the case, I am convinced there are persons among us endowed with spiritual gifts and susceptible of cultivation, that could be exercised, if they chose, to a far greater extent than they are, and who could move much faster in the ways of holiness and get much nearer to the Lord. But the spirit which attends the things of this world is operating upon them to that extent that they do not increase those spiritual powers and blessings; they do not place themselves in that close relationship to the Lord that it is their privilege.[6]

Our character, as Latter-day Saints, should be preserved inviolate, at whatever cost or sacrifice. Character, approved of God is worth securing, even at the expense of a life-time of constant self-denial.

While thus living we may look forward . . . , with full assurance that . . . we shall be crowned with the sons and daughters of God, and possess the wealth and glory of a Celestial kingdom.[7] [See suggestion 5 below.]

Suggestions for Study and Teaching

Consider these ideas as you study the chapter or as you prepare to teach. For additional help, see pages v–vii.

1. As you review the account on pages 117 and 119, what do you learn from the actions of Elder Lorenzo Snow and Elder Franklin D. Richards? Consider how you might share these principles with family members or others.
2. President Snow said, "We must be true men and true women" (page 120). What do you think it means to be a true man or a true woman?
3. Consider President Snow's observations about the examples of Moses and Jonah (pages 121–22). What do you see in each of these accounts that can help us improve our character?
4. Ponder the second full paragraph on page 123. Why do you think we need to be aware of our faults in order to strengthen our character? How can we allow ourselves to see our own shortcomings without becoming discouraged?
5. Review President Snow's counsel in the final section of the chapter (pages 123–25). Consider making time to examine yourself and determine how you stand before the Lord.

Related Scriptures: Psalm 24:3–5; 2 Peter 1:2–11; Mosiah 3:19; Alma 48:11–13, 17; Ether 12:25–28; D&C 11:12–14; 88:63–68

Teaching Help: Ask participants to choose one section in the chapter and read it silently. Invite them to gather in groups of two or three people who chose the same section and discuss what they have learned.

Notes

1. *Deseret Semi-Weekly News,* Dec. 19, 1899, 5.
2. *Deseret News: Semi-Weekly,* Aug. 15, 1882, 1.
3. *Deseret News: Semi-Weekly,* Aug. 15, 1882, 1.
4. *Deseret News: Semi-Weekly,* Aug. 15, 1882, 1.
5. *Deseret News: Semi-Weekly,* Aug. 15, 1882, 1.
6. *Deseret News: Semi-Weekly,* Aug. 15, 1882, 1.
7. *Deseret News: Semi-Weekly,* Feb. 9, 1886, 1.

CHAPTER 9

Sacred Family Relationships

"If we are faithful we will associate with each other in an immortal and glorious state. . . . Those connections formed here, that are of the most enduring character, shall exist in eternity."

From the Life of Lorenzo Snow

Anticipating his 70th birthday, Lorenzo Snow invited all his children and their families to gather in Brigham City, Utah, for a "grand re-union and anniversary celebration." He arranged for their lodging and food and for programs that all, including the young children, would enjoy. "The more I reflect upon this subject [of a family reunion]," he wrote, "the greater are my anxieties and desires for a family gathering, that I may see you all once in my life, and give you a father's blessing." He urged them to let nothing prevent their attendance "except the most serious and insurmountable obstacles."[1]

The Snow family gathered from May 7 to 9, 1884, and enjoyed music, theatrical productions, speeches, poetry, games, food, and friendly conversation.[2] President Snow's sister Eliza reported that throughout the event, he attended "various meetings of the family, and in the capacity of Patriarch, . . . engaged in conferring blessings upon members" and giving "much fatherly counsel, instruction and admonition." As the reunion drew to a close, all the family came together to hear him speak. According to Eliza's record, he expressed "his pleasure and gratitude to God that he now enjoyed the happiness of beholding the pleasant and smiling faces of his large family, and the good he anticipated would result from this reunion." Looking out over his family, President Snow exclaimed: "My heart is filled to overflowing with warmest feelings of gratitude to my Heavenly Father. . . . Language is powerless to express the deep feelings of my heart for this holy and sacred opportunity on

Children are "a precious heritage from the Lord."

this the celebration of my seventieth birthday, of standing here and beholding this glorious and heavenly inspiring spectacle."

President Snow continued: "This is the last family re-union we have reason to expect this side of the spirit world. May the God of our fathers help us to keep His laws, live honorable lives, preserve inviolate our virtue and integrity, listen to the whisperings of the Holy Spirit, and seek diligently to purify ourselves, that not a single member of this family be lost by deviating from the straight and narrow path, but may we all prove ourselves worthy to come forth in the morning of the first resurrection, crowned with glory, perpetuating in immortality the family union, and continue to increase down through the endless ages of eternity."[3] [See suggestion 1 on page 134.]

Teachings of Lorenzo Snow

Family relationships are sacred and can grow stronger in eternity.

Encourage marriage, . . . and impress upon [others] the sacredness of that relation and the obligation they are under to observe that great commandment which was given of God to our first parents, to multiply and replenish the earth [see Genesis 1:28]. This is all the more necessary, in view of the present tendency in the world to disregard that law and to dishonor the marriage covenant. It is saddening to note the frequency of divorces in the land and the growing inclination to look upon children as an encumbrance instead of as a precious heritage from the Lord.[4]

[The Lord] has shown us that if we are faithful we will associate with each other in an immortal and glorious state; that those connections formed here, that are of the most enduring character, shall exist in eternity.[5]

The associations that are formed here, will be possessed by [us] in the eternal worlds. Fathers, mothers, sisters, brothers—yes, mothers who see their lovely ones expiring by their side, know that they will be theirs in the spirit world, and that they will have them as they lay them down. The wife when she sees her husband dying, when his life is ebbing away from him, she knows she will have him again, and she sees comfort, consolation and joy, that is given by the revelations of the Almighty, in that she will possess her husband in the eternal worlds. The same forms of relationship here will still exist beyond the veil; the ties here formed will grow stronger in the other life which is to come. And the Latter-day Saints feel an assurance, because God has given it unto them.[6] [See suggestion 2 on page 134.]

Faithful Latter-day Saints who are unable to marry or raise children in this life will be able to receive all the blessings of exaltation in the life to come.

A lady came into our office the other day and asked to see me on a private matter. She informed me that she felt very badly, because her opportunities for getting a husband had not been favorable. . . . She wanted to know what her condition would be in the other life, if she did not succeed getting a husband in this life. I suppose this question arises in the hearts of our young people. . . . I desire to give a little explanation for the comfort and consolation of parties in this condition. There is no Latter-day Saint who dies after having lived a faithful life who will lose anything because of having failed to do certain things when opportunities were not furnished him or her. In other words, if a young man or a young woman has no opportunity of getting married, and they live faithful lives up to the time of their death, they will have all the blessings, exaltation and glory that any man or woman will have who had this opportunity and improved it. That is sure and positive. . . .

People who have no opportunity of marrying in this life, if they die in the Lord, will have means furnished them by which they can secure all the blessings necessary for persons in the married condition. The Lord is merciful and kind, and He is not unjust. There is no injustice in Him; yet we could scarcely look upon it as being just when a woman or a man dies without having had the opportunity of marrying if it could not be remedied in the other life. There would be injustice in that, and we know that the Lord is not an unjust being. My sister Eliza R. Snow, I believe, was just as good a woman as any Latter-day Saint woman that ever lived, and she lived in an unmarried state until she was beyond the condition of raising a family. . . . I cannot for one moment imagine that she will lose a single thing on that account. It will be made up to her in the other life, and she will have just as great a kingdom as she would have had if she had had the opportunity in this life of raising a family.[7]

When husband and wife enjoy a oneness of feeling, they encourage love and kindness in the home.

See that the little, trifling misunderstandings in domestic concerns do not poison your happiness.[8]

Wives, be faithful to your husbands. I know you have to put up with many unpleasant things, and your husbands have to put up with some things as well. Doubtless you are sometimes tried by your husbands, on account perhaps of the ignorance of your husbands, or perchance at times because of your own ignorance. . . .

. . . I do not say but that your husbands are bad—just as bad as you are, and probably some of them are worse; but, never mind: try to endure the unpleasantnesses which arise at times, and when you meet each other in the next life you will feel glad that you put up with those things.

To the husbands, I say: Many of you do not value your wives as you should. . . . Be kind to them. When they go out to meeting, you carry the baby at least half the time. When it needs rocking, and you have not much to do, rock it. Be kind when sometimes you have to make a little sacrifice to do so; feel kind anyway, no matter what the sacrifice.[9]

The men ought to be more fatherly at home, possessing finer feelings in reference to their wives and children, neighbors and friends, more kindly and godlike. When I go into a family I do admire to see the head of that family administering to it as a man of God, kind and gentle, filled with the Holy Ghost and with the wisdom and understanding of Heaven.[10]

If you ever secure a union in any family in Zion, if you ever secure that heavenly union which is necessary to exist there you have got to bind that family together in one, and there has got to be the Spirit of the Lord in the head of that family and he should possess that light and that intelligence which if carried out in the daily life and conduct of those individuals, will prove the salvation of that family, for he holds their salvation in his hands.

He goes to work and associates his feelings and affections with theirs as far as lies in his power, and endeavors to secure all those things that are necessary for their comfort and welfare, and they on the other part have got to turn round and manifest the same feeling, the same kindness and the same disposition, and to the utmost of their ability manifest feelings of gratitude for the blessings which they receive.

This is necessary that there may be a oneness of feeling, or oneness of sentiment and a corresponding affection, that they being one may be bound together in this way.[11]

When [men] kneel down in the presence of their wives and children they ought to be inspired by the gift and power of the Holy Ghost that the husband may be such a man as a good wife will honor, and that the gift and power of God may be upon them continually. They ought to be one in their families that the Holy Ghost might descend upon them, and they ought to live so that the wife through prayer may become sanctified, that she may see the necessity of sanctifying herself in the presence of her husband and in the presence of her children that they may be one together in order that the man and the wife may be pure element, suitable to occupy a place in the establishment and formation of the kingdom of God, that they may breathe a pure spirit and impart pure instruction to their children and to their children's children.[12] [See suggestion 3 on pages 134–35.]

Children learn the gospel best when their parents seek inspiration and set good examples.

This is not our work that we are engaged in, it is the work of God. We are directed in our movements by a superior intelligence. . . . The future of this kingdom will rest on our offspring; and its power and ultimate triumph, on their education and proper training. If we wish to sway a proper influence over our families, we must show them good examples as well as give them good precepts. We should be able to say, do as I do, as well as to say do as I say.[13]

Parents should strive to "bind [their] family together in one."

Strive to teach your children in such a way, both by example and precept, that they will unhesitatingly follow in your footsteps and become as valiant for the truth as you have been.[14]

Men who wish to retain their standing before God in the holy priesthood must have the spirit of prophecy, and be qualified to administer life and salvation to the people; and [even] if they cannot do it to the world they must do it at home, in their families, in their shops and in the streets that their hearts may be inspired with words of life at their firesides, in teaching the gospel to their children and to their neighbors as much so as when they are speaking to their brethren from this stand. This having a little of the Spirit when before the people and then laying it aside will not do. Some men will speak to the people and then go home . . . , and instead of having the words of life in them they become perfectly dry and dead, but this will not do any longer.

It becomes the duties of fathers in Israel to wake up and become saviors of men, that they may walk before the Lord in that strength of faith and that determined energy that will insure them the inspiration of the Almighty to teach the words of life to their families. . . .

In this we will see a spirit of determination that will enable us to become one, that we may learn how to love each other, and I pray to the Lord that he will deposit that love in each of our hearts which he deposited in Jesus his Son, and that he will continue to deposit a knowledge of that which is good.[15]

It is the business of the father to be qualified to teach and instruct his children, and to lay principles before them, so that by conforming to those instructions they can be the most happy that their natures are susceptible of in a state of childhood, while at the same time they learn the principles upon which they can gain the most happiness and enjoyment in a state of [adult]hood.[16]

Our children, if we are diligent in cultivating in ourselves the pure principles of life and salvation, will grow up in the knowledge of these things and be able with greater facility than ourselves, to promote the order of heaven and establish happiness and peace around them.[17] [See suggestions 4 and 5 on page 135.]

Suggestions for Study and Teaching

Consider these ideas as you study the chapter or as you prepare to teach. For additional help, see pages v–vii.

1. Review President Snow's feelings about bringing his entire family together (pages 127, 129). What are some good results that can come when we bring our families together? How can we help our families stay united?

2. In what ways is the second full paragraph on page 129 relevant today? What can we do to help the youth of the Church understand the sacredness of the marriage covenant? What can we do to help them look forward to marriage and parenthood?

3. President Snow said that "little, trifling misunderstandings" can "poison [our] happiness" in the home (page 131). What are

some specific ideas that can help us avoid this "poison"? (For some examples, see pages 131–34.)

4. Study the section starting on page 132. Why do you think parents need to be able to say "do as I do" in addition to "do as I say"? In what ways can parents teach by example? What are some principles you have learned because of your parents' good examples?

5. President Snow expressed concern about parents who teach with power at church but not at home (pages 133–34). Think about what you can do to share "the words of life" with your family.

Related Scriptures: 1 Nephi 8:10–12; Helaman 5:12; D&C 68:25–28; 93:40–50; 132:19–20

Teaching Help: "You should be careful not to talk more than necessary or to express your opinion too often. These actions can cause learners to lose interest. . . . Your main concern should be helping others learn the gospel, not making an impressive presentation. This includes providing opportunities for learners to teach one another" (*Teaching, No Greater Call,* 64).

Notes

1. See Eliza R. Snow Smith, *Biography and Family Record of Lorenzo Snow* (1884), 453–54.
2. See *Biography and Family Record of Lorenzo Snow,* 461–83.
3. In *Biography and Family Record of Lorenzo Snow,* 484–86.
4. In "Prest. Snow to Relief Societies," *Deseret Evening News,* July 9, 1901, 1; this address was given directly to women in the Relief Society.
5. *Deseret News,* Apr. 11, 1888, 200; from a detailed paraphrase of a discourse Lorenzo Snow delivered in the April 1888 general conference.
6. *Salt Lake Daily Herald,* Oct. 11, 1887, 2.
7. *Millennial Star,* Aug. 31, 1899, 547–48.
8. *Deseret News,* Oct. 21, 1857, 259.
9. "The Grand Destiny of Man," *Deseret Evening News,* July 20, 1901, 22.
10. *Deseret News: Semi-Weekly,* Mar. 31, 1868, 2.
11. *Deseret News,* Mar. 11, 1857, 3; in the original source, page 3 is incorrectly labeled as page 419.
12. *Deseret News,* Jan. 14, 1857, 355.
13. *Deseret News,* July 26, 1865, 338.
14. In "Scandinavians at Saltair," *Deseret Evening News,* Aug. 17, 1901, 8.
15. *Deseret News,* Jan. 14, 1857, 355.
16. *Deseret News,* Jan. 28, 1857, 371.
17. *Deseret News,* Oct. 21, 1857, 259.

On April 6, 1892, thousands of people gathered to witness the capstone being secured on the highest spire of the Salt Lake Temple.

CHAPTER 10

"Come into the Temples"

"The prospects that God has opened up to our view are wonderful and grand; the imagination cannot conceive of them. Come into the Temples and we will show you."

From the Life of Lorenzo Snow

Soon after his baptism and confirmation, Lorenzo Snow began attending meetings in the Kirtland Temple. There, with the Prophet Joseph Smith and other Church leaders, he received great spiritual blessings. In his journal he reported: "There we had the gift of prophecy—the gift of tongues—the interpretation of tongues—visions and marvelous dreams were related—the singing of heavenly choirs was heard, and wonderful manifestations of the healing power, through the administrations of the Elders, were witnessed. The sick were healed—the deaf made to hear—the blind to see and the lame to walk, in very many instances. It was plainly manifest that a sacred and divine influence—a spiritual atmosphere pervaded that holy edifice."[1]

Lorenzo Snow loved the Kirtland Temple, knowing that "the Son of God, in His glory, had honored it with His royal presence." Consequently, he was awestruck when he first stood at a pulpit there to teach. "No language can describe my feelings," he said, "when, for the first time, I stood up in one of those pulpits to address an audience—a pulpit on the breastwork of which, only a short time before, this holy Personage stood—*'his hair as white as pure snow, his eyes as a flame of fire'*—where also Moses, Elias and Elijah came and committed the keys of their dispensations to Joseph Smith." [See D&C 110.][2]

Many years later, on April 6, 1892, President Lorenzo Snow stood before another gathering, this time in front of the almost-completed Salt Lake Temple. About 40,000 Latter-day Saints crowded into the enclosure surrounding Temple Square, and about 10,000 more "occupied the tops of adjoining houses and places from which a view could be obtained."[3] The multitude had gathered for a ceremony in which the capstone would be secured on the temple's highest spire. Later that day the statue of the angel Moroni would be placed on the capstone. By assignment from the First Presidency, President Snow, who was then President of the Quorum of the Twelve Apostles, was to lead the Saints in the Hosanna Shout. As he explained the Hosanna Shout to the multitude, he expressed his love and enthusiasm for temple work.

"The words of the shout, Hosanna!" he said, "to be uttered upon, or after, the laying of the capstone to-day, were introduced by President Joseph Smith at the Kirtland Temple, and were there used at a solemn assemblage where the power of God was manifested and the vision of the Almighty was opened up to the brethren. This is no ordinary order, but is—and we wish it to be distinctly understood—a sacred shout, and employed only on extraordinary occasions like the one now before us. We wish it also to be distinctly understood that we want the brethren and sisters not only to express the words, but that their hearts shall be full of thanksgiving to the God of heaven, who has accomplished, through our agency, this mighty and extraordinary labor. Thirty-nine years ago to-day the foundation-stone—the corner-stone—of this Temple was laid, and in reflecting and meditating upon the wonderful blessings that God has bestowed upon us, His people, during this number of years that have passed since that time, we wish the Saints to feel when they pronounce this shout that it comes from their hearts. Let your hearts be filled with thanksgiving." He demonstrated the Hosanna Shout and then said, "Now when we go before the Temple, and this shout goes forth, we want every man and every woman to shout these words to the very extent of their voices, so that every house in this city may tremble, the people in every portion of this city hear it, and it may reach to the eternal worlds."[4]

The following report of the capstone ceremony illustrates the Saints' reverence and excitement during the event:

"Just as the hour of noon was reached, President Wilford Woodruff stepped to the front of the platform, in full view of the assembled multitude, in whose midst a solemn stillness reigned. A thrill went through the hearts of the people as he spoke:

"'Attention, all ye house of Israel, and all ye nations of the earth! We will now lay the top stone of the Temple of our God, the foundation of which was laid and dedicated by the Prophet, Seer and Revelator Brigham Young.'

"President Woodruff then pressed an electric button, and the Temple capstone moved securely into its position. The scene that followed is beyond the power of language to describe. The venerable President of the Twelve, Apostle Lorenzo Snow, came forward and led forty thousand Saints in shouting in concert:

"'Hosanna! hosanna! hosanna! to God and the Lamb. Amen, amen, and amen!

"'Hosanna! hosanna! hosanna! to God and the Lamb. Amen, amen, and amen!

"'Hosanna! hosanna! hosanna! to God and the Lamb. Amen, amen, and amen!'

"Each shout was accompanied by the waving of handkerchiefs. . . . The eyes of thousands were moistened with tears in the fulness of their joy. The ground seemed to tremble with the volume of sound which sent forth its echoes to the surrounding hills. A grander or more imposing spectacle than this ceremony of laying the Temple capstone is not recorded in history. The hosannas had scarce ceased when the vast congregation burst forth in the glorious inspirational hymn, 'The Spirit of God like a fire is burning.'"[5]

President Woodruff dedicated the Salt Lake Temple exactly one year later, on April 6, 1893, after the Saints had labored 40 years to complete it. President Lorenzo Snow was called to serve as the first president of that temple, and he fulfilled this calling until he became President of the Church in September 1898. A portrait of President Snow hangs in the Salt Lake Temple today, in remembrance of his devotion to what he called the "mighty work that we are accomplishing" in the house of the Lord.[6] [See suggestion 1 on page 144.]

Teachings of Lorenzo Snow

In temples we learn of the marvelous blessings God has prepared for the faithful.

The prospects that God has opened up to our view are wonderful and grand; the imagination cannot conceive of them. Come into the Temples and we will show you. Many of you, I presume, have been there, and have heard the marvelous things that God has prepared for those that love Him and continue faithful to the end. . . .

. . . He has prepared everything for the Latter-day Saints that they could possibly wish or imagine in order to effect their complete happiness throughout the vast eternities.[7] [See suggestion 2 on pages 144–45.]

Through temple ordinances we form sacred ties that can bind families together for time and eternity.

Think of the promises that are made to you in the beautiful and glorious ceremony that is used in the marriage covenant in the Temple. When two Latter-day Saints are united together in marriage, promises are made to them concerning their offspring that reach from eternity to eternity.[8]

We have received much wisdom and knowledge of things which astonish the world when we speak of them. We have learned that, in temples, we are able to form ties which are not dissolved at death, but which reach into eternity; sacred ties which bind families together for time and eternity.[9] [See suggestion 3 on page 145.]

In temples we receive the ordinances of exaltation in behalf of our kindred dead.

Every son and daughter of God will have the opportunity necessary for exaltation and glory. . . . There is but one way by which exaltation and glory can be secured. We have to be baptized for the remission of sins and have hands laid upon us for the reception of the Holy Ghost. These and other ordinances are absolutely necessary for exaltation and glory; and where individuals have lived when the Gospel has not been accessible, these things can be attended to by their friends. We have come into the world now in order to do these things—at least, it is one of the chief objects of our coming. We cannot lay too great stress upon the importance of this work.[10]

We did not come into this world accidentally. We came for a special purpose, and it was undoubtedly through certain arrangements in the other life where we dwelt that we came into this life. Well, in the Temples we are accomplishing a great work in reference to our kindred dead. We have from time to time important manifestations that God approved of this labor that we are performing in our Temples. Most extraordinary manifestations have been experienced by individuals that are laboring for their ancestry. It is a mighty work that we are accomplishing. Thousands of persons have been baptized for their dead during the progress of our labors in the Temples. . . .

Now, in our Temples we allow persons to come in, after they have traced their ancestry, no matter how far back, and to be baptized for their dead father, grandfather, and great grandfather and so on, just as far as they can trace their line. Then we allow them to have the wives sealed to their husbands, all along the ancestry line, as far as they can trace it. Take the case of a virtuous young man who lived before the Gospel was introduced to the children of men. . . . He married a wife, and raised a family; but he never had the privilege of receiving the Gospel, as you and I have. However, he taught his family the principles of morality, and he was affectionate and kind to his wife and children. What more could he do? He should not be condemned because he did not receive the Gospel; for there was no Gospel to receive. He should not lose his wife because when he married her he could not go into a Temple and have her sealed to him for time and eternity. He acted according to the best knowledge that he had, and she was married to him for time, according to the custom of the country. We respect that marriage, solemnized according to the laws of his country. . . . We seal children to their parents and wives to their husbands, all along the line.[11]

The Savior said on a certain occasion, "Verily, verily, I say unto you, the hour is coming, and now is, when the dead shall hear

Parents can help their children prepare to accept the invitation to come into the temple.

the voice of the Son of God;" and He continued and made this remarkable expression: "and they that hear shall live." [John 5:25.] I believe there will be very few who will not receive the truth. They will hear the voice of the Son of God; they will hear the voice of the Priesthood of the Son of God, and they will receive the truth and live. These brethren and sisters that are laboring so industriously in the temples will have the honor of being, as it were, saviors to their kindred and friends in whose favor they administered these ordinances.[12] [See suggestion 4 on page 145.]

We should strive to perform temple and family history work, even if it requires sacrifice on our part.

Now, it should be an object in every man's and woman's mind to come into our Temples and to perform this labor. It is a great labor, and an important one, too. When we go back into the other life and find our dead friends living there, if we have not performed the labor that is necessary for their exaltation and glory we shall not feel very happy and it will not be a very pleasant meeting.

We ought not to wait for opportunities to be pleasant and agreeable always; but we should strive, even if it takes a little sacrifice on our part, to put ourselves in a condition to perform this labor. . . . We desire anxiously that the brethren and sisters should not neglect this important work. Do you know what will be the main labor during the thousand years of rest [the Millennium]? It will be that which we are trying to urge the Latter-day Saints to perform at the present time. Temples will be built all over this land, and the brethren and sisters will go into them and perhaps work day and night in order to hasten the work and accomplish the labors necessary before the Son of Man can present His kingdom to His Father. This work has got to be accomplished before the Son of Man can come and receive His kingdom to present it to His Father.[13] [See suggestion 5 on page 145.]

When we enter the temple with a pure heart, the Lord blesses us according to what He knows is best for us.

We feel when we go into these temples that we enjoy the Spirit of the Lord more fully than in any other place. They are the Lord's buildings, and His most important work is carried on within their walls. . . .

. . . I am satisfied that when persons go into these temples, they do not [leave] without feeling better and with a determination in their minds to do a little better than they have done. That is the feeling we want the Saints to get. . . .

. . . Be faithful, brethren and sisters, and persevering; come to the temple and do your work there, and you will enjoy yourselves, and be better prepared to resist the unpleasantnesses of the world.[14]

Those who [enter the] Temple with a pure heart and a contrite spirit [will] not come out of it without receiving peculiar blessings, although these in some, or possibly many, instances might be different from what some might expect. . . . Some of the Saints might be looking for the appearance of ministering angels . . . or expect to behold the face of God. It might not be profitable for you to impart such manifestations. The Lord knows what is best for every individual, and will adapt His gifts for the production of the greatest good to those who receive them. It may be safely anticipated that every faithful Saint who enters that House will receive a blessing that will give much satisfaction to the recipient. Before those who would enter the Temple [leave] it, something [will] arise in their hearts and understanding which [will] be serviceable to them in their future lives. To this, as true Latter-day Saints, they [are] entitled.[15] [See suggestion 6 on page 145.]

Suggestions for Study and Teaching

Consider these ideas as you study the chapter or as you prepare to teach. For additional help, see pages v–vii.

1. Read the account of the capstone ceremony for the Salt Lake Temple (pages 137–39). If you have participated in a temple dedication, think about how you felt at the time. When we participate in a Hosanna Shout, what are we expressing to the Lord?

2. Review President Snow's invitation to "come into the Temples" (page 140). Think about how you can accept this invitation

and about how you might extend this invitation to family members and friends.

3. As you study the second section on page 140, ponder the blessings that can come through receiving temple ordinances and making temple covenants. How have these blessings influenced you and your family?

4. Read the section beginning at the bottom of page 140. In what ways do we act as "saviors to [our] kindred and friends" when we perform this work? What resources has the Church provided to help us?

5. What can we do to give temple and family history work the attention and time they deserve? (Review the section beginning at the top of page 143.)

6. What are some personal, spiritual blessings we can receive when we participate in temple work? (For some examples, see pages 143–44.)

Related Scriptures: D&C 97:15–17; 109:1–23; 128:15–18; 132:19; 138:57–59

Teaching Help: "You can help those you teach feel more confident about their ability to participate in a discussion if you respond positively to every sincere comment. For example, you might say, 'Thank you for your answer. That was very thoughtful' . . . or 'That is a good example' or 'I appreciate all that you have said today'" (*Teaching, No Greater Call,* 64).

Notes

1. In Eliza R. Snow Smith, *Biography and Family Record of Lorenzo Snow* (1884), 11.
2. In *Biography and Family Record of Lorenzo Snow,* 11–12.
3. See J. H. A., *Millennial Star,* May 2, 1892, 281.
4. *Millennial Star,* July 4, 1892, 418.
5. *Millennial Star,* May 2, 1892, 281–82.
6. *Millennial Star,* June 27, 1895, 403.
7. *Deseret Semi-Weekly News,* Mar. 30, 1897, 1.
8. *Deseret Semi-Weekly News,* Mar. 30, 1897, 1.
9. In "Funeral Services of Apostle Erastus Snow," *Millennial Star,* July 2, 1888, 418.
10. *Millennial Star,* June 27, 1895, 405.
11. *Millennial Star,* June 27, 1895, 403–4; see also *Teachings of Presidents of the Church: Wilford Woodruff* (2004), 177.
12. *Deseret Weekly,* Nov. 4, 1893, 609.
13. *Millennial Star,* June 27, 1895, 404–5.
14. *Deseret Semi-Weekly News,* Mar. 30, 1897, 1.
15. Adapted from a detailed paraphrase of an address by President Snow in *Deseret Weekly,* Apr. 8, 1893, 495.

In the Garden of Gethsemane the Savior said,
"Not my will, but thine, be done" (Luke 22:42).

C H A P T E R 1 1

"I Seek Not Mine Own Will, but the Will of the Father"

"We should bring our wills into subjection to the will of the Father, and feel to say, what is the will of our Father, whom we are here in the world to serve? Then every act that we perform will be a success."

From the Life of Lorenzo Snow

On March 31, 1899, President Lorenzo Snow traveled to Brigham Young Academy (now Brigham Young University), where a large group of Latter-day Saints had gathered to commemorate his 85th birthday. In the morning, he delivered a devotional address to the men in the congregation. At the same time, the women had a similar meeting, conducted by wives of members of the First Presidency and Quorum of the Twelve Apostles. In the afternoon, all met together.

As part of the afternoon meeting, 23 children "marched upon the rostrum, and facing President Snow, sang two songs . . . , after which each child presented the President with a bouquet of flowers." President Snow expressed his gratitude to the children and pronounced a blessing upon them. Then eight Brigham Young Academy students came to the stand, one at a time. Each one, representing an organization in the school, presented a carefully prepared tribute to their prophet. In response to these words of affection and admiration, President Snow said:

"Now brethren and sisters, I do not know what to say about all this. I should like to go home and think about it, but I suppose a few remarks are expected, and I suppose I should say something, but I really don't know what to say. There is this, however. I understand very distinctly that you are not paying this honor to me as

Lorenzo Snow, but because of the cause I represent in connection with my brethren, my counselors and the members of the Quorum of the Twelve. . . . I feel that whatever I have accomplished that it is not Lorenzo Snow, and the scenes that have brought me to this position as President of the Church—it is not Lorenzo Snow, but the Lord has done it. When Jesus was upon the earth He made this remarkable expression; I have thought of it and it is before me constantly in all of my labors: 'I can of myself do nothing; as I hear I judge, and my judgment is just.' Now, why did He say that His judgment was just? He says, because 'I seek not my own will but the will of my Father who sent me.' [See John 5:30.] That is the principle, my brethren and sisters, that I have endeavored to act upon ever since it was revealed to me that my Father in heaven, and your Father in heaven, exists. I have endeavored to do His will. . . .

"It is the Lord that you honor when you honor me and my counselors and the Quorum of the Twelve. We have discovered that a long time since, every one of us, that of ourselves we could do nothing. Only as far as we followed that principle which Jesus followed when He was in the world has success followed our efforts; and it will be so with you."[1]

Teachings of Lorenzo Snow

When we seek God's will, we follow a course in which there will be no failure.

There is a course that men and women may pursue wherein there will be no failure. Whatever disappointments may arise or seeming failures may result, there will be in reality no failure, as a general thing. . . . There have been times when it seemed as though we were moving backward; at least, it has to those who were not fully enlightened in regard to the mind and will of God. The Church has passed through very strange experiences, and the people have made great sacrifices. . . . But we have come along through these sacrifices, and as a people there has been no failure. Why has there been no failure? Because the people, as a whole, have had their minds fixed upon the true principles of life, and they have conformed to their duty. . . . The people generally have had the Spirit of the Lord, and have followed it. Hence there has been no failure. So it may be with individuals. There is a course for every person to pursue in which there will be no failure. It will apply to temporal as well as spiritual matters. The Lord has given us the keyword in these verses that I have read from the Book of Doctrine and Covenants:

"If your eye be single to my glory, your whole bodies shall be filled with light, and there shall be no darkness in you, and that body which is filled with light comprehendeth all things. Therefore sanctify yourselves that your minds become single to God." [D&C 88:67–68.]

That is the key by which a person can always be successful. Paul says:

"I press toward the mark for the prize of the high calling of God in Christ Jesus." [Philippians 3:14.]

A grand object that every Latter-day [Saint] ought to have before him constantly. What is that prize? . . . "All that my Father hath shall be given unto him." [D&C 84:38.]

The Savior on one occasion made an extraordinary statement. It is in the 5th chapter of St. John, and is as follows:

"I can of mine own self do nothing." [John 5:30.]

It is remarkable that the God who made the worlds, who came down here clothed with flesh, performed mighty miracles, and sacrificed his life on Mount Calvary for the salvation of the human family—that He should say, "I can of mine own self do nothing." And He goes on to say:

"As I hear, I judge: and my judgment is just; because I seek not mine own will, but the will of the Father which hath sent me." [John 5:30.]

That is a wonderful saying, and there is a great deal in it. Now, what we want is to have that spirit in every act of our lives and in every undertaking, whether temporal or spiritual, and not think of self. We should try to ascertain how we should spend the money and the information that God has given us. The answer is simple—for the glory of God. Our eye should be single to the glory of God. That is what we left the other life for and [came] into this. We should seek to promote the interests of the Most High God, and to feel as Jesus felt, "I can of mine own self do nothing." Inasmuch as we act today and tomorrow, this week and next week, in the interest of God, and have our eye single to His glory, there can be no failure.[2] [See suggestion 1 on page 154.]

As we obey God's will, He gives us power to succeed in His work.

Of ourselves we can do nothing. As Jesus said: "Verily, verily I say unto you, the Son can do nothing of himself, but what he seeth the Father do; for what things soever he doeth, these also doeth the Son likewise." [John 5:19.] He came into this life to do the will of his Father, and not his own will. Our desire and determination should be the same. When things come up that require an exertion on our part, we should bring our wills into subjection to the will of the Father, and feel to say, what is the will of our Father, whom we are here in the world to serve? Then every act that we perform will be a success. We may not see its success today or tomorrow, nevertheless it will result in success.[3]

"And Moses said unto God, who am I, that I should go unto Pharaoh, and that I should bring forth the children of Israel out of Egypt?" [See Exodus 3:11.] . . .

"And Moses said unto the Lord, O, my Lord, I am not eloquent, neither heretofore nor since thou has spoken unto thy servant, but I am slow of speech, and of a slow tongue." [See Exodus 4:10.] . . .

We see in these passages which I read, that God called upon Moses to accomplish a certain work; Moses felt his inability and incompetency to do that which was required of him. The work was too great. It was too profound in its nature and character, and it required that which Moses felt he did not possess in power and ability; and he felt his weakness, and he asked God to look to others. . . . He objected in his feelings, and so talked to the Lord saying: Who am I that I should be sent forth to accomplish this great work,—for it is impossible that it can be accomplished by any such ability that I possess. . . .

These are the feelings and the notions that Moses possessed and he wished to impress God with the same. So it has been from the beginning; when the Lord called upon individuals, they felt their inability, and so is it when elders are called to address you. So it is with the elders who are called to go forth to the nations of the earth as ministers of the gospel. They feel their inadequacy. They feel their insufficiency. . . .

Now, when Jeremiah was called, he felt the same as did Moses. He said that the Lord had called upon him to be a prophet, not only to the house of Israel, but to all the surrounding nations. He was but a child, like Joseph Smith, when God first appeared unto him. Joseph was only about 14 years of age—but a child as it were—unknown, as far as the wisdom and learning of the world was concerned—so with Jeremiah, when God first called him—he said: "I am but a child. How can I accomplish this great work you require at my hands, to discharge these great responsibilities you propose to lay upon my shoulders?" He set his heart and feelings at the idea of doing this great work. But God told him, . . . for his comfort, "I knew you before I formed you in the belly." He said He knew him in the [premortal] spirit world, that he would accomplish that which the Lord required at his hands; "and before thou camest forth from the womb, I sanctified thee and ordained thee to be a prophet to the nations." [See Jeremiah 1:5–6.] He went forth, and through the power of the Almighty, Jeremiah accomplished that which the Lord required at his hands. . . .

Now the Lord does very different from the doings of men. He works different. The Apostle Paul said that. He said: "You are called. It is not the wise that are called, but God has called the foolish to confound those which are wise." [See 1 Corinthians 1:25–27.] And [the] apostles which God called, which Jesus, the Son of God called, and laid his hands upon them and bestowed upon them his priesthood and his authority to accomplish his work, they were not educated; they did not comprehend the sciences, they did not occupy high positions in Judeah—they were poor and illiterate; of humble callings in life. . . . Well, then, the Lord is different. He makes His calls different from those calls made by men. And people are very apt to be [confused] in regard to the operations of

Moses "ascribed all his success to the Almighty God who called him. And so do we."

God in his callings; the best of men, the wisest of men are ofttimes [confused]. Moses was [confused] in regard to how the Lord would enable him to accomplish what he required but he was informed after. The Lord helped and aided him in a marvelous way, in convincing his brethren, Israel, when he was seen by the great Jehovah. He counseled with them and told them his mission and they finally consented. They accepted and received his counsels and his leadership and he brought them forth out of the land of bondage in Egypt. He was successful, not successful through his own wisdom; but he ascribed all his success to the Almighty God who called him. And so do we. . . .

Now, it may be sufficient to state that God has called us. We don't preach [except] as God requires it. There is scarcely a man that can be pointed out of the elders of Israel but their heart sunk within them when they were called to preach the gospel, to discharge the duties and obligations devolving upon them. I notice that some of the best speakers that have ever spoken from this stand, when they are called upon they are afraid, they feel to ask the faith and support of the congregation. And they have stood forth in the power of Jehovah and proclaimed his will in fear and trembling; but it was not by their own strength and wisdom that they thus addressed the Latter-day Saints. Although they may never have had the benefits of a college education, still, they stand before, not depending upon their own strength but in the strength and might of the gospel.[4]

We cannot always do what we would like to do, but we shall have the power to do that which we should do. The Lord will give us the power to do this.[5] [See suggestion 2 on page 154.]

We have been called to act in God's name, and we acknowledge His hand in all the good we do.

What we do we perform in the name of the Lord God of Israel, and are willing to acknowledge the hand of the Almighty in everything we do. When Moses stood forth as the deliverer of the Children of Israel from their Egyptian bondage, he did not present himself in the manner of a common deliverer, but he went in the name of the Lord God of Israel, having been commanded to accomplish their redemption by the power and authority which he received from God. And from the moment that he appeared before them in this capacity, until he had accomplished his work, he acted in and through the name of the Lord, and not by his own wisdom or ingenuity, nor because he possessed superior intelligence to the rest of mankind. The Lord appeared to him in the burning bush, and commanded him to go forth and accomplish a certain work, which concerned the peace, happiness and salvation of a great people; and its success and prosperity depended upon the carrying out of the order of things revealed to him by the God of Heaven. His success and prosperity were made perfectly sure from the fact that the work to which he was assigned was not a thing of his own invention, but it emanated from Jehovah. . . .

It is so in reference to ourselves. The great work now being accomplished—the gathering of the people from the nations of the earth had not its origin in the mind of any man or any set of men; but it emanated from the Lord Almighty.[6]

We depend upon God; and in all our works and labors, and in all the success that attends us in our labors, we feel that it has been God who has wrought it.[7]

We came into the world for a great purpose, the same as Jesus, our elder brother, to do the will and works of our Father; in this there is peace, joy and happiness, an increase of wisdom, knowledge and the power of God; outside of this are no promised blessings. Thus let us devote ourselves to righteousness, help each and all to be better and happier; do good to all and evil to none; honor God and obey His Priesthood; cultivate and preserve an enlightened conscience and follow the Holy Spirit; faint not, hold fast to what is good, endure to the end, and your cup of joy shall be full even to overflowing, for great shall be your reward for your trials and your sufferings under temptations, your fiery ordeals, your heart yearnings and tears; yea, our God will give you a crown of unfading glory.[8] [See suggestion 3 below.]

Suggestions for Study and Teaching

Consider these ideas as you study the chapter or as you prepare to teach. For additional help, see pages v–vii.

1. Study the section that starts on page 148. How can you know when your eye is single to the glory of God? With so many distractions in the world, how can parents help their children keep their eyes single to the glory of God?
2. Review President Snow's comments about Moses and Jeremiah (pages 150–52). How might these accounts help us in our efforts to serve in priesthood quorums, the Relief Society, and other Church organizations?
3. President Snow taught that we should serve "in the name of the Lord" (page 153). How would you describe a person who acts in the name of the Lord? Think about opportunities you have to serve in the name of the Lord.
4. President Snow uses the words *success* and *successful* several times in this chapter. How does God's definition of success

differ from the world's definition? Why can we be assured of success when we follow God's will?

Related Scriptures: Philippians 4:13; 2 Nephi 10:24; Mosiah 3:19; Helaman 3:35; 10:4–5; 3 Nephi 11:10–11; 13:19–24; D&C 20:77, 79; Moses 4:2

Teaching Help: "Do not be afraid of silence. People often need time to think about and reply to questions or to express what they are feeling. You might pause after you have asked a question, after a spiritual experience has been shared, or when a person is having difficulty expressing himself or herself" (*Teaching, No Greater Call,* 67).

Notes

1. In "Anniversary Exercises," *Deseret Evening News,* Apr. 7, 1899, 9–10.
2. "The Object of This Probation," *Deseret Semi-Weekly News,* May 4, 1894, 7.
3. In Conference Report, Oct. 1899, 2.
4. *Salt Lake Daily Herald,* Oct. 11, 1887, 2.
5. *Deseret News,* May 15, 1861, 82.
6. *Deseret News,* Dec. 8, 1869, 517.
7. *Salt Lake Daily Herald,* Oct. 11, 1887, 2.
8. In Eliza R. Snow Smith, *Biography and Family Record of Lorenzo Snow* (1884), 487.

The St. George Tabernacle. In this building, President Lorenzo Snow gave his first of many discourses on the law of tithing.

CHAPTER 12

Tithing, a Law for Our Protection and Advancement

"The law of tithing is one of the most important ever revealed to man. . . . Through obeying this law the blessings of prosperity and success will be given to the Saints."

From the Life of Lorenzo Snow

In early May 1899, President Lorenzo Snow felt prompted to visit the city of St. George and other settlements in southern Utah. He quickly began organizing a group of people, including several General Authorities, to take the long trip with him.

When President Snow arranged for the journey, he did not tell anyone why they were going—he did not know the reason himself. "When we left Salt Lake," he later said, "we did not know just what we were going to visit these southern settlements for."[1] But on May 17, soon after the travelers arrived in St. George, the Lord's will was "clearly manifested" to His prophet.[2] In a meeting held on May 18, 1899, President Snow declared:

"It is the word of the Lord to you, my brethren and sisters, that you should conform to that which is required of you as a people who have these glorious prospects of exaltation and glory before you. What is it? Why, it is something that has been drummed into your ears from time to time until you perhaps have got tired of hearing it. . . . The word of the Lord to you is not anything new; it is simply this: THE TIME HAS NOW COME FOR EVERY LATTER-DAY SAINT, WHO CALCULATES TO BE PREPARED FOR THE FUTURE AND TO HOLD HIS FEET STRONG UPON A PROPER FOUNDATION, TO DO THE WILL OF THE LORD AND TO PAY HIS TITHING IN FULL. That is the word of the Lord to you, and it will be the word of the Lord to every settlement throughout the land of Zion. After I leave you and you get to thinking about this, you will see yourselves that the time has come when every man should stand up and pay his tithing in full. The Lord has blessed us and has had mercy upon us in the past; but there are times coming when the Lord requires us to stand up and do that which He has commanded and not leave it any longer. What I say to you in this Stake of Zion I will say to every Stake of Zion that has been organized. There is no man or woman that now hears what I am saying who will feel satisfied if he or she fails to pay a full tithing."[3]

In his previous 50 years as an Apostle, President Snow had rarely mentioned the law of tithing in his sermons. That changed in St. George, Utah, because of the revelation he received. "I never had a more perfect revelation," he later said, "than [the revelation] I received on this subject of tithing."[4] From St. George, he and his traveling companions went from town to town in southern Utah and on their way home to Salt Lake City, holding 24 meetings. President Snow delivered 26 sermons. Each time he spoke, he counseled the Saints to obey the law of tithing.

The group returned to Salt Lake City on May 27. A newspaper reporter observed, "The President looks stronger and more active today than the day he left Salt Lake." Responding to a comment that he had "stood the journey remarkably well," the 85-year-old prophet said: "Yes, so they all say. . . . The trip has done me good. I never felt better in my life. I feel that the Lord sustains me in answer to the prayers of the Saints."[5]

In addition to commenting on his own well-being, he shared his feelings about the faith and righteousness of the Saints in southern Utah. He said that he and his company had been received "with the warmest manifestations of joy and appreciation."[6] He reported that when he counseled the Saints to obey the law of tithing, "the Spirit of the Lord fell upon the people, and they rejoiced exceedingly, and in their hearts they decreed that they would observe this principle to the very letter and in the spirit of it."[7] In response to a question about the general condition of the people, he said: "They are living in comfortable homes, they are particularly well dressed, and appear to have plenty of the good things of the earth to eat and drink. In the St. George Stake the people are suffering from [a] severe drought, the severest one that has ever visited the country, but they have faith that they will soon have moisture."[8]

On May 29 and 30, President Snow gave two sermons on the law of tithing, first to the officers of the Young Ladies' Mutual Improvement Association and then to the officers of the Young Men's Mutual Improvement Association.[9] At the conclusion of the second discourse, Elder B. H. Roberts of the Seventy presented the following resolution, which was unanimously supported by all in attendance: "Resolved: That we accept the doctrine of tithing, as now presented by President Snow, as the present word and will of the Lord unto us, and we do accept it with all our hearts; we will ourselves observe it, and we will do all in our power to get the Latter-day Saints to do likewise."[10] On July 2, all the General Authorities and representatives from all the stakes and wards in the Church attended a solemn assembly in the Salt Lake Temple, having fasted and prayed in preparation for the meeting. There they unanimously accepted the same resolution.[11] President Snow was true to this resolution himself, teaching the law of tithing in many stakes and overseeing the same effort by other Church leaders.

In the months after President Snow's visit to southern Utah, he received word of the Latter-day Saints' renewed dedication to obey the law of tithing. This news gave him "the greatest pleasure and satisfaction,"[12] for he knew that through continued obedience to this law, "the blessings of the Almighty [would] be poured out upon this people, and the Church [would] progress with a force and rapidity that [had] never been experienced before."[13]

President Snow had repeatedly assured the Saints that they would be blessed individually, both temporally and spiritually, as they obeyed the law of tithing.[14] That promise was partially fulfilled in August 1899, when the people of St. George enjoyed temporary relief from their drought; their faith was rewarded with 2.93 inches of rain, more than they had received in the previous 13 months combined.[15] President Snow had also promised that obedience to the law of tithing would bring blessings to the Church as a whole. He felt certain that the tithes of the faithful would enable the Church to break free from its indebtedness, which had come largely as a result of persecution.[16] This promise was fulfilled in 1906, five years after he died. In the April 1907 general conference, President Joseph F. Smith announced:

"There never has been a time in the history of the Church, I believe, when the law of tithing was observed more universally and more honestly than it has been observed by the Latter-day Saints of late. The tithes of the people during the year 1906, have surpassed the tithing of any other year. This is a good indication that the Latter-day Saints are doing their duty, that they have faith in the Gospel, that they are willing to keep the commandments of God, and that they are working up to the line more faithfully perhaps than ever before. I want to say another thing to you, and I do so by way of congratulation, and that is, that we have, by the blessing of the Lord and the faithfulness of the Saints in paying their tithing, been able to pay off our bonded indebtedness. Today the Church of Jesus Christ of Latter-day Saints owes not a dollar that it cannot pay at once. At last we are in a position that we can pay as we go. We do not have to borrow any more, and we won't have to if the Latter-day Saints continue to live their religion and observe this law of tithing."[17] [See suggestion 1 on page 164.]

Teachings of Lorenzo Snow

The law of tithing is easy to understand and can be obeyed by all.

I plead with you in the name of the Lord, and I pray that every man, woman and child . . . shall pay one-tenth of their income as a tithing.[18]

[Tithing] is not a difficult law. . . . If a man receives ten dollars, his tithing is one dollar; if he receives one hundred, his tithing is ten. . . . It is very easy to comprehend.[19]

[A man might ask himself] How much of this tithing shall I give? Cannot I reserve a portion to myself? The Lord is very rich and I doubt if He will be troubled at all if I withhold a little for myself; and so a little to oneself is withheld. But that very little that is reserved will trouble that man, if his conscience is like the consciences of most of the Latter-day Saints. It will trouble him more

President Snow counseled parents and teachers to teach children to pay tithing.

or less in the day time, and also when he thinks of it at night. He does not have that happiness that it is his privilege to enjoy—it goes from him.[20]

A part of a tithing is no tithing at all, no more than immersing only half a person's body is baptism.[21]

There is no man or woman who can not pay one tenth of what he or she receives.[22]

Brethren and sisters, we want you to make this matter a subject of prayer. . . . Instead of having such groveling ideas as some have in regard to money, we should pay our tithing. . . . What the Lord requires of us is to pay our tithing now. And He expects every person in the future to pay his or her tithing. We know what one-tenth is; let us pay that to the Lord. Then we can go to the Bishop with an open face and ask him for a recommend to go to the temple.[23]

I say to you in the name of the Lord God of Israel, if you will pay tithing from now on, the Lord will forgive you for all the past [nonpayment of tithing] and the blessings of the Almighty will be poured out upon this people.[24]

I want to have this principle so fixed upon our hearts that we shall never forget it. As I have said more than once, I know that the Lord will forgive the Latter-day Saints for their past negligence in paying tithing, if they will now repent and pay a conscientious tithing from this time on.[25] [See suggestion 2 on page 165.]

When we pay tithing, we contribute to the work of the Church.

This Church could not go on unless there was revenue, and this revenue God has provided for [through the law of tithing]. Our temples, in which we receive the highest blessings ever conferred on mortal man, are built through revenue. We never could send the . . . Elders out into the world to preach the Gospel, as we are now doing, unless there was revenue to do it. . . . Then there are a thousand other things constantly occurring for which means are required. . . .

If some of the Latter-day Saints had not paid tithing our four Temples here [in 1899] never would have been erected, and the judgments and statutes of God pertaining unto exaltation and glory never could have been kept. The first principle of action to the Latter-day Saints is to sanctify the land by keeping this law of tithing and placing themselves in a position where they can receive the ordinances that pertain unto exaltation and glory of our dead.[26] [See suggestion 3 on page 165.]

The Lord will bless us temporally and spiritually as we obey the law of tithing.

The law of tithing is one of the most important ever revealed to man. . . . Through obeying this law the blessings of prosperity and success will be given unto the Saints.[27]

If we will keep that law . . . the land will be sanctified, and we shall be counted worthy to receive the blessings of the Lord and to be sustained and supported in our financial affairs and in everything we do, temporal as well as spiritual.[28]

The temporal salvation of this Church . . . depends upon obedience to this law.[29]

Tithing funds are used to help pay for the construction and maintenance of temples.

Poverty exists among the Latter-day Saints, and always will exist until we at least obey the law of tithing.[30]

I believe truly if the Latter-day Saints will conform with this law we can claim deliverance from every evil that may come upon us.[31]

Here is a law revealed specially for our protection and safety, as well as for our advancement in the path of righteousness and holiness; a law by which the land on which we dwell might become sanctified; a law by which Zion might be built up and established never more to be thrown down or removed out of her place by wicked and ungodly men.[32]

We have temples, and we receive blessings pertaining to them, even the highest ordinances ever administered to man on the earth, by reason of our obedience to this law.[33]

We can never be prepared to see the face of God until we are conscientious in the payment of tithes and other duties.[34]

I have spoken plainly, and I say it comes from the Lord what I have said to you in regard to tithing. You act now according to the Spirit of the Lord, and your eyes will be opened.[35] [See suggestion 4 on page 165.]

Parents and teachers have a responsibility to pay tithing and then teach children to do the same.

Teach [children] to pay their tithing while they are young. You mothers, teach your children that when they get any money they should pay one-tenth of it to the Lord, however little it may be. Educate them to pay their tithing in full.[36]

It is meet and proper that . . . officers and teachers [in the Church] should receive in their hearts and very souls the spirit of this law, so that they may be fully qualified to impart the same, and to impress the rising generation with its importance and sacredness. It is required of you, my brethren and sisters, to not only obey the law yourselves, but to teach it to others, even to the rising generation, . . . and in proportion as you are able to receive the spirit of it, you will be able to impart it, and teach it. . . .

. . . I require it at your hands, not only to obey it, but to teach it to the children of the Latter-day Saints, and to impress it upon the tablets of their memories, so that when they shall grow into years of discretion, it may be said they were taught it, and that they obeyed it from their youth up.[37] [See suggestion 5 on page 165.]

Suggestions for Study and Teaching

Consider these ideas as you study the chapter or as you prepare to teach. For additional help, see pages v–vii.

1. Review the account of President Snow receiving the revelation about tithing (pages 157–60). Think about his willingness to travel to St. George and the people's readiness to obey the law of tithing. What can we gain from this account?

2. In what ways is tithing "not a difficult law"? (For some examples, see pages 160–61.) Why might some people think the law of tithing is difficult to obey? How might President Snow's teachings help someone gain a testimony of paying tithing?
3. Study the first section that begins on page 162. What are some blessings you and loved ones have received through the buildings and programs funded by tithing? Why is it a privilege to pay tithing?
4. President Snow testified that we will be blessed as we obey the law of tithing (pages 162–64). What are some blessings the law of tithing has brought into your life? into the lives of your family members and friends?
5. Consider President Snow's counsel to parents and teachers (page 164). Why do you think it is important for children to pay their tithing, "however little it may be"? What are some ways to teach children to pay tithes and offerings?

Related Scriptures: Malachi 3:8–10; D&C 64:23; 119:1–7

Teaching Help: "Be careful not to end good discussions too soon in an attempt to present all the material you have prepared. Although it is important to cover the material, it is more important to help learners feel the influence of the Spirit, resolve their questions, increase their understanding of the gospel, and deepen their commitment to keep the commandments" (*Teaching, No Greater Call,* 64).

Notes

1. In "In Juab and Millard Stakes," *Deseret Evening News,* May 29, 1899, 5.
2. In "In Juab and Millard Stakes," 5.
3. *Millennial Star,* Aug. 24, 1899, 532–33; see also *Deseret Evening News,* May 17, 1899, 2; *Deseret Evening News,* May 18, 1899, 2. The *Millennial Star* says that President Snow delivered this discourse on May 8, but other contemporary sources show that he delivered it on May 18. President Snow also spoke about tithing on May 17.
4. In "President Snow in Cache Valley," *Deseret Evening News,* Aug. 7, 1899, 1.
5. In "Pres. Snow Is Home Again," *Deseret Evening News,* May 27, 1899, 1. The Church had 40 stakes at the time.
6. In "Pres. Snow Is Home Again," 1.
7. *Deseret Evening News,* June 24, 1899, 3.
8. In "Pres. Snow Is Home Again," 1.
9. See "The Annual Conference of the Young Men's and Young Ladies' Mutual Improvement Associations," *Improvement Era,* Aug. 1899, 792–95; see also Ann M. Cannon, "President Lorenzo Snow's Message on Tithing," *Young Woman's Journal,* Apr. 1924, 184–86.

10. B. H. Roberts, quoted in "The Annual Conference of the Young Men's and Young Ladies' Mutual Improvement Associations," 795.
11. See B. H. Roberts, *Comprehensive History of the Church,* 6:359–60.
12. In Conference Report, Oct. 1899, 28.
13. In "President Snow in Cache Valley," *Deseret Evening News,* Aug. 7, 1899, 2.
14. See, for example, *Deseret Evening News,* June 24, 1899, 3. Contemporary transcripts of President Snow's discourses and contemporary newspaper articles about his travels show that while he promised the Saints that they would be blessed temporally as well as spiritually as they obeyed the law of tithing, he did not specifically promise an end to the drought in southern Utah.
15. See Western Regional Climate Center, http://www.wrcc.dri.edu/cgi-bin/cliMONtpre.pl?utstge.
16. See, for example, "The Annual Conference of the Young Men's and Young Ladies' Mutual Improvement Associations," 793.
17. In Conference Report, Apr. 1907, 7.
18. In Conference Report, Oct. 1899, 28.
19. *Deseret Semi-Weekly News,* July 28, 1899, 10.
20. In Conference Report, Apr. 1899, 51.
21. *Deseret Evening News,* June 24, 1899, 3.
22. In "President Lorenzo Snow's Message on Tithing," 185; from the minutes of a meeting held in the Assembly Hall in Salt Lake City on May 29, 1899.
23. *Deseret Semi-Weekly News,* July 28, 1899, 10.
24. In "President Snow in Cache Valley," 2.
25. In Conference Report, Oct. 1899, 28.
26. In Conference Report, Oct. 1899, 27–28.
27. In "In Juab and Millard Stakes," 5.
28. *Deseret Evening News,* June 24, 1899, 3.
29. In "The Annual Conference of the Young Men's and Young Ladies' Mutual Improvement Associations," 794.
30. *Deseret Semi-Weekly News,* July 28, 1899, 10.
31. In "President Lorenzo Snow's Message on Tithing," 185.
32. "Tithing," *Juvenile Instructor,* Apr. 1901, 216.
33. "Tithing," 215.
34. In "Conference of Granite Stake," *Deseret Evening News,* May 21, 1900, 2; from a detailed paraphrase of a discourse President Snow gave at the Granite Stake conference on May 20, 1900.
35. *Deseret Semi-Weekly News,* July 28, 1899, 10.
36. *Millennial Star,* Aug. 31, 1899, 546.
37. "Tithing," 215–16.

CHAPTER 13

Relief Society: True Charity and Pure Religion

"No institution was ever founded with a nobler aim. Its basis is true charity, which is the pure love of Christ."

From the Life of Lorenzo Snow

In the summer of 1901, the general Relief Society presidency organized a day-long activity for the Relief Society sisters in the Salt Lake Valley. President Lorenzo Snow accepted an invitation to attend and to speak to the group. He began his address by saying: "I appreciate the privilege of being able to spend an hour or two in your company this afternoon, and I trust you are all enjoying yourselves today. Proper recreation and amusement are good things, and I am glad to see you sisters indulging in a little rest and recreation, for you who work so hard day after day in your homes and in the Relief Society certainly deserve all the enjoyment you can get."

President Snow, whose sister Eliza R. Snow had served as the second Relief Society general president, expressed gratitude for the work of the Relief Society. Speaking of the women of the Church, he said, "It is difficult to imagine what we should have done, or what progress the work of the Lord would have made, without them." To cite one example, he referred to the Church's missionary program at the time, in which married men often were called to serve full-time missions: "When we have been absent on foreign missions, their missions at home have generally been no less arduous than ours abroad; and in the midst of trial and privation they have exhibited a patience, a fortitude and a self-help that has been truly inspiring. Thank God for the women of this Church! That is the way I feel today as I join in this assembly."[1] [See suggestion 1 on page 172.]

From the early days of the Church, Relief Society sisters have worked together and strengthened one another temporally and spiritually.

Teachings of Lorenzo Snow

Members of the Relief Society exemplify true charity and pure religion.

The Relief Society was organized . . . by the Prophet Joseph Smith, under the inspiration of the Lord. . . . Today it is recognized as one of the most powerful forces for good in the Church. . . .

The mission of the Relief Society is to succor the distressed, to minister to the sick and feeble, to feed the poor, to clothe the naked, and to bless all the sons and daughters of God. No institution was ever founded with a nobler aim. Its basis is true charity, which is the pure love of Christ [see Moroni 7:47], and that spirit has been manifested in all the ministrations of the Society among the people. The Apostle James said that "pure religion and undefiled before God and the Father is this: To visit the fatherless and widows in their affliction, and to keep himself unspotted from the world." [James 1:27.] Accepting that as true, the members of the Relief Society have most surely exemplified in their lives pure and undefiled religion; for they have ministered to those in affliction, they have thrown their arms of love around the fatherless and the widows, and they have kept themselves unspotted from the world. I can testify that there are no purer and more God-fearing women in the world than are to be found within the ranks of the Relief Society.[2] [See suggestion 2 on page 172.]

Relief Society sisters work with priesthood holders to advance the interests of the kingdom of God.

It has always been a source of pleasure to me to notice how faithfully you sisters of the Relief Society have stood by the servants of the Lord under all circumstances. You have ever been found at the side of the Priesthood, ready to strengthen their hands and to do your part in helping to advance the interests of the kingdom of God; and as you have shared in these labors, so you will most certainly share in the triumph of the work and in the exaltation and glory which the Lord will give to His faithful children.

. . . No wise Bishop will fail to appreciate the labors of the Relief Society in his ward. What could a Bishop do without a Relief Society? I would say to all the Bishops in the Church, encourage the sisters of the Relief Society, and support them in their work of charity and benevolence, and they will prove a blessing to you and to the people.[3] [See suggestion 3 on page 173.]

It is good to have the influence of the Relief Society in every home.

I would advise the brethren to encourage their wives to [participate in] the society . . . ; for it would be a good thing to have the influence of this organization in every home. I ask you, my sisters, in your visits to the homes of the Latter-day Saints, to carry this influence wherever you go. The Lord has clearly shown to you the nature of your relationship to Him and what is expected of you as wives and mothers. Teach these things to those whom you visit, especially to the young ladies. . . .

You, my sisters, as members of the Relief Society and as mothers in Israel, should exercise all your influence . . . in favor of pure motherhood and faithfulness to the marriage covenant.[4] [See suggestion 4 on page 173.]

As the Church grows, Relief Society sisters will have greater opportunities to serve.

It is not necessary for me to detail what the Relief Society has done in the past; its splendid work is known throughout Zion, and in many parts of the world. Suffice it to say, it has been true to its mission, and its record is not surpassed, if equaled, by any other charitable organization. The Latter-day Saints are proud of it and of its achievements, and are grateful to our Father in Heaven that He inspired His servant the Prophet to establish such an institution. The future of the Society is full of promise. As the Church grows, its field of usefulness will be correspondingly enlarged, and it will be even more potent for good than it has been in the past. If all the sisters will rally to the support of the society, it will accomplish a mighty work and be a continued blessing unto the Church. It

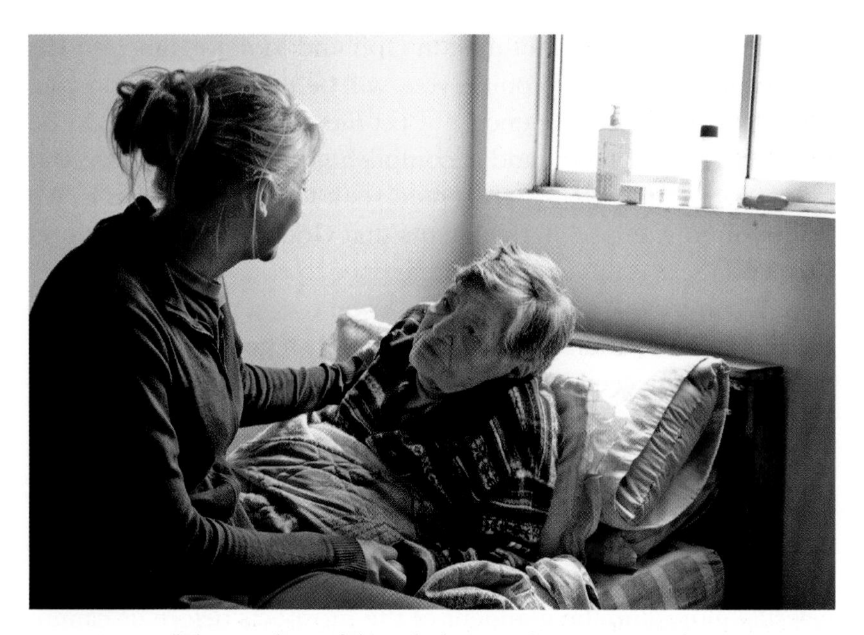

"The members of the Relief Society have most surely exemplified in their lives pure and undefiled religion."

would be gratifying to see the middle-aged as interested in this institution as the aged, and by becoming so they will find that it will strengthen their faith, give them broader ideas of life and its responsibilities, and advance them materially along the path of progress and perfection.[5]

From the beginning of their work the blessing of God has been bestowed upon [the women of the Church], and I have watched with a great deal of delight and pleasure and deep interest their progress. . . . They have succeeded astonishingly, and it is marvelous how God has blessed them and poured out upon them His Spirit. They have become, I might almost say with propriety, as angels standing in the presence of the people of the world.[6] [See suggestion 5 on page 173.]

Relief Society sisters who trust in God and serve Him will be blessed in this life and in the eternities.

This is what we desire to instill into the hearts of the sisters—to be useful in their sphere and not be discouraged because of difficulties in the way, but trust in God and look to Him, and His marvelous blessings, I promise you, will be poured out upon you. This shall be your experience. . . . Let me reiterate again, don't be discouraged, but go on and accomplish good, exercise faith, and every opportunity that is presented seek to improve upon it. We want you to exercise all the talents that God has bestowed upon you. And there is this about it in reference to your prospects of success. When a person commences to travel over a path that the Lord has marked out, and by which to accomplish good in His interest, he is sure to succeed. He is precisely where God wants him to be, and there is the place that you may, with the greatest propriety, ask God for His blessing.[7]

I feel to say, God bless the officers and members of the Relief Society. You are performing a grand mission, and I would exhort you to not weary in well doing [see D&C 64:33]. We are all aiming for celestial glory, and the grandeur of the prospects before us cannot be expressed in human language. If you will continue faithful to the work in which you are engaged, you will attain unto this glory, and rejoice evermore in the presence of God and the Lamb. This is worth striving for; it is worth sacrificing for, and blessed is the man or woman who is faithful unto the obtaining of it. God bless you all.[8] [See suggestion 6 on page 173.]

Suggestions for Study and Teaching

Consider these ideas as you study the chapter or as you prepare to teach. For additional help, see pages v–vii.

1. President Snow declared that it would be difficult to imagine the progress of the work of the Lord without the women of the Church (page 167). In what ways do women contribute to the work of the Lord today?
2. Ponder President Snow's words about the mission of the Relief Society (page 169). Think of a time when Relief Society sisters fulfilled this mission by helping you or your family. How have such actions influenced your life?

3. Review the section that begins at the bottom of page 169. In what ways do Relief Society sisters "advance the interests of the kingdom of God"? What examples have you witnessed of Relief Society sisters and priesthood holders working together?
4. Ponder President Snow's plea for Relief Society sisters to exercise their influence "in favor of pure motherhood and faithfulness to the marriage covenant" (page 170). Why is this influence needed in the world today? In what ways can Relief Society sisters help young women prepare for temple marriage and motherhood?
5. President Snow said, "As the Church grows, [the Relief Society's] field of usefulness will be correspondingly enlarged, and it will be even more potent for good than it has been in the past" (page 170). In the world today, what can Relief Society sisters do to increase in their influence for good?
6. Study the section that begins on page 171. Ponder ways you have been led to be "where God wants [you] to be." How has God helped you in these efforts?

Related Scriptures: Isaiah 1:17; Matthew 25:34–40; Mosiah 4:26–27; Alma 1:29–30; Moroni 7:44–48

Teaching Help: "As you prepare to teach, ensure that you use a variety of teaching methods from lesson to lesson. This may mean using something as simple as a colorful poster or wall chart in one lesson and a list of questions on the chalkboard in another" (*Teaching, No Greater Call,* 89).

Notes

1. In "Prest. Snow to Relief Societies," *Deseret Evening News,* July 9, 1901, 1.
2. In "Prest. Snow to Relief Societies," 1.
3. In "Prest. Snow to Relief Societies," 1.
4. In "Prest. Snow to Relief Societies," 1.
5. In "Prest. Snow to Relief Societies," 1.
6. *Young Woman's Journal,* Sept. 1895, 577–78.
7. *Young Woman's Journal,* Sept. 1895, 578.
8. In "Prest. Snow to Relief Societies," 1.

Before healing a blind man, the Savior said, "I must work the works of him that sent me" (John 9:4).

CHAPTER 14

"With God All Things Are Possible"

"The nature of those demands upon us [is] such that no person can comply with them, unless by assistance from the Almighty. . . . He has promised this aid."

From the Life of Lorenzo Snow

President Lorenzo Snow was a worker, following his own often-repeated counsel: "We have to exert ourselves. . . . Remaining idle without putting ourselves into action is of no use."[1] But he acknowledged that in his desire to build up the kingdom of God, his own exertions would never be enough without the grace of God—or "supernatural aid,"[2] as he often called it. Therefore, while he encouraged Church members to work hard in "the development of [righteous] principles," in the same breath he declared that "we, as Latter-day Saints, should understand and bear in mind that salvation comes through the grace of God."[3] He testified that God will add His strength to our efforts: "Where the Lord plants us, there we are to stand; when he requires us to exert ourselves for the support of these holy principles, that we are to do; that is all we need to trouble ourselves about; the rest our Heavenly Father will take care of."[4]

President Snow's sister Eliza observed that he lived true to this teaching. She described him as a man who had "unshaken confidence in [God's] assisting power and grace." She said that he "knew in whom he trusted" and therefore was able to endure "every hardship, every opposition" and "overcome every obstacle."[5]

Lorenzo Snow showed his confidence in God's assisting power when he journeyed to serve a mission in England in 1840. On the 42-day voyage across the Atlantic Ocean, he and his fellow travelers suffered through three large storms. He later reported that these were "terrible storms—storms which those accustomed to the ocean pronounced very dangerous." He noticed a difference between his response to the storms and the response of some of the other travelers: "In a number of instances, to say the least of it, the scene was fearfully terrific. I did not feel surprised that men, women and children who had not learned to trust in God, wrung their hands in an agony of fear, and wept. My trust was in Him who created the seas and defined their bounds. I was on His errand—I knew that I was sent on this mission by the authority He recognizes, and, although the elements raged and the ship swayed and trembled amid the heaving billows, He was at the helm, and my life was safe in His keeping."[6]

Many years later, when Lorenzo Snow became President of the Church, he again found comfort in his knowledge that the Lord was at the helm. In a meeting held on September 13, 1898, the Quorum of the Twelve Apostles unanimously expressed their commitment to sustain him as President of the Church. A record of the meeting states that he then stood and said that "there was no use in his making excuses as to inability etc., to assume the vast responsibilities involved in the position. . . . He felt that it was for him to do the very best he could and depend upon the Lord."[7] [See suggestion 1 on page 181.]

Teachings of Lorenzo Snow

With God's help, we can do anything required of us.

I wish to speak in a manner that will be for our edification and mutual improvement in those things that pertain to our salvation. For this purpose I desire the faith and prayers of all those who believe in looking to the Lord for instruction and intelligence.

We should realize the relationship that we sustain to the Lord our God, and the peculiar position we occupy. To properly discharge the obligations devolving upon us, we require supernatural aid. . . .

. . . Jesus told [a] young man who came to him and wished to know what he should do to inherit eternal life, to "keep the commandments." The young man replied that he had kept these commandments referred to from his youth upward. The Savior, looking upon him, saw there was still something lacking. The young man had kept the moral law, the law given to Moses, and for this Jesus loved him, but saw that there was one thing lacking. He was a rich man, and held influence in the world in consequence of his superior wealth. Jesus knew that before he could elevate him, or any other man, to the celestial world, it was necessary that he should be submissive in all things, and view obedience to the celestial law of the utmost importance. Jesus knew what was required of every man to gain a celestial crown—that nothing should be held dearer than obedience to the requirements of heaven. The Savior saw in this young man a cleaving to something that was not in accordance with the law of the celestial kingdom. He saw, peradventure, a disposition in him to adhere in his feelings to that which was injurious to him, and would render a compliance to all the demands of the gospel disagreeable or impossible, therefore he told him that he should go and sell all that he had "and give to the poor, and follow him."

This commandment made the young man feel sad and sorrowful. He looked upon riches as the great object in life, as bringing him the influence of the world, and all things that were desirable; as procuring him the blessings and enjoyments of life, and as the means of lifting him to high positions in society. He could not conceive the idea of a person's securing the blessings, enjoyments and privileges of life, and such things as his nature craved, independent of his wealth. But the gospel was of a nature that provided for everything that was necessary to fulfil the wants and requirements of man and to make him happy. Riches were not so calculated; and the Lord desired him to give up these ideas, and to dislodge them from his mind and feelings, so he might secure him as his servant in all things. He desired this man to be wholly devoted to his service, and to go into his work with full purpose of heart, and follow the dictates of the Holy Spirit, and prepare himself for celestial glory. But this young man was not willing; it was too great a sacrifice. And the Savior said upon this occasion, "How hardly shall they that have riches enter into the kingdom of heaven. It is easier for a camel to go through the eye of a needle, than for a rich man to enter into the kingdom of God."

The disciples "were astonished out of measure" at this, "saying among themselves, who then can be saved?" They thought that no man could possess riches and be saved in the kingdom of God. This was the idea they received from the remarks of the Savior. But Jesus answered, "With men it is impossible, but not with God: for with God all things are possible." [See Matthew 19:16–26; see also the Joseph Smith Translation in Matthew 19:26, footnote *a,* and Mark 10:27, footnote *a*.][8] [See suggestion 2 on page 181.]

God has promised to help us in our personal efforts to live the gospel.

In and of ourselves we cannot possibly comply with all the commandments that God has given unto us. Jesus himself could not without divine aid from His Father accomplish His work. He said on one occasion, "I can of mine own self do nothing, as I hear I judge and my judgment is just because I seek not my own will but the will of the Father who sent me." [John 5:30.] And we, if it was necessary for Him, our Lord, to have divine assistance, will find it all the more important to receive His assistance. And in every circumstance and condition surrounding the Latter-day Saints, while in the performance of their duties, they are entitled to supernatural aid from the Holy Spirit, to help in the various conditions surrounding them, and in the duties that they are required to perform.

. . . I cannot imagine anything that is so vastly important as to work for and obtain one's own individual exaltation and glory. That undoubtedly is one great purpose for which we came into the world. . . . No man or woman should be discouraged when they feel that they cannot complete what they would like to perform, but we all should do what we can toward carrying out the grand work for which we are here.[9]

The character of the religion that we have espoused demands a certain course of conduct that no other religion that we know of requires of its adherents; and the nature of those demands upon us [is] such that no person can comply with them, unless by assistance from the Almighty. It is necessary that we comprehend, at least in part, the great and important blessings that we are to derive, eventually, by complying with the requirements of the religion or

"The work in which you and I are engaged can only prosper and be forwarded through the blessings of God upon our faithful and honest exertions."

gospel that we have received. The sacrifices that are required of us are of that nature that no man or woman could make them, unless aided by a supernatural power; and the Lord, in proposing these conditions, never intended that his people should ever be required to comply with them unless by supernatural aid, and of that kind that is not professed by any other class of religious people. He has promised this aid. . . .

These demands . . . were required in every age and period when God called a people to serve him, and to receive his laws. They were required in the days of Israel, in the beginning of that people. They were required of Abraham, Isaac and Jacob. They were required of Moses, and of the people that he led from Egyptian bondage. They were required by all the prophets that existed from the days of Adam to the present period of time. They were required by the apostles that received their commission by the laying on of hands of Jesus Christ, the Son of the living God, and by the adherents of the religion that the apostles proclaimed and taught to the people, in their day and no man or set of men or class of people from the day of Adam to the present time, could comply with these requirements, except the people of God, as they were endowed with power from on high, which could proceed only from the Lord our God.[10] [See suggestion 3 on page 181.]

When we participate in God's work, we need God's help.

Whatever you may undertake for the furtherance of the interests of Zion, you must depend upon the Lord for its success.[11]

A man's mind should be single to the glory of God in everything that he starts to accomplish. We should consider that of ourselves we can do nothing. We are the children of God. We are in darkness, [unless] God enlightens our understanding. We are powerless, [unless] God helps us. The work that we have to do here is of that nature that we cannot do it unless we have the assistance of the Almighty. . . . Here is the great trouble with men of the world, and too much so with the Elders of Israel; we forget that we are working for God; we forget that we are here in order to carry out certain purposes that we have promised the Lord that we would carry out. It is a glorious work that we are engaged in. It is the work of the Almighty; and He has selected the men and the women whom He knows from past experience will carry out His purposes.[12]

This work in which you and I are engaged can only prosper and be forwarded through the blessings of God upon our faithful and honest exertions and our determination to accomplish the labors for which we have come into this existence. When we look back upon the experiences through which we have passed, we easily understand that our prosperity has been dependent upon our honest endeavors to accomplish the work of God, to labor in the interest of the people, and to rid ourselves as far as possible of selfishness. This having been so in the past, we can well believe that our future progress will depend upon our determination to do the will of God under all circumstances and the aid which He shall give to us.[13] [See suggestion 4 on page 181.]

Suggestions for Study and Teaching

Consider these ideas as you study the chapter or as you prepare to teach. For additional help, see pages v–vii.

1. Review the account on pages 175–76. Why do you think people who trust in God respond to trials so differently from people who do not trust in God?
2. Ponder the story of the Savior and the rich young man (pages 176–78). What are some things people set their hearts on that can lead them to "go away sorrowing"? Why do we need to "dislodge" such things from our lives before we can receive the Lord's greatest blessings?
3. President Snow taught that even the Savior needed "divine aid" to "accomplish His work" (page 178). How might you use President Snow's words to help someone who feels inadequate to meet the requirements of gospel living?
4. Search the final section of this chapter. Why do you think we sometimes do not ask God for His help? Think about what you can do to receive His help more in your life.

Related Scriptures: Philippians 4:13; 2 Nephi 10:23–24; 25:23; Jacob 4:6–7; Mosiah 24:8–22; Articles of Faith 1:3

Teaching Help: "Assign participants to read selected questions from the end of the chapter (either individually or in small groups). Ask them to look for teachings in the chapter that relate to the questions. Then invite them to share their thoughts and insights with the rest of the group" (page vii in this book).

Notes

1. *Deseret News,* Jan. 28, 1857, 371.
2. *Deseret News,* Jan. 14, 1880, 786.
3. *Deseret News: Semi-Weekly,* Aug. 15, 1882, 1.
4. *Deseret News,* Oct. 28, 1857, 270.
5. Eliza R. Snow Smith, *Biography and Family Record of Lorenzo Snow* (1884), 116–17.
6. In *Biography and Family Record of Lorenzo Snow,* 49.
7. In Journal History, Sept. 13, 1898, 4.
8. *Deseret News,* Jan. 14, 1880, 786.
9. In Conference Report, Apr. 1898, 12.
10. *Deseret News,* Jan. 14, 1880, 786.
11. *Improvement Era,* July 1899, 708.
12. *Deseret Weekly,* May 12, 1894, 638.
13. In Conference Report, Apr. 1901, 1.

Elder Lorenzo Snow

CHAPTER 15

Faithful, Energetic Service in the Kingdom of God

"Knowing our religion to be true we ought to be the most devoted people on the face of the earth to the cause we have embraced."

From the Life of Lorenzo Snow

Toward the end of 1851, the First Presidency published an epistle in which they requested that all members of the Quorum of the Twelve Apostles "arrange the affairs of their various missions" and return to Salt Lake City by April 1853.[1] Thus Elder Lorenzo Snow's mission in Italy began to draw to a close. In February 1852, he placed the work there under the leadership of Brother John Daniel Malan, a recent convert, and journeyed with Elder Jabez Woodard to the island nation of Malta. From Malta, Elder Snow hoped to board a ship to India. The first missionaries in that land were working under his supervision, and he felt a great desire to join them. From there he planned to "accomplish the circumnavigation of the globe," returning home by way of the Pacific Ocean to the western United States.[2]

Elder Snow's plans changed when he and Elder Woodard reached Malta. He learned that he would be delayed on the island several weeks because a steamer had broken down in the Red Sea. Rather than complain about the delay, he decided to go to work. In a letter dated March 10, 1852, he wrote, "I feel that much good will result from the manner in which the Lord may direct the employment of the time now at my command, as I am surrounded by an interesting people, and in a most important field of labour, where a great work will be accomplished, extending to adjacent nations." He reported that he had sent for Elder Thomas Obray, a missionary in Italy, "to come immediately, and bring a good supply of pamphlets and books." While Elder Snow did not know exactly what he and his companions would do in Malta, he expressed a desire to establish a branch of the Church there. This action, he said, "would loosen the spiritual fetters of many nations, as the Maltese in their commercial relations, are spread along the shores of Europe, Asia, and Africa."[3]

On May 1, 1852, Elder Snow sent a letter reporting the progress of the work in Malta. He wrote: "People are now constantly making calls to inquire concerning this 'strange religion;' a few evenings since, we had at one time, at our private lodgings, gentlemen from eight different nations, having come from various parts of the city to hold conversation in reference to our doctrines: among the number were those from Poland and Greece, who are now reading our works with peculiar interest. Two intelligent and enterprising young men, the firstfruits of our ministry upon this island, will ably assist in moving forward the cause in which we are engaged; one of whom we have ordained an Elder who speaks with fluency several languages."[4]

Elder Snow never realized his dream of serving in India and circumnavigating the globe. Instead, he diligently followed the will of the Lord during his unexpected stay in Malta, building a foundation for missionary work there. When he was finally able to board a ship in May 1852, he went west rather than east, following his leaders' instructions to return to Salt Lake City. About two months later, Elders Woodard and Obray organized a branch of the Church in Malta.[5] [See suggestion 1 on page 192.]

Teachings of Lorenzo Snow

Because we have received the fulness of the gospel, we serve as ambassadors of Christ.

We testify to the whole world that we know, by divine revelation, even through the manifestations of the Holy Ghost, that Jesus is the Christ, the Son of the living God, and that he revealed himself to Joseph Smith as personally as he did to his apostles anciently, after he arose from the tomb, and that he made known unto him [the] heavenly truths by which alone mankind can be saved. This . . . is assuming a very important and responsible position, knowing, as we do, that God will hold us accountable for the disposition we make of this sacred trust which he has committed to us.

As the apostles appeared before the world, after they had received their commission from the risen Redeemer, to preach the gospel of the kingdom to all nations, promising all who believed on their word, the Gift of the Holy Ghost through the laying on of hands, so we appear. As they by virtue of their commission, declared with all assurance, amidst persecution and opposition, the gospel to be the power of God unto salvation to all those who believed and obeyed, so declare we. As they preached faith in the Lord Jesus Christ, baptism for the remission of sins, and the laying on of hands, by those duly authorized, for the reception of the Holy Ghost, as being essential to salvation, so preach we. As they by the power of the Holy Ghost became witnesses of the Lord Jesus Christ, and the faithful bearers of his gospel message to the whole Gentile world, so, by and through the same Holy Spirit, we have become witnesses of him, and, having been called by the same divine and holy calling, we therefore assume the same position.

Then, having assumed this position, we assume all the responsibilities of ambassadors of Christ, we become answerable for our individual acts and for the manner in which we use the talents and ability the Lord has given us.[6] [See suggestion 2 on page 192.]

Membership in the Church is a call to help others receive salvation.

When the Lord calls an individual or a class of individuals out from the world, it is not always with an object to benefit that particular individual or individuals. The Lord has not in view merely the salvation of a few people called Latter-day Saints . . . , but the salvation of all men, the living and the dead. When the Lord called Abraham He made him certain promises concerning the glory that should come upon him and his posterity, and in these promises we find this remarkable saying: that in him and in his seed all the nations of the earth should be blessed [see Genesis 22:15–18;

Abraham 2:9–11]. . . . The design of the Lord was to bless not only him and his posterity, but all the families of the earth. . . .

. . . When Jesus came, He came as a sacrifice not simply in the interest of Israel, or the posterity of Abraham, Isaac and Jacob, but in the interest of the whole human family, that in Him all men might be blessed, that in Him all men might be saved; and His mission was to make provision by which the whole human family might receive the benefits of the everlasting Gospel, not, as I say, Israel alone, but the whole human race; and not alone those dwelling upon the earth, but those also in the spirit world. . . .

. . . We have the same Priesthood that Jesus had, and we have got to do as He did, to make sacrifice of our own desires and feelings as He did, perhaps not to die martyrs as He did, but we have got to make sacrifices in order to carry out the purposes of God, or we shall not be worthy of this holy Priesthood, and be saviors of the world. God intends to make us saviors not only of many that now dwell on the earth, but of many in the spirit world: He will not only place us in a position to save ourselves, but He will make us competent to assist in the redemption of many of the offspring of the Almighty.[7] [See suggestion 3 on page 192.]

Every calling and responsibility is important in the Lord's work.

Now the question is, do we sense our position, do we comprehend fully the nature of the work we have undertaken to consummate? I am sometimes led to believe that some of our brethren, Elders in Israel, are too ready and willing to shirk the obligations they are under by reason of their covenants, the faith they once possessed seems to be almost exhausted, and they appear to settle down into the quiet satisfaction of a mere nominal membership in the Church.

There are others who think because their names are not very widely known, because they are perhaps . . . occupying narrow spheres, that it does not matter much what habits they contract, or what kind of examples they set before their brethren. But then, if they held responsible positions, such as the Presidency of the

"If you are in the line of your duty you are in possession of that which the world cannot give nor take away."

Church, or a counsellorship, or if they belonged to the Quorum of the Twelve, or were they President of the High Council, or of the High Priests or Seventies, then they would consider it important how they conducted themselves. Herein they manifest great weakness or gross ignorance, their lamp is either growing dim or they never sensed the position they assumed in taking upon themselves the responsibilities of the gospel.

We are told in the parable of the Saviour that the kingdom of heaven is as a householder who delivered his goods to his servants as he was about to travel into a far country. To one he gave five talents, to another two, and to another one. The one that received the five talents went and traded, and made other five talents, doubling the portion that had been entrusted to him, and he also that received two talents went and gained other two. But he that received the one talent, went and digged in the earth, and hid his lord's money. He doubtless considered that his responsibility was so small that he could not do much, and consequently he would not exercise a talent so inferior. [See Matthew 25:14–30.] Does not this apply directly to the condition of some of our elders? Says one, "I am only a carpenter, or a tailor, or peradventure only a hod-carrier [an assistant to a bricklayer], therefore it cannot matter much how I deport myself, whether I do or do not honestly discharge my duties in my humble sphere. But it would be *very different* if I were acting in some more responsible and prominent position."

Stop, my brother; do not allow yourself to be deceived by such alluring sentiments. It is true you may only be a hod-carrier, but remember you are an elder in Israel, you are an ambassador of the Lord Jesus Christ, and if you are in the line of your duty you are in possession of that which the world cannot give nor take away; and you are held accountable to God for the honest use of the talent over which he has made you steward, whether it be large or small.

Again, you exert a certain degree of influence, and be it ever so small it affects some person or persons, and for the results of the influence you exert you are held more or less accountable. You, therefore, whether you acknowledge it or not, have assumed an importance before God and man that cannot be overlooked and from which you cannot be released if you wish to sustain the name you bear.

And what of the prospects of that individual? I say that if he honors his calling, and is found faithful to the trust reposed in him, his prospects for salvation and exaltation in the kingdom of God are just as good as any other man's. If he comprehends his position and lives accordingly, his prospects are equally good with any man that ever lived since the days of father Adam to the present moment; and it is just as important that he deport himself properly according to the sphere in which he walks, as it is that any other individual should, who may be called to act in a higher position; or, in other words, who may have been made steward over a larger number of talents. . . .

. . . The Lord does not require so much of the man who possesses but one talent, as of him who possesses more than one; but, according to that which he hath, so shall it be required of him. Let all, therefore, be encouraged, and seek to improve the talents they severally possess; and let him who may have the one talent use it and not hide it in the earth; that is, let him who may be endowed with little ability improve himself, and not complain because nature may not have been so propitious to him as to his more fortunate brother. Let us all be satisfied with our lot in life, and should it not be so desirable as we could wish, we should seek with becoming diligence to improve it, ever feeling grateful for our earthly being, and more especially for the Spirit of God we have received through obedience to the Gospel. . . .

I remember reading an anecdote . . . of a man who, through his wisdom and patriotism, had gained great renown, but who through envy was assigned to a position which was considered very degrading. On entering upon its duties it was said that he made this significant remark: "If the office does not honor me I will honor the office." Much difficulty would be avoided, and our condition and situation would be much more encouraging if we all honored the office in which we are called to act. We are told that the Lord himself made clothes for our first parents, or, in other words, on that occasion, acted as tailor; also that Jesus Christ was a carpenter. Now, the Saviour must have been an honorable and honest carpenter, or he never could have merited the position he afterwards occupied. If we could get the brethren and sisters to see the importance of acting honestly and faithfully in their respective callings, much of the annoyances and troubles we now experience would be averted, and the work of God would roll on with redoubled rapidity, and all his purposes would be more rapidly and speedily accomplished; and besides, as a people, we would be better prepared than we now are for the dispensation of his will. . . .

May God bless you, my brethren and sisters, and enable you to act always as wise stewards over that with which you have been entrusted.[8] [See suggestion 4 on page 192.]

When we serve God with faith, energy, and cheerfulness, He strengthens us and helps us succeed.

I say, let men serve God faithfully and energetically, and be cheerful. . . . There are times when persons are brought into conditions where it would be very difficult, if not impossible, to assume a cheerful aspect. But such times are very few.[9]

Knowing our religion to be true we ought to be the most devoted people on the face of the earth to the cause we have embraced. Knowing as we do, or should know, that the gospel we have received promises all our hearts can wish or desire, if we are faithful, we ought to be very faithful, devoted, energetic and ambitious in carrying out the designs and wishes of the Lord as He reveals them from time to time through His servants. We ought not to be lukewarm or negligent in attending to our duties, but with all our might, strength and souls we should try to understand the spirit of our calling and the nature of the work in which we are engaged.

When Jesus was upon the earth, he commanded His disciples to go forth and preach the gospel without purse or scrip, taking no thought beforehand as to what they should eat, or drink, or wherewithal they should be clothed; but simply to go forth and to testify of those things which had been revealed to them. In doing this they secured to themselves the blessings of the Almighty, and success attended all their exertions. They were bound to succeed; no power could cross their path and prevent them reaping the most sanguine success because they went forth in the strength of the Almighty to perform His will, and it was His business to sustain and support them and to furnish them all the means of success. Through obedience to the commands of the Lord they secured to themselves the blessings of life with the privilege of coming forth in the morning of the first resurrection, and they had the assurance that in their labors no power on earth could successfully oppose them. These were the kind of prospects I should have liked had I been in their position, or in any other position, for to the thoughtful mind the idea of ultimate success in any pursuit is very pleasing.

Now had the apostles, instead of doing as they were commanded, imagined that by doing something else they could have answered the same purpose, they would not have succeeded so well in their operations, neither would they have possessed that assurance of success which under all the trials and persecutions to which they were exposed was doubtless to them a source of constant pleasure and satisfaction.

. . . Had the apostles or seventies in the days of Jesus imagined that they could have fulfilled the missions given them by building an ark as Noah did, or building granaries and storing grain as Joseph did they would have been grandly mistaken.

Joseph in the land of Egypt was called upon to perform a certain class of duties, which were made incumbent upon him. He was not called to preach the gospel without purse or scrip; but to build granaries, and to use all his influence with the King, nobles and people of Egypt to store their grain against a day of famine. . . . Now supposing that Joseph had gone to work and built an ark, he would not have been accepted of the Lord, neither could he have saved the people of Egypt nor his father's house. When Noah was commanded to build an ark, supposing he had established granaries, he and his house could not have been saved. So in regard to ourselves, when duties are required at our hands, . . . whatever we may be required to do within the pale of the kingdom of the Almighty, we have to walk in the spirit of these requirements and perform them if we would gain power and influence with our God.[10] [See suggestion 5 on page 192.]

The work of the Lord is sometimes difficult, but it brings great joy.

We meet many things associated with this labor that are not pleasant, but there is a great pleasure connected with it. When we look back upon our determinations to devote ourselves to the cause of truth and keep our covenants, we have great joy, because the spirit of our callings rests mightily upon us, without which spirit we cannot keep pace with the kingdom of God.[11]

We should renew our covenants before God and the holy angels, that we will, God being our helper, serve him more faithfully during the ensuing year than we have in the past, that our public and private life, our actions and the spirit and influence we wield may be in keeping with the motto, "The Kingdom of God or nothing." I trust . . . that we may devote ourselves entirely to the service of our God in the establishing of his Zion on the earth, zealously laboring in the interest of truth and righteousness on the earth, until it shall become a joy to us to be so engaged, that it may become second nature to us to serve God and keep his commandments, and to observe the celestial law, and that we may so enjoy the Holy Spirit in our hearts that we may overcome the world and establish the celestial law in our minds and establish it in our practice; that we may so understand ourselves and our privileges that we may in this life secure a considerable portion of the blessings that pertain to the celestial law, and which are to be enjoyed in the celestial glory.[12] [See suggestion 6 on page 193.]

Suggestions for Study and Teaching

Consider these ideas as you study the chapter or as you prepare to teach. For additional help, see pages v–vii.

1. Review the account on pages 183–84. What words would you use to describe Lorenzo Snow's attitude about serving the Lord? Think about what you can do to follow his example.

2. Consider the section that begins on page 184. Why do you think membership in the Church brings such great responsibilities? What does it mean to you to be an ambassador of Christ?

3. President Snow taught that our callings in the Church are opportunities to "assist in the redemption" of God's children (pages 185–86). How might this understanding affect the way we serve in the Church?

4. President Snow said that we should serve diligently, no matter how small our responsibility may seem (pages 186–89). When have you seen someone honor a seemingly small calling or assignment?

5. Read the section that begins on page 190. In what ways do faith, energy, and cheerfulness influence our service?

6. Read the final section in the chapter (pages 191–92). When have you experienced the joy of serving in the Lord's kingdom? How can we find pleasure in our service even when our tasks are not pleasant? What can we do to help children and youth serve the Lord faithfully?

Related Scriptures: Psalm 100:2; 1 Corinthians 12:12–31; Jacob 1:6–7; 2:3; Mosiah 4:26–27; D&C 64:33–34; 72:3; 76:5–6; 107:99–100; 121:34–36

Teaching Help: "Listen sincerely to learners' comments. Your example will encourage them to listen carefully to one another. If you do not understand someone's comment, ask a question. You might say, 'I'm not sure I understand. Could you explain that again?' or 'Could you give me an example of what you mean?'" (*Teaching, No Greater Call,* 64).

Notes

1. See Brigham Young, Heber C. Kimball, and Willard Richards, "Sixth General Epistle of the Presidency of The Church of Jesus Christ of Latter-day Saints," *Millennial Star,* Jan. 15, 1852, 25.
2. See "Address to the Saints in Great Britain," *Millennial Star,* Dec. 1, 1851, 365.
3. "The Gospel in Malta," *Millennial Star,* Apr. 24, 1852, 141–42.
4. "The Malta Mission," *Millennial Star,* June 5, 1852, 236.
5. See Jabez Woodard, "Italian Correspondence," *Millennial Star,* Sept. 18, 1852, 476.
6. *Deseret News: Semi-Weekly,* Jan. 23, 1877, 1.
7. *Deseret News: Semi-Weekly,* Jan. 23, 1883, 1.
8. *Deseret News: Semi-Weekly,* Jan. 23, 1877, 1.
9. *Deseret Semi-Weekly News,* Mar. 30, 1897, 1.
10. *Deseret News: Semi-Weekly,* Mar. 31, 1868, 2.
11. *Millennial Star,* Oct. 29, 1888, 690.
12. In Conference Report, Apr. 1880, 81.

Before the Saints left Nauvoo, priesthood leaders covenanted to help all the Saints who wanted to join the emigration.

CHAPTER 16

"That We May Become One"

"The voice of the Almighty called us out from the midst of confusion . . . to form a union and a lovely brotherhood, in which we should love one another as we love ourselves."

From the Life of Lorenzo Snow

Before the Saints were driven from Nauvoo, the leading Brethren of the Church met in the temple. They covenanted that they would "never cease [their] exertions, by all the means and influence within [their] reach, till all the Saints who were obliged to leave Nauvoo should be located at some gathering place of the Saints."[1] Determined to keep this covenant, President Brigham Young established the Perpetual Emigrating Fund in 1849. Under this program, the Church loaned money to emigrating Saints with the understanding that the people would repay their loans after they arrived in Utah and found employment.

President Young called Elder Lorenzo Snow and others to raise funds for this effort. It was difficult for Elder Snow to ask the Saints for donations—they were poor themselves, having been driven from place to place before settling in the Salt Lake Valley. He wrote in his journal: "In performing the mission of soliciting means from the Saints who, after having been robbed and plundered, had performed a journey of more than one thousand miles, and just located in an unwatered, desolate recess of the great 'American Desert,' I found myself inducted into an uphill business. With very few exceptions, the people had very little, or nothing they could possibly spare." However, everywhere Elder Snow went, people gave all they could. He reported: "The efforts and willingness, everywhere manifested, to eke out a portion of the little—the feeling of liberality and greatness of soul, which everywhere I met in the midst of poverty, the warm-hearted greetings I received even where comparative indigence held court, filled my heart with exceeding great joy. One man insisted that I should take his only cow, saying that the Lord had delivered him, and blessed him in leaving the old country and coming to a land of peace; and in giving his only cow, he felt that he would only do what duty demanded, and what he would expect from others, were the situation reversed."

After collecting donations in northern Utah, Elder Snow observed, "The hearts of the Saints were open, and, considering their circumstances, they donated liberally and amply, and I need not say cheerfully."[2]

Although the people had little to give individually, their unified efforts blessed many lives. The Perpetual Emigrating Fund expanded beyond its original purpose, helping more than just the members of the Church who had been in Nauvoo. It continued for 38 years, helping tens of thousands of converts from many lands gather with their fellow Saints. [See suggestion 1 on page 202.]

Teachings of Lorenzo Snow

When we are united in the gospel, the Lord shows the world His character through us.

Jesus prayed to his Father that those he had given him out of the world might be one as he and the Father were one, and says he, I pray that thou wilt give them the same love which thou hast for me, that I may be in them and thou in me, that all may be one. There is something very important in this, and we have got to practice ourselves until we become like the Father and the Son, one in all things.[3]

From the verses which I have read [John 17:19–21] the importance and the necessity of the Apostles being united, was shown, in order that the purposes of the Lord might be effective in the world. For unless the Apostles and those that believed on them were united, the world could not believe in the mission and purposes of the Savior. Therefore Jesus prayed to the Father that all those whom the Father had given Him might be one as He and the Father were one, that the world might believe that the Father had sent Him. In fact this is what the Lord designed to effect through Israel in bringing them out from Egyptian bondage; He wished to make of them a united people, a peculiar nation, a nation of people whom God could honor and respect in order that the world might believe, and that they might receive the blessings which He wished to bestow upon them, inasmuch as the human race are all the offspring of God; and if Israel had carried out His requirements, the world, no doubt would have been greatly benefited thereby, and the purposes of God more fully effected. The Lord wished to show His character, and the character of the heavens, and wished to extend His love and blessings through Israel to the whole human family; but Israel was disobedient and would not hearken to His voice. . . .

If we have division in our midst; if we be divided either spiritually or temporally, we never can be the people that God designs us to become, nor can we ever become instruments in His hands of making the world believe that the holy Priesthood has been restored, and that we have the everlasting Gospel. In order for us to effect the purposes of God we shall have to do as Jesus did—conform our individual will to the will of God, not only in one thing, but in all things, and to live so that the will of God shall be in us.[4] [See suggestion 2 on page 203.]

Unity is essential in the Church and in our families.

There should be greater union in our midst than we find today. There is a perfect union in the quorum of the Twelve. Should there not be a perfect union in that quorum? Most assuredly, every one would say Yes, a perfect union in the quorum of the Twelve Apostles. . . . And there is also a perfect union with the First Presidency, and should there not be? Every one will say, certainly, there should be. And should there not be a perfect union with the seven presidents of the Seventies? There most assuredly should be; we all say Yes. Should there not be a perfect union with the High Councils of the various Stakes of Zion? Certainly there should be, and there is a way to accomplish that union. And the same way with the various other organizations and quorums. Should there not be a perfect union with the presidencies of Stakes? Certainly, and if I were a president of a Stake, I would not rest day or night until I had union with my counselors. Should there not be a union with the Bishop and his Counselors? Most assuredly there should be.

Well, what is more important? Should there not be union in the family? . . . Most assuredly there should. And why should any man be satisfied, why should any husband and father of a family rest satisfied until he effects a perfect union, that is, just as far as a perfect union can be accomplished? And in this matter the father should make himself just as perfect as a man can in this life be made perfect before his family. And the wife should make herself just as perfect as a woman can possibly do in this life. And then they are prepared to make their children just as perfect as they are willing and are capable of being made perfect. And the father and the mother should be very careful. The wife should never in the presence of her children speak disrespectfully of her husband. If she thinks her husband has done wrong (he might have done), she should never speak of it in the presence of her children. She should take him out of the presence of her children and there tell him of his faults, in a pleasant way, but never in the presence of the children speak disrespectfully of the father. And the father the same. He has no right to speak disrespectfully of his wife in the presence of her children. And I pray God to give the husband and wife the spirit and the understanding to correct themselves in such matters. I know that a great many of the difficulties that now appear, and the disrespect that we find in reference to the Priesthood, among young people, arises from this fact, that there have been difficulties in the home circle, and there has been disrespect expressed in their presence, of the father by the mother, or of the mother by the father. Now I know these things are so.[5] [See suggestion 3 on page 203.]

We become united as we help each other secure peace and happiness.

We talk considerably in regard to the principle of loving our neighbors as well as we love ourselves; we talk about it and we sometimes think about it, but how much do we really enter into the spirit of these things, and see that the difficulty lies within ourselves? We must understand that we have got to act upon certain principles by which we can bind ourselves together as a people, to bind our

"Should there not be union in the family? . . . Most assuredly there should."

feelings together that we may become one, and this never can be accomplished unless certain things are done, and things that require an exertion on our part.

How would you go to work to bind yourselves together? How would a man go to work to unite himself with his neighbor? If two men were associated together who had never been acquainted, how would they go to work to secure each other's friendship, attachment and affection one towards another? Why something would have to be done, and that not by one party only, but would have to be done by one as well as by the other. It would not answer for one to do the business alone; it would not do for one to answer those feelings and do the work himself, but in order to become as one in their sentiments and affection—the action of both would be requisite. . . .

. . . Something has to be done by [each] party in order to secure each other's friendship and to bind us together as a community. . . .

. . . Let your minds be expanded to comprehend and look after the interest of your friends that are around you, and where it is in your power to secure benefits to your friends do so, and in so doing you will find that those things which you need will come into your hands quicker than if you labor entirely to secure them to yourselves independent of regarding the interests of your friends. I know this is a good and important principle. . . .

. . . We have got to know that it is our business to learn to secure the peace and happiness of those that are around us, and never take a course to trample upon the feelings and rights of our neighbors. Let a man go and trample upon the rights of a brother and how long would it take him to destroy that feeling of confidence that had heretofore existed between them? And when once destroyed how long will it take to establish that feeling which once existed between them? It will take a great while. This is what we have to place our eye upon; I feel it so; in all our thinking, in all our movements and in our secret meditations we want to let our minds reflect upon the interests of all around; and to consider that they have rights and privileges as well as ourselves; we ought to have this firmly established in our minds.

Now you take a man that is continually looking after the interests of the people around him, and let him feel to bless anything and all things that belong to his brethren, and he will in this way establish happiness in himself and around him. Let a man take the opposite course and instead of blessing and laboring for the benefit of others, find fault and pull down, will he make the same improvement? Assuredly he will not.

. . . If we feel that it is our duty to go to work more ambitiously than what we have done to secure confidence, we will proceed if it is in our power to yield temporal blessings and favors to secure the friendship of those around us. In this way and in no other can we be bound together and manifest that we have a kind and brotherly feeling.—We must exhibit this feeling by our works . . . instead of shaking a person by the hand and saying God bless you my good fellow, and the next day pay[ing] no regard to what we have previously said but trampl[ing] upon his best feelings.[6]

When a man is not willing to sacrifice for the benefit of his brethren, and when he knows that he trespasses upon the feelings of his brethren, . . . that man is not right before the Lord, and where is the love of that individual for his brother?

When one brother is not willing to suffer for his brother, how is it in his power to manifest that he has love for his brother? I tell you it is in our folly and weakness that we will not bear with our brethren, but if they trespass upon our rights we immediately retaliate, and if they tread upon our toes we immediately jump upon theirs. . . . When I see a brother that has been trespassed against, and then he turns round and jumps upon the offender, then I say how far is that brother from the path of duty, and I say to him you must learn to govern yourself or you never will be saved in the kingdom of God.[7]

I will read some paragraphs in the Book of Doctrine and Covenants:

"My disciples, in days of old, sought occasion against one another, and forgave not one another in their hearts, and for this evil they were afflicted, and sorely chastened;

"Wherefore I say unto you, that ye ought to forgive one another, for he that forgiveth not his brother his trespasses, standeth condemned before the Lord, for there remaineth in him the greater sin." [D&C 64:8–9.] . . .

As I read here, there was one thing that the disciples of the Savior did not accomplish—they did not succeed in establishing that union of spirit and feeling that they ought to have had, and the Lord chastened them for it. The Lord requires that men should forgive one another, even seventy times seven. And even if the party does not ask forgiveness, we are to forgive. . . . He that forgives not his brother, we are told, there remaineth in him the greater sin—that is, he is a greater sinner than the person that offended him. The Lord requires us to love our neighbor as we do ourselves—a pretty difficult matter under many circumstances; but we will have to reach that point of perfection, and we will reach it.[8] [See suggestion 4 on page 203.]

As we become united in the gospel, we increase in light and intelligence and prepare to dwell in God's presence.

We should be bound together and act like David and Jonathan as the heart of one [see 1 Samuel 18:1], and sooner let our arm be severed from our bodies than injure each other. What a mighty people we would be if we were in this condition, and we have got to go into it, however little feelings of friendship we may have in exercise at the present time. I can just tell you that the day will come when we must become united in this way if we ever see the presence of God. We shall have to learn to love our neighbors as we love ourselves. We must go into this, however far we are from it at the present time, yet no matter, we must learn these principles and establish them in our bosoms. Now this I can see clearly, and that is the reason why I talk about these matters in the style in which I do, for I wish to plant them in the minds of the Saints, and to have these things among their every day feelings.[9]

The voice of the Almighty called us out from the midst of confusion, which is Babylon, to form a union and a lovely brotherhood, in which we should love one another as we love ourselves. When we depart from this purpose, the Spirit of God withdraws from us to the extent of that departure. But if we continue in the extent of those covenants which we made when we received the Gospel, there is a corresponding increase of light and intelligence, and there is a powerful preparation for that which is to come. And because of our faithfulness and our adherence to the covenants we have made, the foundation upon which we stand becomes like the pillars of heaven—immovable.[10] [See suggestion 5 on page 203.]

Suggestions for Study and Teaching

Consider these ideas as you study the chapter or as you prepare to teach. For additional help, see pages v–vii.

1. Review Lorenzo Snow's experience with the Perpetual Emigrating Fund (pages 195–96). In the Church today, what opportunities do we have to give money or goods to help others? In what ways can these efforts help us become one?

2. Ponder President Snow's teachings about why the Lord wants us to be unified (pages 196–97). Why do you think other people will be more likely to gain a testimony of the Lord and His restored Church when they see that we are unified? How might their feelings change if they see that we are divided?
3. Examine the section that begins at the bottom of page 197. How does this counsel apply in our homes? Consider what you can do to encourage more unity in your family relationships.
4. How can we experience unity in our Relief Society or priesthood quorum, even when we have different interests and ideas? (For some examples, see pages 198–201.) In what ways have you benefited from unity in your family? in the Church? in the community?
5. Why do you think love for one another can make us "a mighty people"? How does love for others influence the way we live? As you ponder or discuss these questions, review the last two paragraphs in the chapter.

Related Scriptures: Psalm 133; John 13:34–35; Romans 12:5; Mosiah 18:21; 4 Nephi 1:15–17; D&C 51:9; Moses 7:18

Teaching Help: "The crowning, convincing, converting power of gospel teaching is manifest when an inspired teacher says, 'I know by the power of the Holy Ghost, by the revelations of the Holy Spirit to my soul, that the doctrines I have taught are true'" (Bruce R. McConkie, quoted in *Teaching, No Greater Call,* 43).

Notes

1. Quoted in Brigham Young, Heber C. Kimball, and Willard Richards, "Important from Salt Lake City," *Millennial Star,* Apr. 15, 1850, 120; see also Eliza R. Snow Smith, *Biography and Family Record of Lorenzo Snow* (1884), 107.
2. In *Biography and Family Record of Lorenzo Snow,* 108.
3. *Deseret News,* Jan. 14, 1857, 355.
4. *Deseret News: Semi-Weekly,* Jan. 23, 1883, 1.
5. In Conference Report, Oct. 1897, 32–33.
6. *Deseret News,* Mar. 11, 1857, 3–4; in the original source, page 3 is incorrectly labeled as page 419.
7. *Deseret News,* Jan. 14, 1857, 355.
8. In Conference Report, Apr. 1898, 61, 63.
9. *Deseret News,* Mar. 11, 1857, 4.
10. *Deseret Semi-Weekly News,* June 4, 1889, 4.

A modern-day photograph of the Piedmont region of Italy, where Elder Lorenzo Snow served as a missionary in the early 1850s.

CHAPTER 17

Priesthood—"for the Salvation of the Human Family"

"The priesthood we hold has been revealed for the salvation of the human family. We must be lively in our minds in reference to it."

From the Life of Lorenzo Snow

Elder Lorenzo Snow was ordained an Apostle on February 12, 1849. Eight months later he was called to establish a mission in Italy. With other brethren who had been called to serve, he left for this mission on October 19, 1849. He and his companions made the long journey by foot, on horseback, and by boat.

Arriving in Italy in June 1850, he and his companions found that the people in the major Italian cities were not yet ready to receive the gospel. But a people known as the Waldenses attracted his attention, and he felt inspired to work among them. The Waldenses had lived for centuries in the secluded Piedmont region—a mountain valley just south of the Italy-Switzerland border and east of the Italy-France border. Having formed their society because of a desire for religious reform, they were dedicated to studying the Bible and following the example of the Savior's Apostles.

Elder Snow said that when he considered preaching the gospel among the Waldenses, "a flood of light seemed to burst upon my mind."[1] But despite these assurances, he felt that it was unwise to begin active missionary work immediately because enemies of the Church had distributed publications among the people, spreading lies about the Church.[2] Elder Snow reported, "As I felt it was the mind of the Spirit that we should proceed at first, by slow and cautious steps, I submitted to the will of heaven."[3]

Although the missionaries did not begin preaching right away, Elder Snow oversaw the publication of pamphlets in Italian and French. In addition, he and his companions befriended the people around them. "We endeavoured to lay a foundation for future usefulness," he said, "in silently preparing the minds of the people for the reception of the Gospel, by cultivating friendly feelings in the bosoms of those by whom we were surrounded. Yet I felt it rather singular, and no small tax upon patience, to be weeks, and months, in the midst of an interesting people, without being actively and publicly engaged in communicating the great principles which I had come to promulgate."[4]

The Waldenses' feelings about the Church began to change significantly after Elder Snow administered a priesthood blessing to a boy who had become very ill. Elder Snow wrote the following in his journal:

"Sept. 6th.—This morning my attention was directed to Joseph Guy, a boy three years of age, the youngest child of our host. Many friends had been to see the child, as to all human appearance, his end was nigh at hand. I went to see him in the afternoon: death was making havoc of his body; his former healthy frame was now reduced to a skeleton, and it was only by close observation we could discern he was alive."

Troubled by the opposition to the preaching of the gospel and concerned about little Joseph Guy, Elder Snow turned to the Lord for help that evening. He later recalled: "For some hours before I retired to rest, I called upon the Lord to assist us at this time. My feelings on this occasion will not be easily erased from memory.

"Sept. 7th.—This morning, I proposed . . . that we should fast, and retire to the mountains, and pray. As we departed, we called and saw the child; his eyeballs turned upwards: his eyelids fell and closed: his face and ears were thin, and wore the pale marble hue, indicative of approaching dissolution. The cold perspiration of death covered his body, and the principle of life was nearly exhausted. Madame Guy and other females were sobbing, while Monsieur Guy hung his head." Whispering to Elder Snow and the other missionaries, Monsieur Guy said, "He dies. He dies."

Elder Snow continued: "After a little rest upon the mountains, aside from any likelihood of interruption, we there called upon the Lord in solemn prayer, to spare the life of the child. As I contemplated the course we wished to pursue and the claims we should soon advance to the world, I regarded this circumstance as one of vast importance. I know not any sacrifice which I could possibly make, that I was not willing to offer that the Lord might grant our requests."

When they returned to the Guy family that afternoon, Elder Snow gave Joseph a priesthood blessing. They went to see the family a few hours later, and Joseph's father, "with a smile of thankfulness," told them the boy was much better.

"Sept. 8.—The child had been so well, the parents were enabled to betake themselves to rest, which they had not done for some time previous. To-day, they were enabled to leave him, and attend to their business." When Joseph's mother expressed her joy at the boy's recovery, Elder Snow responded, "The God of heaven has done this for you."

"From that hour he began to amend," recounted Elder Snow, "and with a heart filled with gratitude to our heavenly Father, I am happy to say, that in a few days he left his bed, and joined his little companions."[5]

After this experience, Elder Snow felt that circumstances were "as favourable as could be expected" for the work of the Lord to progress among the people. On September 19, 1850, exactly 11 months after he had left home to serve in Italy, he told his companions that they should "commence [their] public business." They again ascended a mountain, where Elder Snow dedicated the land for the preaching of the restored gospel.[6]

Elder Snow's words to Madame Guy—"the God of heaven has done this for you"—reflected his lifelong teachings about the priesthood. He reminded the Saints that through the work of priesthood holders, "the glory and power of God [is] made manifest" for the benefit of others.[7] [See suggestion 1 on page 213.]

Teachings of Lorenzo Snow

Priesthood bearers are messengers of the Almighty, with authority delegated from heaven to administer holy ordinances.

We, the Latter-day Saints, profess to have received from God the fulness of the everlasting gospel; we profess to be in possession of the holy Priesthood—the delegated authority of God to man, by virtue of which we administer in its ordinances acceptably to him.[8]

Any man who will humble himself before God and will be immersed in water, after repentance, for the remission of his sins, shall receive, through the laying on of hands, the gift of the Holy Ghost. Can I give this to him? No, I, simply as a messenger of the Almighty to whom has been delegated authority, administer immersion for the remission of sins; I simply immerse him in water, having authority so to do. I simply lay my hands upon him for the reception of the Holy Ghost, then God, from his presence, acknowledges my authority, acknowledges that I am his messenger, and confers the Holy Ghost upon the individual.[9]

When [I have] baptiz[ed] people and administer[ed] the ordinances of this holy priesthood, God has confirmed those administrations by imparting the Holy Ghost, giving a knowledge to the individuals to whom I administered, convincing them that the authority was delegated from heaven. And every Elder who has gone forth to preach this everlasting Gospel, and acted in the spirit of his calling, can bear the same testimony, that through their administrations in these holy ordinances the glory and power of God has been made manifest in a convincing manner upon the heads of those to whom they have administered. This is our testimony; this was the testimony [in 1830] of a certain individual who stood forth and claimed that God had authorized him to baptize people for the remission of sins, and lay hands upon them for the reception of the Holy Ghost, which should impart unto them a knowledge from the eternal worlds that he had this authority. This person was Joseph Smith; and he conferred this authority, which was given unto him by holy angels, upon others who were sent forth to bear testimony to the world that those who would receive those holy

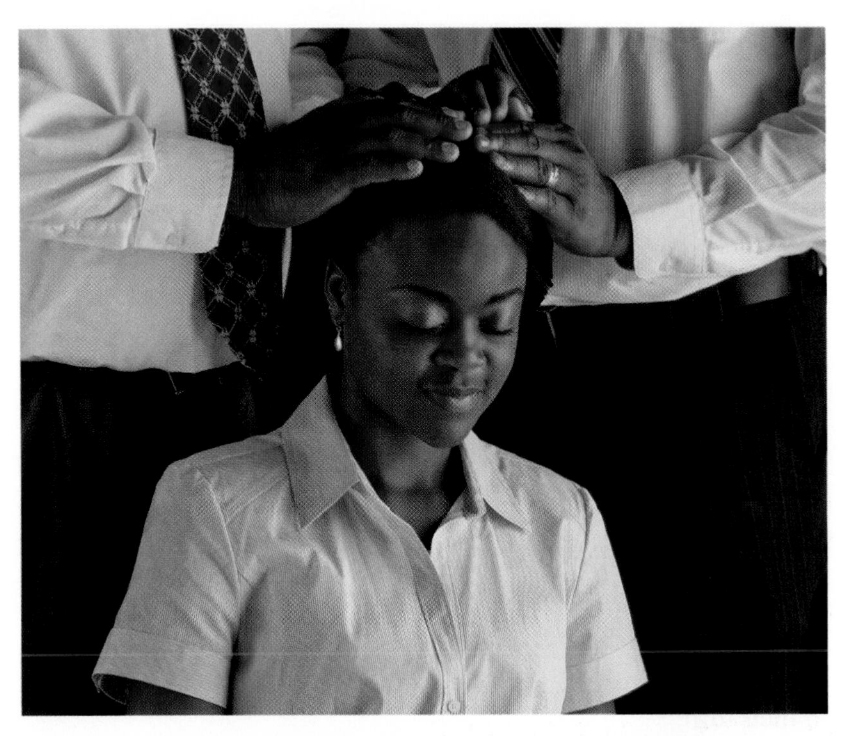

All faithful members of the Church are blessed through priesthood ordinances and covenants.

ordinances, should receive the testimony from the Almighty that they were thus authorized to so administer. And this is our testimony; and this is my testimony before this people and before the world.[10]

Where in all the world can you find a class of ministers that dare take the position our Elders do? Where is the man or the set of men that can be found that dare to present themselves before the world and say that they have been authorized of God to administer certain ordinances to the people through which they may receive revelation from God? Any one announcing a doctrine of this kind would soon be found out if he was an impostor—he would place himself in a very dangerous position, and would soon be discovered if he held no such authority. Our Elders, however, dare take this position. . . . God has sent his holy angels from heaven and restored the authority to man to administer the ordinance[s] of the gospel.[11] [See suggestion 2 on page 213.]

The priesthood helps us find happiness in this life and throughout eternity.

The Priesthood has been restored; it has been bestowed upon man that through that medium, all who would like to be good and happy, might have the privilege. The gospel tells us how to be great, good and happy. The spirit of the gospel of Christ teaches all things that are necessary for our present and future welfare.

We have these objects in view today, and we should continually keep them before us. Look back for twenty-five years, or look back ten years only, and a great many have been in the church that length of time, and see what we have accomplished. We see farther and comprehend things better, hence we are better prepared for the things that are coming on the earth than we were ten, fifteen, twenty or twenty-five years ago to know how to be useful, to know how to do things as they should be done. . . .

. . . The object of the priesthood is to make all [people] happy, to diffuse information, to make all partakers of the same blessings in their turn.[12]

For this very purpose the Holy Priesthood has been bestowed in this our day, to guide and perfect the saints of God here, and just in proportion as we attain to intelligence in this world and to integrity and faithfulness . . . , so will be the exalted condition in which we shall appear behind the veil.[13]

The Lord has said that He will give us all that He hath—and this according to the oath and covenant which belongs to the Priesthood [see D&C 84:33–44]. Nobody ought to doubt what Jesus says, and He declares, as recorded in the Revelations of St. John, "To him that overcometh will I grant to sit with me in my throne, even as I also overcame, and am set down with my Father in His throne." [Revelation 3:21.] Can anything be said greater than that? Does not that comprehend everything?[14]

This gospel we have received has been revealed from heaven, and the priesthood we hold has been revealed for the salvation of the human family. We must be lively in our minds in reference to it.[15] [See suggestion 3 on page 213.]

The ancient Apostles Peter, James, and John conferred the Melchizedek Priesthood upon Joseph Smith and Oliver Cowdery.

Righteous priesthood holders seek diligently and energetically for spiritual gifts to help them serve others.

To my brethren in the Priesthood I beg to offer a few words of counsel, instruction and exhortation. Upon you rest high and sacred responsibilities, which relate not only to the salvation of this generation, but of many past generations, and many to come. The glorious ensign of Emanuel's kingdom once again established in the world must be unfurled in every nation, kingdom, and empire; the voice of warning . . . must be carried forth unto all people; you are the ones whom the Lord has selected for this purpose, even the horn of Joseph, to push together the people [see Deuteronomy 33:13–17]. Surely you cannot be too anxiously, nor too industriously engaged, seeking how best, the manner most useful to yourselves and mankind, to magnify your holy and sacred offices.[16]

There are men in this Church who are as good in their hearts and feelings as men ever were, but lack faith and energy, and do not obtain really what is their privilege to receive. If their faith, their energy and determination were equal to their good feelings and desires, their honesty and goodness, they would indeed be mighty men in Israel; and sickness and disease and the power of the evil one would flee before them as chaff before the wind. Yet, we say we are a good people and that we are not only holding our own but making great advances in righteousness before God; and no doubt, we are. But I wish to impress upon you, my brethren and sisters that there are Elders among us endowed with spiritual gifts that may be brought into exercise through the aid of the Holy Ghost. The gifts of the Gospel must be cultivated by diligence and perseverance. The ancient Prophets when desiring some peculiar blessing, or important knowledge, revelation or vision, would sometimes fast and pray for days and even weeks for that purpose.[17]

My young brethren, when things go against you, when everything seems black, do your duty and you will become strong men, powerful men; the sick will be healed under your ministrations; devils will flee from you; the dead will rise; and everything that was ever done by man since the days of Adam, you will be able to do through the power of God and through a proper ambition.[18]

Purity, virtue, fidelity, godliness must be sought ambitiously, or the crown cannot be won. Those principles must be incorporated with[in] ourselves, woven into our constitutions, becoming a part of us, making us a centre, a fountain of truth, of equity, justice, and mercy, of all that is good and great, that from us may proceed the light, the life, the power, and the law to direct, to govern and assist to save a wandering world; acting as the sons of God, for and in behalf of our Father in heaven. We expect in the resurrection to exercise the powers of our priesthood—we can exercise them only in proportion as we secure its righteousness and perfections; these qualifications can be had only as they are sought and obtained, so that in the morning of the resurrection we will possess those acquisitions only which we secured in this world! Godliness cannot be *conferred* but must be *acquired,* a fact of which the religious world seem[s] strangely and lamentably unconscious. Seek to benefit others, and others will seek to benefit you; and he that would be great, let him be good, studying the interests of the whole, becoming the servant of all.[19]

As Saints of God, Elders of Israel, we should be willing to devote time and labor, making every necessary sacrifice in order to obtain the proper spiritual qualifications to be highly useful in our several callings. And may the Lord inspire every heart with the importance of these matters that we may seek diligently and energetically for the gifts and powers promised in the Gospel we have obeyed.[20] [See suggestion 4 below.]

Suggestions for Study and Teaching

Consider these ideas as you study the chapter or as you prepare to teach. For additional help, see pages v–vii.

1. Review the account on pages 205–7. In what ways can Melchizedek Priesthood holders prepare themselves to give priesthood blessings? What can we all do to prepare ourselves to receive priesthood blessings?
2. Read the paragraph at the bottom of page 208. In what ways do priesthood ordinances manifest the power of God in our lives?
3. In what ways do priesthood ordinances and blessings help us all find happiness in this life? How do they help us secure eternal happiness? In connection with these questions, ponder President Snow's teachings on page 210.
4. On pages 211–13, examine the spiritual gifts that President Snow encouraged priesthood holders to cultivate. What do you think it means to cultivate a spiritual gift? How does this counsel relate to the efforts of all members of the Church?

Related Scriptures: James 5:14–15; Alma 13:2–16; D&C 84:19–22; 128:8–14; Articles of Faith 1:3, 5

Teaching Help: "To help learners prepare to answer questions, you may want to tell them before something is read or presented that you will be asking for their responses. . . . For example, you could say, 'Listen as I read this passage so that you can share what most interests you about it' or 'As this scripture is read, see if you can understand what the Lord is telling us about faith'" (*Teaching, No Greater Call,* 69).

Notes

1. See letter to Brigham Young, in *The Italian Mission* (1851), 11.
2. See "Organization of the Church in Italy," *Millennial Star,* Dec. 15, 1850, 371.
3. Letter to Brigham Young, in *The Italian Mission,* 14.
4. Letter to Brigham Young, in *The Italian Mission,* 14.
5. Quoted in "Organization of the Church in Italy," 371.
6. See letter to Brigham Young, in *The Italian Mission,* 15.
7. In Conference Report, Apr. 1880, 81.
8. *Deseret News: Semi-Weekly,* Jan. 23, 1877, 1.
9. *Deseret News,* Jan. 24, 1872, 598.
10. In Conference Report, Apr. 1880, 81–82.
11. *Deseret News: Semi-Weekly,* Dec. 2, 1879, 1.
12. *Deseret News,* May 15, 1861, 81–82.
13. *Deseret Evening News,* Oct. 6, 1880, 2; from a detailed paraphrase of a discourse Lorenzo Snow delivered at the October 1880 general conference.
14. "The Object of This Probation," *Deseret Semi-Weekly News,* May 4, 1894, 7.
15. In Journal History, July 11, 1865, 2.
16. "Address to the Saints in Great Britain," *Millennial Star,* Dec. 1, 1851, 362.
17. *Deseret News: Semi-Weekly,* Aug. 15, 1882, 1.
18. In "Anniversary Exercises," *Deseret Evening News,* Apr. 7, 1899, 9.
19. "Address to the Saints in Great Britain," 362–63.
20. *Deseret News: Semi-Weekly,* Aug. 15, 1882, 1.

CHAPTER 18

Church Leadership and Selfless Service

"We are your servants in the Lord and desire your welfare and the welfare of all mankind."

From the Life of Lorenzo Snow

From October 1840 to January 1843, Lorenzo Snow presided over the Church in London, England, and the surrounding area. He watched over priesthood leaders there, sometimes teaching them in person and sometimes writing letters to offer counsel. Shortly before the end of his mission in England, he wrote to two "Presiding Elders of London Branches," who served much like branch presidents do today. In his letter, he told of an experience he had with another branch leader in the area.

Elder Snow described this leader as having "no external faults." The man was "ambitious in promoting the cause" and had the ability to ensure "that everyone [was] in his place, and doing his duty." He was diligent, "labour[ing] in the work himself more industriously than they all." But despite this man's outward appearances of faithfulness, the branch consistently had problems that seemed to center on him. Elder Snow tried for some time to identify the source of the problems, and he gently rebuked the branch members for not supporting their leader. Then he began to wonder if the leader "may possibly possess some secret, internal working spirit that he [was] not aware of, that [did] not manifest itself openly" but that led somehow to the difficulties in the branch. Elder Snow recounted:

"I accordingly prayed that the Lord would give me a spirit of discernment in the case. My prayer was answered; I found the brother possessed of a kind of half-hidden, concealed spirit of self-exaltation which was directing him in many of his movements. He would

Faithful Church leaders follow the Lord's admonition to Peter: "Feed my sheep" (John 21:16–17).

send out a brother to fill an appointment but had a suppressed wish to have the honor of it himself; if the appointment was not attended to, he would chasten the delinquent, not because the work of the Lord was in any degree frustrated or that the brother lost a blessing, but because [he] himself was so despised in being disobeyed. In [a] case where a number were baptized by a brother, his heart rejoiced not so much because the persons were brought into the covenant but because it was done under his superintendency, secretly wishing no person under his charge to obtain much honor unless his own name were brought into connection."

Elder Snow observed that if a member of the branch succeeded in a task but did not follow the leader's counsel in every particular, the leader had "a spirit of envy . . . lurking underneath of an expressed approbation." He continued: "This spirit was concealed; its fruits were not openly manifest, but would be if not checked; it was an inherent working evil that would eventually destroy his usefulness. It brought upon him unnecessary trouble in conducting the affairs of his charge; it likewise originated a source of continued unpleasantness in his own mind. Anxious to promote the cause of God, but always in such a way that his own hand might be plainly seen in all things. Ambitious to give good instructions but careful to put his whole name in full length at the bottom of them."

Elder Snow did not write this letter to condemn the local leader. His purpose in writing was to help other leaders—that the prideful spirit he described "may be seen, known, and avoided" among them. He warned that many people "who sincerely believe themselves entirely devoid of this spirit of exaltation, would on close examination of their motives which inspire them in their conduct, discover to their surprise that this spirit was urging them forward to perform many of their movements."

Having shared this warning, he counseled: "To become as God would wish us, we must accustom our minds to rejoice in seeing others prospered as ourselves; rejoice in seeing the cause of Zion exalted by whatsoever hands Providence may order; and have our bosoms closed against the entrance of envy when a weaker instrument than ourselves is called to greater honor; be content in magnifying a lesser office till called to a higher; be satisfied in doing small things and not claim the honor of doing great ones." He compared the Church to a great building, with individual Saints as parts of that building, saying that we should "never feel too lofty to be sometimes cut down, squared, scored, and hewed to be fitted into the place we are to occupy in the spiritual building."

Elder Snow concluded the letter with these words: "If a presiding elder will only seek to become as he may be and ought to be, ridding himself of selfish principles, and always act for the good of his people, and be humble, and not seek to do too much in a little time, or be too great until grown, he will never be at a loss how to magnify his office properly, nor will ever lack the power of God to bring about His wise purposes."[1] [See suggestion 1 on page 222.]

Teachings of Lorenzo Snow

The Lord has given leaders in His Church a divine mandate: "Feed my sheep."

Let every man who stands in an official station, on whom God has bestowed his holy and divine priesthood think of what the Savior said to the Twelve Apostles just before he went into the presence of his Father—"Feed my sheep." [John 21:16–17.] And he continued to say this until his apostles felt sorrowful that he should continue to call upon them in this manner. But said he—"Feed my sheep." That is, "Go forth with your whole heart, be devoted wholly to my cause. These people in the world are my brethren and sisters. My feelings are exercised towards them. Take care of my people. Feed my flock. Go forth and preach the gospel. I will reward you for all your sacrifices. Do not think that you can make too great a sacrifice in accomplishing this work." He called upon them in the fervor of his heart to do this work. And now I call upon all who hold this priesthood, the presiding officers of [the] stake, and the Bishops, and the High Council, to go forth and feed the flock. Take an interest in them. . . . Work for them, and do not confine your thoughts and feelings to your personal aggrandizement. Then God will give you revelation upon revelation, inspiration upon inspiration, and teach you how to secure the interests of the Saints in matters pertaining to their temporal and spiritual welfare.[2] [See suggestion 2 on page 222.]

Leaders and teachers are called to follow the Savior's example and serve with love, not to aggrandize themselves.

Why is [a] man called to act as president over a people? Is it in order to acquire an influence and then to use that influence directly for his own aggrandizement? No, but on the contrary, he is called to act in such a position on the same principle as the priesthood was given to the Son of God, that he should make sacrifices. For himself? No, but in the interests of the people over whom he presides. Would he be required to offer himself up on the cross as did the Saviour? No, but to become the servant of his brethren, not their master, and to work in their interest and welfare. Not to exercise the influence thus obtained to benefit himself, his family and relatives and personal friends, but esteeming all as his brethren, having rights in common with himself and, therefore, seeking to bless and benefit all equally according to the talents and worthiness they may possess, and thus by so doing develop in himself that fatherly feeling which always exists in the bosom of the Father. . . .

. . . Let those who preach in the midst of [the] Saints, realize what the Priesthood was placed upon them for; let them know and fully sense why they were appointed to fill such and such an office, viz., that they should act in the spirit of our Master, a servant of all, that they learn to consider and esteem in the same affectionate interest, the welfare of all, as they do that of themselves. . . . Then will they enter into the spirit of the two great commands upon which, said the Saviour, "hang the law and the prophets," namely, loving the Lord with all our might, mind and strength, and our neighbor as ourselves [see Matthew 22:37–40].[3]

Make one prayer before [teaching], and that is this: Ask the Lord that you may say something during your remarks that will be beneficial to those whom you address. Never mind whether it will be something that will add to your own glory or not, but simply bear in mind that you are called upon to address the audience and that they desire to receive something that will benefit them. This can only come from the Lord. Do not worry as to whether . . . those

"You will find, as a general thing, that talent is diffused through the many and rarely combined in single individuals."

who hear you may say you spoke beautifully. Do not mind about that at all, but remove every selfishness that may be in your mind that the Lord may dictate unto you something that will be of benefit to the people.[4] [See suggestion 3 on page 222.]

Wise leaders appreciate the talents of others and give people opportunities to serve.

From the fact of [a leader] having established himself in the hearts of the people, and his being known by them for his integrity and honesty, and his disposition to work for the interests of God and the people, willing to make any sacrifice that might be required of him, he possesses their confidence, and when once in possession of so sacred a trust, what then might he do in order to satisfy the minds of the people, which are, more or less, inclined to be progressive? Let such a man call to his aid those of his brethren who are the most capable, letting them share his responsibilities. Because you will find, as a general thing, that talent is diffused through the many and rarely combined in single individuals; and it only needs opportunity in order to be developed. He might say to one, "Here,

Brother So and so, you are better adapted to fill this or that position than I am;" or, to another, "You are the man best fitted for this department;" and so on until he gets the talents of all brought out, and instead of diminishing the public confidence in himself, such a course would add to it.[5] [See suggestion 4 on page 222.]

The proper way to lead is by humility, good example, and devotion to the welfare of others.

Authorita[rian] rule is not the proper rule by which to govern Saints, but rather seek to administer in the spirit of humility, wisdom, and goodness, teaching not so much by theory as practice. Though one teach with the eloquence of an angel, yet one's good practices, good examples, one's acts, constantly manifesting wholeheartedness for the interests of the people, teach much more eloquently, much more effectually.[6]

If you will be as faithful and united as the First Presidency and Twelve are faithful and united, and will follow us as we follow Christ, all will be well with you. We are determined to perform our duty and to serve the Lord and labor for the benefit of His people and the accomplishment of His work. We are your servants in the Lord and desire your welfare and the welfare of all mankind.

The Lord has not chosen the great and learned of the world to perform His work on the earth. It is not those who have been trained and educated in the colleges and seminaries of learning, but humble men devoted to His cause whom He has chosen to take charge of the affairs of His Church, men who are willing to be led and guided by the Holy Spirit, and who will of necessity give the glory unto Him, knowing that of themselves they can do nothing. I can assure you, brethren and sisters, that I had no ambition to assume the responsibility which now rests upon me. If I could have escaped it honorably I should never have been found in my present position. I have never asked for it, nor have I ever asked the assistance of any of my brethren that I might attain to this position, but the Lord revealed to me and to my brethren that this was His will, and I have no disposition to shirk any responsibility nor to decline to occupy any position that the Lord requires me to fill.[7]

I will endeavor to be devoted to your interests and the interests of the kingdom of God. I will serve you to the best of my knowledge and understanding, in reference to that which will promote your interests in connection with the interests of the Almighty. I will do this, the Lord being my helper.[8] [See suggestion 5 below.]

Suggestions for Study and Teaching

Consider these ideas as you study the chapter or as you prepare to teach. For additional help, see pages v–vii.

1. How might Lorenzo Snow's letter to leaders in England (pages 215, 217–18) apply to us? For example, what can result when we have a "spirit of self-exaltation" in our Church callings? How can we magnify our callings without magnifying ourselves?
2. Study the section that begins on page 218. In what ways can leaders "feed the flock" of Christ? What have Church leaders done to "feed" you? What character traits do you admire in these leaders?
3. Read President Snow's warnings about self-aggrandizement (pages 219–20). Then review the second full paragraph on page 217. Why should we examine our motives as we give service? Prayerfully consider your motives for serving in the Church.
4. Ponder the paragraph that begins at the bottom of page 220. How is a ward or branch influenced when leaders share some responsibilities with other members? What results have you seen when Church members with different talents and experiences have worked together toward a common goal?
5. President Snow counseled, "Authorita[rian] rule is not the proper rule by which to govern Saints" (page 221). What are some possible results of authoritarian rule by Church leaders? by parents? What are some possible results of humble leadership?

Related Scriptures: Matthew 6:24; 20:25–28; 23:5; Mark 10:42–45; John 13:13–17; 2 Nephi 26:29; 28:30–31; Mosiah 2:11–19; 3 Nephi 27:27; D&C 46:7–11; 50:26; 121:34–46

Teaching Help: "Questions written on the chalkboard before class will help learners begin to think about topics even before the lesson begins" (*Teaching, No Greater Call,* 93).

Notes

1. Letter from Lorenzo Snow to William Lewzey and William Major, Nov. 1842, in Lorenzo Snow, Letterbook, 1839–1846, Church History Library.
2. *Deseret News,* Jan. 14, 1880, 787.
3. *Deseret News,* June 13, 1877, 290–91.
4. *Improvement Era,* July 1899, 709.
5. *Deseret News,* June 13, 1877, 290.
6. "Address to the Saints in Great Britain," *Millennial Star,* Dec. 1, 1851, 362.
7. *Deseret Semi-Weekly News,* Oct. 4, 1898, 1.
8. In Conference Report, Oct. 1898, 54.

"When a man receives knowledge, he is prompted to impart it to others; when a man becomes happy, the spirit that surrounds him teaches him to strive to make others happy."

CHAPTER 19

Missionary Work: "To Reach Every Human Heart"

"There is a way to reach every human heart, and it is your business to find the way to the hearts of those to whom you are called."

From the Life of Lorenzo Snow

Lorenzo Snow was baptized in Kirtland, Ohio, where he studied Hebrew in a class with the Prophet Joseph Smith and other Church leaders. He hoped to someday pursue a "classical education" at a college in the eastern United States.[1] But as he worked toward this goal, he began to feel a pull toward another purpose. He later recalled:

"I received [the truths of the gospel] with an open heart, and I was determined not to rest there. . . . I began to be a little worried in my mind whether, after having received this wonderful knowledge, it was proper for me to remain without testifying in reference to it. Young men who had been sent out upon missions were returning and testifying of the blessings that had attended them . . . , and I began to think that, instead of preparing myself for an eastern college or university, I ought to start out and bear testimony to what the Lord had so fully given me a knowledge of. At the same time I did not like to give up my prospects of an education, because I had had it in mind for a long time, and I then had the opportunity and the means to accomplish it."

Struggling with his feelings, he asked a trusted friend for advice: "I told him what I wanted, and he said, 'Brother Snow, I would not give anyone else such counsel as I feel to give you, under the circumstances. If I were in your place, I would go on with my intentions and get an education.' That was just the very thing I wanted him to say, and it pleased me. I was contented for a time; but in the winter season, hearing these young Elders testify of their success in preaching the Gospel, I began to think about it still more. The Lord had given me a knowledge that He was coming upon the earth, and that there was a preparation necessary to be made: He had given me all that I had asked for, and more; for the baptism which I received of the Holy Ghost and the perfect knowledge then given to me was more real and convincing than my immersion in the cold water; and I felt that there was a responsibility resting upon me. So I shut up my books [and] laid my Latin and Greek aside."[2]

After making this decision, Lorenzo Snow served a mission in the state of Ohio in 1837. He later served other missions—first in the states of Missouri, Illinois, Kentucky, and Ohio, and then in England, Italy, the Hawaiian Islands, the northwestern United States, and the state of Wyoming. While he was in England, he wrote a letter to his aunt, explaining why he was willing to leave home and serve as a missionary:"The thought that I am between four and five thousand miles from the home of my childhood and all of my early, fond associations, very naturally prompts the question, *Why am I here?* . . . I am here because God has spoken, and raised up a Prophet, through whom He has restored the fulness of the everlasting Gospel, with all its gifts, powers, ordinances, and blessings; with a proclamation to all peoples, '*Repent, for the kingdom of heaven is at hand.*' In the providence of God, I have been called as an ambassador, to bear this message to the nations of the earth, which I realize devolves on me a great responsibility which I cannot discharge without the aid of the Almighty."[3]

President Snow was always grateful for the decision he made to serve the Lord as a missionary. In September 1901, at the age of 87, he said: "I have joy even now in contemplating the days of my missionary labors. The feelings produced by these peculiar experiences have become part and parcel of my very being."[4] [See suggestion 1 on page 234.]

Teachings of Lorenzo Snow

Having received the fulness of the gospel, we desire to help others rejoice in the same blessings.

When a man receives knowledge, he is prompted to impart it to others; when a man becomes happy, the spirit that surrounds him teaches him to strive to make others happy. . . . Is there any chance of a man becoming happy without a knowledge of the gospel of Christ? . . . Though in the world [people] try to make themselves happy, still they are not successful in what they strive to accomplish. They cannot be happy, except upon one principle, and that is by embracing the fulness of the gospel, which teaches us not to wait till we get into eternity before we begin to make ourselves happy, but it teaches us to strive here to make ourselves and those around us rejoice in the blessings of the Almighty.

This, then, should be our aim and object: to learn to make ourselves useful; to be saviors to our fellow man; to learn how to save them; to communicate to them a knowledge of the principles that are necessary to raise them to the same degree of intelligence that we have ourselves.[5]

Go and make friends among the individuals by whom you are surrounded; or select one and try to start his feelings, his faith, his circumstances and his mind and try to enlighten them and if they are sinners, endeavor to save them from their sins, and bring them from their bondage in which they are placed to participate in the light and liberty which you participate in, for in this way you can do good through the information which the Lord has imparted to you.[6] [See suggestion 2 on page 234.]

Missionaries are willing to make sacrifices to help others come to a knowledge of the truth.

No sooner had the Saints become fairly settled in these valleys [in Utah] than the servants of the Lord turned their attention again to the great missionary work which rested upon the Church.

We were in the midst of poverty and struggling to make the land habitable, but we could not neglect the obligation we were under to spread the Gospel abroad; for the Lord had given forth the command that it should be preached in all the world. It is one of the evidences of the divinity of this work that in the midst of all their drivings and persecutions the Latter-day Saints have faithfully sought to carry out this command of the Lord.

At the general conference of the Church held in October, 1849—only two years after the pioneers entered [the Salt Lake] valley—a number of Elders were called to open up missions in different parts of the earth. Four of the Twelve Apostles were appointed to take the lead. Apostle Erastus Snow was called to go to Scandinavia, Apostle John Taylor to France, myself to Italy, and Apostle Franklin D. Richards to England, where a mission had already been established. Under the adverse circumstances in which we were then situated, with our families almost destitute, this was a great undertaking for us; but the Lord had called, and we felt to respond, no matter what sacrifice it involved.[7]

We dedicate our lives which we hold as not dear to us, in order that the world may understand that there is a God in the eternal worlds; in order that they may understand that God has something to do at the present time with the affairs of the children of men. The world is passing into feelings and opinions of infidelity. Even among the Christian portions of the human family, thousands and tens of thousands, though they are not willing to confess it because of being unpopular, do not believe that God has anything to do with the children of men. We have to stand forth and make sacrifices in order that that belief and knowledge may come to the children of men.[8]

When we call our young missionaries to go to the nations of the earth, they take the matter into consideration, and having heard the experience of those that have been in the world as missionaries, it is not one of the most delightful things for a person to anticipate to go through the trials and difficulties that they can see they will have to pass through. But the virtue lies in their willingness to start forth, and to comply with the requirements.[9]

There are things about a mission which are not altogether agreeable to our young Elders. They realize that they have to sacrifice the pleasures of home, and they understand that they are going among people who will not always feel gratified at what they have

"Sink your own interests, and your success will be grand and glorious, and the whole Church will feel the effects of your labors."

to say to them; yet, on the other hand, they feel that they have the seeds of life in their possession, and that if they can find an honest man or woman, the Spirit of the Lord will operate upon their hearts and they will perchance receive this glorious message which they have to deliver. This affords them pleasure and satisfaction. Another thing, they see in this experience a chance for them to secure that which will be of great value to them in their future duties. It is a strange thing that among the thousands of letters which I have received from those who have been called to go upon missions—mostly young men—I do not think of but one case where a refusal was given. Why is this? It is because the spirit of love and of immortality, the Spirit of the Almighty, is upon these young Elders, and they have received manifestations which inspire them to do that which otherwise no inducement could prompt them to do.[10] [See suggestion 3 on page 234.]

Missionaries should never forget that they are ambassadors of heaven, bearers of good and glad tidings.

We send our Elders to preach the Gospel. Who sends them? . . . The God of Israel sends them. It is His work. There is no mortal man that is so much interested in the success of an Elder when he is preaching the Gospel as the Lord that sent him to preach to the people who are the Lord's children. He begot them in yonder world, and they came here because the Lord wanted them to come.[11]

We feel that you [missionaries] will make a grand success, because we sense and know that you have been called of God. The wisdom of man would never have thought of such a work as this. I am surprised when I think of its greatness. I can say that it is the very work that is necessary at this time: and I feel that you will enter upon it with your whole souls. Cultivate the Spirit of Jesus when he said he could do nothing except that which his Father gave him to do [see John 5:30].

Never mind your difficulties and apparent losses; sink your own interests, and your success will be grand and glorious, and the whole Church will feel the effects of your labors.

Never mind the indifference of some of those amongst whom you will labor, and the little disappointments you will meet with; the Spirit of the Lord will be upon you, and you will stir up the spirits of those to whom you minister, and conquer their indifference; . . . you will be satisfied you have accomplished the work you have been sent to perform. . . .

You have the fullest authority conferred upon you, but you need not talk about this at all. You will discover that there is no need to talk about it; the Spirit of the Lord will confirm it, and the people will feel that you bear it, and this confirmation and feeling will be your authority.

You will find some that think they know more than you do, but if you will do your duty as suggested, before you leave them, they will feel that you have a little more than they have, and that you have blessed them and helped them. . . .

Try to make yourselves agreeable to those to whom you are sent. The humility you display and the Spirit of the Lord resting upon you, will show your fitness for the position you are called to occupy. Try to understand human nature and act accordingly, in order to make everyone happy and everything agreeable. . . .

There is a way to reach every human heart, and it is your business to find the way to the hearts of those to whom you are called. . . .

I feel in my heart to say, God bless you. You will be set apart before you go, and we shall pray for you and shall take a deep interest in you. Be meek of heart and humble. When you look upon an audience, two motives may inspire you; first, that you may speak well and make a good impression upon the audience as an orator; and, next, the question will arise, what am I here for? To sow the seeds of life in the hearts of those who are in this audience; and the prayer should arise in your heart, "O Lord, may it be so; may I have power through thy Spirit to touch the hearts of these thy people?" That very short prayer is all that an elder needs to make. It is all you need to make. "May I say something to save these souls?" This is what the First Presidency . . . and all your brethren want you to do.[12]

Turn your attention to brightening up your spiritual armor. I find that when my temporal matters are all laid aside, my eye is single to spiritual things. Pray, brethren, and not think it harm to fast. . . . Do not joke too much, [and] be careful to grieve not the Spirit. I found when on my mission, after a week or two I could forget home, and the Spirit of God buoyed me up. The Spirit tends to freedom and jollity, but don't be too jollified. . . . Continue prayerful that you may have the Spirit of God to be upon you from the crown of your head to the soles of your feet.[13]

The Elders laboring in the vineyard should never lose sight of the fact that they are ambassadors of heaven, bearers of good and glad tidings to peoples who know not the Lord. . . .

When the Prophet Joseph Smith sent out the first Elders to a foreign land, he foresaw the reception that would be accorded them, and he told them that while a comparative few would receive them as God's servants, the masses would reject them, and pay heedless regard to their message. This has been the lot of God's servants from the beginning of time, and we must be content with the results of faithful labors, even if but few through us are brought to a knowledge of the truth. . . .

I do hope and pray that no Elder laboring . . . will so far forget himself as to fall a prey to the allurements of the world. There is but one safe way to steer clear of them, and that is to shun evil, yea, even the very appearance of evil. Temptation in some form or other will be presented to them. This is the business of the enemy of our salvation; but it is the business of the Elders of Israel to rise above temptation, and in order to do this successfully they must keep themselves unspotted from the world. . . . Inasmuch as they cultivate and cherish the spirit of their mission, and realize the importance of their high calling in Christ Jesus, and live in the spirit of the same, they will be able to stand as guides and saviors to the people, reflecting to them the light of heaven, and be unlike other men; but if they trespass on the ground of the enemy and partake of the spirit of the world, they will be shorn of their strength and become like other men, fit only to return home to sup the sorrow of the fallen, and to cause the hearts of their loved ones to mourn because of their condition. . . . Inasmuch as they shall continually seek unto the Lord in humility, having an eye single to His honor and glory, and desiring in their hearts the salvation of the souls of men, and doing all they can to bring about their salvation, they shall have joy beyond expression in their labors in the flesh, and shall at last be made partakers with the Father and the Son of things too great and glorious for mortality to conceive or contemplate.[14] [See suggestions 4 and 5 on page 234.]

Our hearts rejoice as we help others receive the fulness of the gospel.

We expect . . . on our part, in order to accomplish this work, much patience, faith, diligence, perseverance, and long-suffering will necessarily have to be exercised and experienced; but in the cities . . . in which thousands ultimately received the Gospel, in several instances many months were spent in seemingly fruitless labors before a proper attention and observance to those principles could be procured. . . . We may in some [cases] have not only to employ months, but perhaps even years; but we feel assured, that through faith, prayer, works, and the blessing of the Lord, we shall ultimately overcome and triumph over all these difficulties to the honour and glory of God; and besides, we also ourselves shall have the gratification that we have *done our duty,* and cleared our garments of the blood of all men.[15]

On [one] occasion, before proceeding to Italy, I visited Manchester, Macclesfield, Birmingham, Cheltenham, London, Southampton and South Conferences [in England]. . . . I had the pleasure of meeting with many whom I had been the means of bringing into the Church [eight years earlier]; and I need not say to you that meeting again with these people was truly a joy that has always been delightful to contemplate. The Apostle John remarked in his day, "We know that we have passed from death unto life, because we love the brethren." [1 John 3:14.] This love begotten in the hearts of the missionary Elders of our Church for the peoples of the earth, comparative strangers to them, and in the hearts of the people for the Elders who bear to them the Gospel message, is in itself testimony sufficient to convince the honest heart that its source is divine, and that God is with us. This sacred and holy feeling, awakened within us by the Holy Ghost, has already distinguished us as a community from the rest of the human family; and this is the feeling that will yet revolutionize the whole world, and convince unbelieving man that God is not only the Father of us all, but that we are His friends and servants.[16]

To the service of the Lord I have devoted my life; my *all* has been placed upon the altar of sacrifice, that I may honour him, do his will acceptably, and spread the principles of life among the children of men. When I reflect upon the past, and trace the hand of the Lord marvellously opening my way, and prospering me in every thing relative to these missions beyond my highest expectations, I feel doubly encouraged to press forward to the future; language indeed fails to express the deep gratitude of my heart for his blessings. Those brethren and Saints whose liberality of soul and interest for the work of God have been particularly manifested in these missions upon them, may the blessings of the Most High be poured with equal liberality, and when in after years they shall hear the sweet sound of thousands, and tens of thousands of those nations shouting the praises of the Almighty for the light of revelation, then will their hearts also rejoice in the glad consciousness that they likewise took a part in bringing to pass this glorious redemption.[17] [See suggestion 6 below.]

Suggestions for Study and Teaching

Consider these ideas as you study the chapter or as you prepare to teach. For additional help, see pages v–vii.

1. Read pages 225–26, and consider Lorenzo Snow's answers to the question "Why am I here?" In what ways might this question influence all Church members in our opportunities to share the gospel?
2. Ponder President Snow's counsel in the section beginning at the top of page 227. Think about how you might follow this counsel to help someone be truly happy.
3. President Snow told of sacrifices he and others made so they could share the gospel (pages 227–29). What examples have you seen of people making sacrifices to share the gospel? Why do you think people are willing to make these sacrifices?
4. How might the assurances on pages 230–32 help a full-time missionary? How can they help each of us as we share the gospel? In what ways might we use these teachings to help someone who is hesitating to serve a mission?
5. As you review President Snow's counsel on pages 230–32, think about how it applies in the lives of all Church members. For example: What do you think it means to "sink your own interests"? What are some different ways we might find to "reach every human heart"?
6. Read the final paragraph in the chapter, in which President Snow tells of the lasting joy of missionary work. When have you experienced the joy of missionary work? Why do we sometimes need to be patient before we can fully experience this joy?

Related Scriptures: Alma 26:1–8, 35–37; D&C 12:7–8; 18:10–16; 84:88

Teaching Help: "Ask participants to choose one section and read it silently. Invite them to gather in groups of two or three people who chose the same section and discuss what they have learned" (from page vii in this book).

Notes

1. Journal and Letterbook, 1836–1845, Church History Library, 33; see also "The Grand Destiny of Man," *Deseret Evening News,* July 20, 1901, 22.
2. "The Grand Destiny of Man," 22.
3. In Eliza R. Snow Smith, *Biography and Family Record of Lorenzo Snow* (1884), 48.
4. "Letter from President Snow," *Millennial Star,* Sept. 12, 1901, 595.
5. *Deseret News,* May 15, 1861, 82.
6. *Deseret News,* Mar. 11, 1857, 3; in the original source, page 3 is incorrectly labeled as page 419.
7. In "Scandinavians at Saltair," *Deseret Evening News,* Aug. 17, 1901, 8.
8. In "Laid to Rest: The Remains of President John Taylor Consigned to the Grave," *Millennial Star,* Aug. 29, 1887, 549.
9. In "Report of the Funeral Services Held over the Remains of Daniel Wells Grant," *Millennial Star,* June 20, 1895, 386.
10. In Conference Report, Apr. 1901, 2–3.
11. *Deseret Weekly,* May 12, 1894, 637.
12. "Instructions to Missionaries," *Improvement Era,* Dec. 1899, 126–29; Lorenzo Snow gave this counsel to brethren who had recently been called to serve as missionaries for the Mutual Improvement Association. His sermon was included in the *Improvement Era* with the explanation that it was "full of helpful counsel and advice to every worker in the cause."
13. In Journal History, Apr. 9, 1862, 4.
14. "Letter from President Snow," 595–96.
15. "The Malta Mission," *Millennial Star,* June 5, 1852, 237.
16. "Letter from President Snow," 595.
17. "Address to the Saints in Great Britain," *Millennial Star,* Dec. 1, 1851, 365.

President Lorenzo Snow testified of the Restoration of the gospel through the Prophet Joseph Smith.

CHAPTER 20

The Kingdom of God Moves Forward

"It is the business of those who profess to be engaged in [God's] work to move on, to go forward. . . . So long as there remains a step forward to be taken, that step should be taken."

From the Life of Lorenzo Snow

In 1844, while fulfilling an assignment in the eastern United States, Lorenzo Snow learned that the Prophet Joseph Smith and his brother Hyrum had been martyred. He said: "The news of this sad event, of course, came wholly unexpected, and struck me with profound astonishment and grief, which no language can portray." Obeying instructions from the Quorum of the Twelve Apostles, he made preparations to return to his home in Nauvoo, Illinois.[1]

He later recalled: "It was thought by some in the days of Joseph that this Church could not prosper except Joseph guided its destinies, and when the time came when he was to pass away from this world as a martyr into the spirit world, the Saints throughout the kingdom of God were greatly agitated. It was something unexpected. They hardly knew how things would then move. The responsibility [to lead the Church] then devolved upon the Quorum of the Twelve Apostles; and through the blessings of God upon them and the spirit of inspiration that dwelt in their bosoms, and under the guidance of the Almighty, the kingdom moved forward."[2]

The second President of the Church, Brigham Young, died in 1877, after having led the Church for 33 years. Elder Lorenzo Snow, then a member of the Quorum of the Twelve, once again witnessed a change in the Church's earthly leadership. He later said that President Young "passed away almost unexpectedly. The Saints were hardly prepared for it. And yet the kingdom of God moved forward."[3]

When John Taylor, the third President of the Church, died in 1887, Elder Snow reassured the Saints, "The Lord has seen proper now to call our beloved brother, President Taylor, away from these scenes of suffering, these scenes of martyrdom; and the Church still moves forward."[4]

In 1898, about 11 years after reassuring the Saints at President Taylor's funeral, Lorenzo Snow found himself in need of such reassurance. He was serving as President of the Quorum of the Twelve at the time. President Wilford Woodruff was serving as President of the Church, and his physical health was failing. President Snow knew that according to the established line of succession, he would preside over the Church if he outlived President Woodruff. One evening he felt especially burdened by this possibility. Considering himself inadequate to assume the leadership of the Church, he went alone to a room in the Salt Lake Temple to pray. He asked God to spare President Woodruff's life, but he also promised that he would perform any duty God required of him.

President Woodruff died on September 2, 1898, not long after President Snow's fervent prayer in the temple. President Snow was in Brigham City, about 60 miles (100 kilometers) north of Salt Lake City, when he received the news. He made arrangements to travel to Salt Lake City by train that same evening. Upon his arrival, he again went to a private room in the temple to pray. He acknowledged his feelings of inadequacy but expressed his willingness to do the Lord's will. He asked for guidance and waited for an answer, but none came. So he left the room.

Entering a large hallway, he received the answer—and the reassurance—he had sought. Before him stood the resurrected Savior, who told him what he needed to do. President Snow later told his granddaughter Alice Pond about this experience. Alice recorded the conversation she had with her grandfather in the Salt Lake Temple:

"In the large corridor leading into the celestial room, I was walking several steps ahead of grand-pa when he stopped me and said: 'Wait a moment, Allie, I want to tell you something. It was right here that the Lord Jesus Christ appeared to me at the time of the death of President Woodruff. He instructed me to go right ahead and reorganize the First Presidency of the Church at once and not wait as had been done after the death of the previous presidents, and that I was to succeed President Woodruff.'

"Then grand-pa came a step nearer and held out his left hand and said: 'He stood right here, about three feet above the floor. It looked as though He stood on a plate of solid gold.'

"Grand-pa told me what a glorious personage the Savior is and described His hands, feet, countenance and beautiful white robes, all of which were of such a glory of whiteness and brightness that he could hardly gaze upon Him.

"Then [grand-pa] came another step nearer and put his right hand on my head and said: 'Now, grand-daughter, I want you to remember that this is the testimony of your grand-father, that he told you with his own lips that he actually saw the Savior, here in the Temple, and talked with Him face to face.'"[5]

President Snow's visit with the Savior was a sacred confirmation of a truth he had known for many years—that Jesus Christ is the head of the Church. Inspired by this truth, President Snow frequently testified that the Church would continue to progress in spite of opposition. He expressed his gratitude for the privilege of participating in the forward movement of the Lord's latter-day work. In the October 1898 general conference, in which he was sustained as President of the Church, he said: "Let us decree in our hearts, let us inwardly testify to the Lord, that we will be a better people, a more united people at our next Conference than we are today. This should be the feeling and determination of every man and woman present in this solemn assembly. I feel in my heart that I will try to be more devoted than I have been in the past to the interests of the kingdom of God and the carrying out of His purposes."[6] [See suggestion 1 on page 246.]

Teachings of Lorenzo Snow

In fulfillment of prophecy, the Lord has restored His Church on the earth.

As a servant of God I bear witness to the revelation of His will in the nineteenth century. It came by His own voice from the heavens, by the personal manifestation of His Son and by the ministration of holy angels. He commands all people everywhere to repent, to turn from their evil ways and unrighteous desires, to be baptized for the remission of their sins, that they may receive the Holy Ghost and come into communion with Him. He has commenced the work of redemption spoken of by all the holy prophets, sages and seers of all the ages and all the races of mankind.[7]

Mormonism, a nickname for the real religion of the Latter-day Saints, does not profess to be a new thing, except to this generation. It proclaims itself as the original plan of salvation, instituted in the heavens before the world was, and revealed from God to man in different ages. That Adam, Enoch, Noah, Abraham, Moses, and other ancient worthies had this religion successively, in a series of dispensations, we, as a people, verily believe. . . . Mormonism, in short, is the primitive Christian faith restored, the ancient Gospel brought back again—this time to usher in the last dispensation, introduce the Millennium, and wind up the work of redemption as pertaining to this planet.[8]

We can see the hand of the Almighty establishing a kingdom spoken of in ages long past by Daniel the Prophet,—a kingdom which shall grow and spread until it fills the whole earth [see Daniel 2:44], when light and intelligence shall be so generally diffused that it shall no longer be necessary for any man to say to his fellows, "Know ye the Lord, but all shall know him, from the least unto the greatest;" [see Jeremiah 31:34] and when the Spirit of the Lord shall be poured out upon all flesh to such a degree that their sons and their daughters shall prophesy, their old men shall dream dreams, their young men see visions [see Joel 2:28], and when there shall be nothing to hurt or destroy in all the holy mountain of the Lord [see Isaiah 11:9].[9] [See suggestion 2 on page 246.]

"Brethren and sisters, God has set up His Church and Kingdom on the earth for the benefit and blessing of the human family."

The Church of Jesus Christ of Latter-day Saints is built on a sure foundation, and it will continue to move forward in spite of opposition.

Brethren and sisters, God has set up His Church and Kingdom on the earth for the benefit and blessing of the human family, to guide them in the way of truth, to prepare them for exaltation in His presence and for His glorious coming and kingdom on the earth. His purposes will be accomplished in spite of all the opposition which may be brought against them by wicked men and the powers of darkness. Everything that stands in the way of this work will be removed. Nothing will be able to withstand His power, but everything that He has decreed will be fully and perfectly accomplished. The love of God for His people will continue and abide and they will triumph in His might.[10]

Now talk about this kingdom being destroyed! . . . Why, you might as well try to pluck the stars from the firmament or the moon or the sun from its orbit! It never can be accomplished, for it is the work of the Almighty.[11]

The kingdom of God moves on with force and power, and with grand and glorious success.[12]

This work is built on a sure foundation, being founded on the rock of ages. . . . No matter who are lost by the way and make shipwreck of their faith, the Church will go on.[13]

This Church will stand, because it is upon a firm basis. It is not from man; it is not from the study of the New Testament or the Old Testament; it is not the result of the learning that we received in colleges nor seminaries, but it has come directly from the Lord. The Lord has shown it to us by the revealing principle of the Holy Spirit of light and every man can receive this same spirit.

. . . He gives us a knowledge of what we shall do, inasmuch as we are willing to sacrifice our lives rather than go contrary to that knowledge. He opens to us the secrets of the celestial kingdom, and he is constantly communicating to us things that we never knew before. This knowledge and intelligence is growing upon us continually.

. . . We have received too much knowledge to be thwarted in our purposes. Those who desire to persecute and overthrow Mormonism, let them go on and do their work. . . . Our work is to grow in the knowledge of God, to keep the commandments of God, to be faithful and to continue to increase and to become more and more perfect as we advance in years.[14] [See suggestion 3 on page 246.]

We are the people of God, and He will protect us as we go forward and do all that He requires.

In many instances . . . where the destruction of the people of God seemed imminent, and there appeared no way of escape, . . . suddenly there arose something or another that had been prepared for their salvation to avert the impending destruction. We find this in the case of the Israelites when led by Moses. When they came to the Red Sea, and the Egyptian army in their rear threatened their destruction, there seemed no way of escape, but at the very moment when deliverance was required, behold, it appeared and they were delivered [see Exodus 14:10–25].

So it has been and so it ever will be with us. Notwithstanding our difficulties may appear very great, yet there will be means provided for our escape if we ourselves perform the duties incumbent upon us as the children of God. But it may become necessary in the future—and this is the point I wish to make—for some of the Saints to act the part of Esther, the queen, and be willing to sacrifice anything and everything that is required at their hands for the purpose of working out the deliverance of the Latter-day Saints.

First we should know that we are the people of God. . . . It is our business to step forward as did Esther, and be willing to risk all for the salvation of the people. In undertaking her task, Esther said, "If I perish, I perish." [See Esther 4:3–16.] . . . But the people of God will not perish. There will always be a ram caught in the thicket for their deliverance [see Genesis 22:13]. . . .

. . . The Lord has said, "I have decreed in my heart, that I will prove you in all things, whether you will abide in my covenant, even unto death, that you may be found worthy; for if ye will not abide in my covenant, ye are not worthy of me." [See D&C

98:14–15.] We have something to live for; we have everything to die for. But there is no death in these matters. There is salvation and there is life if the people of God—those that call themselves after the name of the Lord Jesus Christ—will keep His commandments and do that which is acceptable in His sight. It is not in the economy of the Almighty to permit His people to be destroyed. If we will do right and keep His commandments He will surely deliver us from every difficulty.[15] [See suggestion 4 on page 246.]

It is time for us to humble ourselves before God and accomplish the work He has entrusted to us.

It is the business of those who profess to be engaged in His work to move on, to go forward, . . . without murmuring or having to be urged; so long as there remains a step forward to be taken, that step should be taken.[16]

It is now time for the Latter-day Saints to humble themselves before the Almighty. . . . It is time now for the Latter-day Saints to find out wherein they have committed themselves; it is time for the Latter-day Saints to repent of their sins and follies and call upon the Almighty, that His aid may be given; . . . that we may go forward and accomplish the great work entrusted to our care.[17]

We are engaged in the work of God. The prospects before us are glorious, but let us be impressed, in every work of our hands, that we are the servants of God and doing His will. Let not our integrity be impaired, but our faith be continually increased as we proceed through life. I would be satisfied to act where Providence has placed me, and ask the Lord what I can do to aid in building up the kingdom of God in that place, and to assist me to obtain a subsistence for my family.[18]

We may increase in knowledge and power, and in our ability to build up the kingdom of God upon the earth, and that, too, by our diligence, our humility and faithfulness to the covenants we have made.[19]

It may appear through our ignorance in not understanding fully the ways of the Lord and His purposes, that in our onward march in carrying out the programme before us, we sometimes come to a stopping place for the time being, but the fact is, there is no such thing in the programme, and there cannot be, providing the people continue their labors putting their trust in the promises of God. . . .

. . . Let every man be faithful and very diligent in keeping the commandments of God, and cultivate the desire to do good to those around him; and if, in reflecting on the past, we find we have not acted strictly in accordance with the dictates of our consciences and duty, let us make ourselves right before God and man, that we may be prepared for every event that may transpire. Let the work of building temples and houses of worship go on; let [us] continue to educate [our] children and bring them up in the fear of the Lord, and let the Gospel still be carried to the nations afar. . . .

This is the work of God, and He is directing its course and progress in the earth, and this work should ever be uppermost in our mind; and so long as we are found in the path of duty we can surely remain fixed and unmoved and determined in our purpose, and thus exhibit to the world our faith and devotion to the principles of truth which God has revealed. . . .

The Lord very possibly may cause a heavy pressure to bear upon us, such as will require great sacrifice at the hands of his people. The question with us is, will we make that sacrifice? This work is the work of the Almighty and the blessings we look for which have been promised, will come after we have proven ourselves and passed through the ordeal. I have no special word to this people that there is, or that there is not, before them a fiery ordeal through which they will be called to pass; the question with me is, am I prepared to receive and put to a right and proper use any blessing the Lord has in store for me in common with His people; or, on the other hand, am I prepared to make any sacrifice that He may require at my hands? I would not give the ashes of a rye straw for any religion that was not worth living for and that was not worth dying for; and I would not give much for the man that was not willing to sacrifice his all for the sake of his religion.

Well, I [say] to one and all, Move on! move on, and see the salvation of the Lord, and not stand still.[20] [See suggestion 5 on page 246.]

Suggestions for Study and Teaching

Consider these ideas as you study the chapter or as you prepare to teach. For additional help, see pages v–vii.

1. Review the accounts on pages 237–39. What do you think it means to say that the kingdom of God moves forward? What experiences have helped you see the kingdom of God moving forward?
2. In the final paragraph on page 240, President Snow refers to four prophecies in the Old Testament. In what ways are these prophecies being fulfilled today?
3. Study President Snow's teachings about the Church moving forward in spite of opposition (pages 242–43). How might these teachings help us when people persecute us because of our faith? How have you dealt with opposition to your testimony?
4. Examine the third and fourth paragraphs on page 243. When we are required to make sacrifices, what can we learn from the example of Esther? In such situations, how do you think it will help us to "know that we are the people of God"?
5. In the final section of the chapter, President Snow counsels members to build up the kingdom of God wherever the Lord has placed them. In what ways do parents' efforts at home help to build up the kingdom of God throughout the earth? How can home teachers and visiting teachers build up the kingdom of God?

Related Scriptures: Matthew 24:14; Ether 12:27; Moroni 7:33; D&C 12:7–9; 65:1–6; 128:19–23

Teaching Help: "It is often helpful to begin thinking about an upcoming lesson soon after you have taught the preceding lesson. You will probably be most aware of those you teach and their needs and interests immediately after you have been with them" (*Teaching, No Greater Call,* 97).

Notes

1. See Eliza R. Snow Smith, *Biography and Family Record of Lorenzo Snow* (1884), 79–82.
2. In "Laid to Rest: The Remains of President John Taylor Consigned to the Grave," *Millennial Star,* Aug. 29, 1887, 549.
3. In "Laid to Rest: The Remains of President John Taylor Consigned to the Grave," 549.
4. In "Laid to Rest: The Remains of President John Taylor Consigned to the Grave," 549.
5. Alice Pond, in LeRoi C. Snow, "An Experience of My Father's," *Improvement Era,* Sept. 1933, 677; see also correspondence between Elder John A. Widtsoe and Noah S. Pond, husband of Alice Armeda Snow Young Pond, Oct. 30, 1945, and Nov. 12, 1946, Church History Library. Alice was in her early twenties, endowed, and sealed to her husband when President Snow shared this experience with her in the temple.
6. In Conference Report, Oct. 1898, 55.
7. "Greeting to the World by President Lorenzo Snow," *Deseret Evening News,* Jan. 1, 1901, 5.
8. "'Mormonism' by Its Head," *Land of Sunshine,* Oct. 1901, 252.
9. *Deseret News,* Jan. 24, 1872, 597.
10. *Deseret Semi-Weekly News,* Oct. 4, 1898, 1.
11. *Deseret News,* Jan. 24, 1872, 598.
12. *Deseret Weekly,* Nov. 4, 1893, 609.
13. *Millennial Star,* May 12, 1890, 293; from a detailed paraphrase of a discourse Lorenzo Snow delivered in the April 1890 general conference.
14. In Conference Report, Apr. 1900, 3–4.
15. *Deseret News,* Nov. 22, 1882, 690.
16. *Deseret News: Semi-Weekly,* June 27, 1882, 1.
17. *Deseret News,* Nov. 22, 1882, 690.
18. In Journal History, July 11, 1865, 2.
19. *Deseret News,* May 15, 1861, 82.
20. *Deseret News: Semi-Weekly,* June 27, 1882, 1.

Even after the great manifestations in the Kirtland Temple, many Saints in Kirtland fell into apostasy.

C H A P T E R 2 1

Loving God More Than We Love the World

"We have got to reach . . . a higher plane: we have got to love God more than we love the world."

From the Life of Lorenzo Snow

Shortly after Lorenzo Snow was baptized and confirmed in Kirtland, Ohio, a number of Latter-day Saints, including some Church leaders, turned against the Prophet Joseph Smith. According to Lorenzo Snow, this apostasy was fueled by speculation, or, in other words, unusual business risks in hopes of getting rich quickly. Blinded by a desire for the temporary things of the world, people turned away from the eternal blessings of the gospel.

About 50 years later, President Snow, serving as President of the Quorum of the Twelve Apostles, spoke to a group of Latter-day Saints in Logan, Utah. He told them about the adversity he had witnessed in Kirtland and warned them that they would soon experience similar trials. "There is rapidly coming something that will try you, perhaps as you have never been tried before," he said. "All, however, that is necessary for us to do now is to see where our faults and weaknesses lie, if we have any. If we have been unfaithful in the past, let us renew our covenants with God and determine, by fasting and prayer, that we will get forgiveness of our sins, that the Spirit of the Almighty may rest upon us, that peradventure we may escape those powerful temptations that are approaching. The cloud is gathering in blackness. You see what were the results in Kirtland of this spirit of speculation. Therefore, take warning."[1]

Because President Snow's warning continues to apply to Latter-day Saints today, much of his sermon to the Saints in Logan is included in this chapter. He said, "Perhaps a few words in regard to our condition at that time [in Kirtland] might prove of some service to us in the future—might give us some useful lessons."[2] [See suggestion 1 on page 255.]

Teachings of Lorenzo Snow

When people allow worldliness to pervade their minds and hearts, they turn their backs on eternal principles.

I remember very clearly the troublous times which were experienced in Kirtland . . . , where the Prophet of God resided, where God Himself, even Jesus, the Son of God, appeared and showed Himself in His glory. He stood upon the breastwork of the pulpit of the Temple, built by commandment. There was under His feet a pavework of pure gold, in color like amber. His hair was white as the pure snow. His countenance shone as the sun in its strength. His voice was as the sound of rushing waters. [See D&C 110.] This wonderful manifestation was in the temple which had been reared to His honor. I was in Kirtland at that time, where we passed through scenes which, I sometimes think, we are now beginning to repeat. The circumstances which surrounded the Latter-day Saints at that time were of a peculiar nature; at least, the effects upon the people were of a peculiar character. . . . At that time a spirit of speculation pervaded the minds of the people of this nation. There were money speculations, bank speculations, speculations in lands, speculations in city lots, speculations in numerous other directions. That spirit of speculation rose out of the world, and swept over the hearts of the Saints like a mighty wave or rushing torrent, and many fell, and apostatized.[3]

Some of them [the Saints in Kirtland] began speculating; they forgot their religion, they forgot the principles that had been revealed to them, and many of them fell into the spirit of the times and were carried away with speculating. Difficulties arose—envy and strife—and the Lord, being displeased with them, brought destruction into their midst and they were broken to pieces as a settlement.[4]

Just previous to this great apostasy the Lord had poured out wonderful blessings upon the people. The gifts of the Gospel had been poured out to a remarkable extent—the riches of eternity.

Angels had visited them. The Son of God, as I before remarked, had talked with His servants. At the dedication of the Temple the blessings which the people received were marvelous. During that rich time of God's favors I, myself, attended the various meetings which were held in the Temple. We had prayer meetings, and testimony meetings, and such testimonies as the brethren and sisters could bear were wonderful. They prophesied, they spake in tongues, and had the interpretation of tongues to a remarkable degree. These blessings were almost universal upon the people in Kirtland. Their hearts were then devoted; they felt as though they could sacrifice anything they possessed. They felt that they were dwelling almost in the presence of God, and it was natural that they should have that feeling under such marvelous influences.

All these blessings, and many others that I have not time to enumerate, were enjoyed by the Latter-day Saints just previous to the time when this spirit of speculation began to pervade the hearts of the people. One would have imagined that after receiving these wonderful manifestations no temptation could have overthrown the Saints. But it did, and it scattered them, as it were, to the four winds.

Singular as it may appear, this spirit of speculation pervaded the quorum of the Twelve Apostles and the quorum of the Seven Presidents of Seventies; indeed, there was not a quorum in the Church but was more or less touched with this spirit of speculation. As that spirit increased, disunion followed. Brethren and sisters began to slander and quarrel one with the other, because their interests were not in harmony.

Will this be the case with the Latter-day Saints I am now addressing? I fear it is coming, but how far it will affect you it is not for me to say. You will have the experience, however; and perhaps it is very necessary that you should.

. . . One-half the quorum of the Apostles, in the days of Kirtland, fell beneath these evil influences. It was this speculation, this love of gold—the god of the world—which produced this doleful effect. And if it had this effect upon those who held the highest priesthood upon the earth, how would it affect us who, perhaps, have not had the intelligence, the information and the experience they possessed? . . .

Now, you are a good people. . . . God loves you. He delights in your righteousness, and He would not like to see the scenes enacted . . . that were in Kirtland. There is no need of it. We hold in our own hands the power to preserve ourselves from those things that divided the Saints in Kirtland and overthrew one-half of the Twelve. The Lord does not wish that, at this late day, these scenes should again be witnessed.[5]

The Latter-day Saints ought to be too far along in wisdom and intelligence to fall into snares of this character. It does not pay. It will pay no man to turn his back upon these glorious principles and those things which have been received from the eternal worlds—to turn our backs upon these things and mix up and devote ourselves to the beggarly things of the world. It will not pay us. Whatever temptation may come upon us or to which we are now exposed we should listen to the history of the past and not allow ourselves to be overcome, or we will much regret it.[6] [See suggestion 2 on page 255.]

We have covenanted to separate ourselves from worldliness and devote ourselves to the kingdom of God.

The god of the world is the gold and the silver. The world worships this god. It is all-powerful to them, though they might not be willing to acknowledge it. Now, it is designed, in the providence of God, that the Latter-day Saints should show whether they have so far advanced in the knowledge, in the wisdom and in the power of God that they cannot be overcome by the god of the world. We must come to that point. We have also got to reach another standard, a higher plane: we have got to love God more than we love the world, more than we love gold or silver, and love our neighbor as ourselves.[7]

If we . . . fail to keep the covenants we have made, namely, to use our time, talent and ability for the upbuilding of the kingdom of God upon the earth, how can we reasonably expect to come forth in the morning of the first resurrection, identified with the great work of redemption? If we, in our manner, habits and deal[ings], imitate the . . . world, thereby identifying ourselves with the world, do you think, my brethren, that God will bestow upon us the blessings we desire to inherit? I tell you no, he will not! . . . We must build ourselves up in the righteousness of heaven and plant in our hearts the righteousness of God. Said the Lord, through the prophet Jeremiah, "I will put my law in their inward parts, and write it in their hearts; and will be their God, and they shall be my people." [Jeremiah 31:33.] This is what the Lord is endeavoring to do, and this he will accomplish in us if we conform to his will.[8]

I thank God that in these times of corruption and wickedness in the world, we have holy and righteous men and women who can devote those superior talents which God has bestowed upon them to His praise and glory. And I might say further, that there are thousands of virtuous and honorable men and women, whom the Lord has gathered out from the nations, that are also willing to devote their time and talents to aid in accomplishing the work of God in the interest of His children.[9] [See suggestion 3 on page 255.]

We follow the Savior's example when we refuse to trade the glories of eternity for the riches of the world.

You may expect . . . to encounter obstacles in the path of life, which will task to the uttermost your best resolutions, and some of you may be tempted to swerve from the path of truth and honor, and, like Esau, feel to relinquish the glories of eternity for a few passing moments of gratification and pleasure [see Genesis 25:29–34]; then . . . seize your opportunity to emulate the example of our Savior when offered the glory of this world, if he would stoop to an act of folly; he replied to his tempter, *"Get behind me, Satan!"* [See Luke 4:5–8.][10]

I find in reflecting on life, that this world is short compared with eternity; that our intelligence, the divinity within us, has always existed, was never created, and will always exist through all eternity [see D&C 93:29]. In view of these facts, it becomes us as intelligent beings, to realize that this life closes in a few days, then comes the life which is eternal; and in proportion as we have kept commandments, we have the advantage of those who failed to make those improvements.[11]

Like the rich young man who spoke with the Savior (see Matthew 19:16–22), some people today are tempted to turn away from those in need.

The gospel binds together the hearts of all its adherents, it makes no difference, it knows no difference between the rich and the poor; we are all bound as one individual to perform the duties which devolve upon us. . . . Now let me ask the question, Who [does] possess anything, who can really and truly call any of this world's goods his own? I do not presume to, I am merely a steward over a very little, and unto God I am held accountable for its use and disposition. The Latter-day Saints have received the law of the gospel through the revelations of God, and it is so plainly written that all can understand. And if we understood and comprehended the position we assumed in subscribing to it when we entered into its covenant through baptism for the remission of sins, we must still be conscious of the fact that that law requires us to seek *first* the kingdom of God, and that our time, talent and ability must be held subservient to its interest [see Matthew 6:33; 3 Nephi 13:33]. If this were not so, how could we expect hereafter, when this earth shall have been made the dwelling place of God and his Son, to inherit eternal lives and to live and reign with him?

Who shall say that the rich, or those that possess many talents, have any better hope or prospect to inherit these blessings than the poor, or those who have but one talent? As I understand it, the man who works in the shop, whether as tailor, carpenter, shoemaker or in any other industrial department, and who lives according to the law of the Gospel, and is honest and faithful in his calling, that man is just as eligible to the receiving of these and all the blessings of the New and Everlasting Covenant as any other man; through his faithfulness he shall possess thrones, principalities and powers, his children becoming as numerous as the stars in the firmament or the sands on the sea shore. Who, I ask, has any greater prospect than this?[12] [See suggestions 3 and 4 below.]

Suggestions for Study and Teaching

Consider these ideas as you study the chapter or as you prepare to teach. For additional help, see pages v–vii.

1. Consider the account on pages 249–50. What is it about worldliness that leads people to forget their religion? How can we take care of our temporal needs without being overcome by worldliness?
2. Ponder the section beginning on page 250. How can our love for God help us avoid being overcome by worldliness?
3. President Snow taught that we have covenanted to "use our time, talent and ability for the upbuilding of the kingdom of God upon the earth" (page 252). Think about what you can do to keep this covenant.
4. Review the final section in the chapter. In what ways can the following truths help us keep our covenants? "This world is short compared with eternity." No one can "really and truly call any of this world's goods his own."

Related Scriptures: Matthew 6:19–24; John 17:15; 1 John 2:15–17; Jacob 2:13–19; Mormon 8:35–39; D&C 38:39; 63:47–48; 104:13–18

Teaching Help: Discussions in small groups "give a large number of people the opportunity to participate in a lesson. Individuals who are usually hesitant to participate might share ideas in small groups that they would not express in front of the entire group" (*Teaching, No Greater Call,* 161).

Notes

1. *Deseret Semi-Weekly News,* June 4, 1889, 4.
2. *Deseret Semi-Weekly News,* June 4, 1889, 4.
3. *Deseret Semi-Weekly News,* June 4, 1889, 4.
4. *Deseret News,* Apr. 11, 1888, 200; from a detailed paraphrase of a discourse Lorenzo Snow delivered in the April 1888 general conference.
5. *Deseret Semi-Weekly News,* June 4, 1889, 4.
6. *Deseret News,* Apr. 11, 1888, 200.
7. *Deseret Semi-Weekly News,* June 4, 1889, 4.
8. *Deseret News: Semi-Weekly,* Jan. 23, 1877, 1.
9. *Deseret Semi-Weekly News,* June 4, 1889, 4.
10. In Eliza R. Snow Smith, *Biography and Family Record of Lorenzo Snow* (1884), 486.
11. *Brigham City Bugler, Supplement,* Aug. 1, 1891, 2.
12. *Deseret News: Semi-Weekly,* Jan. 23, 1877, 1.

CHAPTER 22

Doing Good to Others

"Cultivate a spirit of charity; be ready to do for others more than you would expect from them if circumstances were reversed."

From the Life of Lorenzo Snow

Lorenzo Snow and his family were part of the Latter-day Saints' initial exodus from Nauvoo, Illinois. With a group of other families, they headed west in the state of Iowa in February 1846. Weather conditions made their trek difficult—day after day they struggled through rain, snow, and mud.

As the Snow family traveled one day, a member of the company asked them for help. Lorenzo Snow wrote in his journal that a man "requested that I would let him put his trunk in my wagon, said he could not get it carried anywhere else." The wagon was "perfectly crowded and as much as seemed we could possibly get along with," Lorenzo recalled, but "still I told him to put it in and come along and share with us."

The next night the family experienced what Lorenzo called "a very unpleasant affair": an axle on their wagon broke. He recounted: "It was then raining very hard and [was] quite cold. We immediately pitched our tent [and] made a good hickory fire. . . . The water and mud was very deep and we could not get to the wagon without wading. . . . We were now about fifteen miles from the camp and nine or ten to the first house, and none of us being mechanics, the prospect of getting our wagon repaired was not very encouraging."

Unexpectedly, relief came from the man they had helped the day before. "I was lamenting over my misfortune," said Lorenzo, "when he came up to me and informed me that his trade was wagon

While traveling across the state of Iowa, the Snow family received assistance from someone they had helped a day earlier.

making and could very easily repair my wagon. . . . As soon as the weather would admit, brother Wilson (that being the name of the aforementioned person) went to work and made an axletree much better than the one I broke. Our wagon being repaired, we left this place, having stayed several days on account of rain and mud."

For Lorenzo Snow, this experience reinforced a valuable lesson about service and fellowship. He wrote in his journal, "Granting one favor often leads to obtaining another."[1] [See suggestion 1 on page 264.]

Teachings of Lorenzo Snow

We are children of the same Heavenly Father, and we have been sent into the world to do good to one another.

We are of the same Father in the celestial worlds. . . . If we knew each other as we should, . . . our sympathies would be excited more than they are at the present time, and there would be a desire on the part of every individual to study in their own minds how they might do their brethren good, how they might alleviate their sorrows and build them up in truth, how [they might] remove the darkness from their minds. If we understand each other and the real relationship which we hold to each other, we should feel different from what we do; but this knowledge can be obtained only as we obtain the Spirit of life, and as we are desirous of building each other up in righteousness.[2]

We have been sent into the world to do good to others; and in doing good to others we do good to ourselves. We should always keep this in view, the husband in reference to his wife, the wife in reference to her husband, the children in reference to their parents, and the parents in reference to their children. There is always opportunity to do good to one another.[3]

I pray to God, in the name of Jesus, that you and I may try every day to keep a little more faithful, that we may try to be a little better to-day than yesterday, that we may try and have a little more love and affection toward our neighbors, as we are told that upon this hangs the law and the prophets, "to love the Lord, our God, with all our might, with all our mind, and with all our strength, and our neighbor as ourself." [See Matthew 22:37–40.] "To do unto others as we would have others do unto us." This is according to the law and the prophets. [See Matthew 7:12.] These are principles we should and must learn. . . . We should be friends everywhere and to everybody. There is no Latter-day Saint that hates the world: but we are friends to the world, we are obliged to be, so far as they are concerned. We must learn to extend our charity and labor in the interests of all mankind. This is the mission of the Latter-day Saints—not simply confine it to ourselves, but to spread it abroad, as it of necessity must be extended to all mankind.[4]

Be upright, just and merciful, exercising a spirit of nobility and godliness in all your intentions and resolutions—in all your acts and dealings. Cultivate a spirit of charity; be ready to do for others more than you would expect from them if circumstances were reversed. Be ambitious to be great, not in the estimation of the worldly minded, but in the eyes of God, and to be great in this sense, *"Love the Lord our God with all your might, mind and strength, and your neighbor as yourself."* You must love mankind because they are your brethren, the offspring of God. Pray diligently for this spirit of philanthropy, this expansion of thought and feeling, and for power and ability to labor earnestly in the interest of Messiah's kingdom.[5] [See suggestion 2 on page 264.]

Our happiness increases when we help others find happiness.

We should have before us a strong desire to do good to others. Never mind so much about ourselves. Good will come to us all right if we keep our minds outside of ourselves to a certain extent, and try to make others happier and draw them a little nearer to the Lord. . . . When you find yourselves a little gloomy, look around you and find somebody that is in a worse plight than yourself; go to him and find out what the trouble is, then try to remove it with the wisdom which the Lord bestows upon you; and the first thing you know, your gloom is gone, you feel light, the Spirit of the Lord is upon you, and everything seems illuminated.[6] [See suggestion 3 on page 264.]

When we look first to the interests of others, we improve more rapidly ourselves.

One of the best things a young man or a young woman can have in view, in trying to be great, is to have others great also; and not mind spending a little time to improve others. The best way to improve ourselves is to exercise ourselves in doing good to others. Keep this in mind constantly.[7]

In pursuing any kind of study a man has to continue to work, and after going through one course he has to go through again, and keep to work in order to make himself master of them, and he never will master them near so well as by communicating his information while engaged in gaining it. Let him go to work and gather up his friends and endeavor to give them the same knowledge that he has received, and he then begins to find himself being enlightened upon those things which he never would have known unless by pursuing that course of teaching and imparting the information he is in possession of unto others. Any one that has been a school teacher will understand me well upon this point. . . .

Let a man remember that there are others that are in darkness and that have not advanced so far in knowledge, wisdom and intelligence, and let him impart that knowledge, intelligence and power unto his friends and brethren, inasmuch as he is farther advanced than they are, and by so doing he will soon discover that his mind will expand, and that light and knowledge which he had gained would increase and multiply more rapidly. . . .

If you want to secure the friendship and affections of your friends go to work and comfort them with that light which you have received, remembering those blessings came down from God, and that by doing this you are only doing what every man should do. . . .

Now an individual in order to secure the highest and greatest blessings to himself, in order to secure the approbation of the Almighty, and in order to continually improve in the things pertaining to righteousness he must do all things to the best advantage. Let him go to work and be willing to sacrifice for the benefit of his

"Let your minds be expanded to comprehend and look after the interest of your friends that are around you."

friends. If he wants to build himself up, the best principle he can do it upon is to build up his friends. . . .

. . . Let your minds be expanded to comprehend and look after the interest of your friends that are around you, and where it is in your power to secure benefits to your friends do so, and in so doing you will find that those things which you need will come into your hands quicker than if you labor entirely to secure them to yourselves independent of regarding the interests of your friends. I know this is a good and important principle.[8] [See suggestion 4 on page 264.]

When we sacrifice for the good of others, we get heaven within us.

We have just got to feel . . . that there are other people besides ourselves; we have got to look into the hearts and feelings of others, and become more godly than what we are now.

. . . There is a self sacrifice to be made for the interests of those with whom we are associated. We see this in the Savior, and in brother Joseph, and we see it in our President [Brigham Young]. Jesus, brother Joseph, and brother Brigham have always been willing to sacrifice all they possess for the good of the people; that is what gives brother Brigham power with God and power with the people, it is the self-sacrificing feeling that he is all the time exhibiting. It is so with others; just in proportion as they are willing to sacrifice for others, so they get God in them, and the blessings of the eternal worlds are upon them, and they are the ones that will secure not only the rights of this world but will secure the blessings of eternity. Just in proportion as you . . . sacrifice one for another, just in that proportion you will advance in the things of God. Now if you want to get heaven within you and to get into heaven you want to pursue that course that angels do who are in heaven. If you want to know how you are to increase, I will tell you, it is by getting godliness within you.

. . . Individuals can enjoy heaven around them in all places. We have got to go to work and do this; we must go to work and establish heaven upon this earth, notwithstanding the evils that are around us, the devils that are around us, and notwithstanding the wickedness that exists, still we have got to go to work and establish heaven upon this earth.

A person never can enjoy heaven until he learns how to get it, and to act upon its principles. Now you take some individuals, and you refer back to the circumstances that surrounded them 20 years ago, . . . when they had a certain amount of joy, of peace, of happiness at that time though things were uncomfortable. Now they may have secured comfortable circumstances and temporal means that would administer to their temporal wants and necessities, but if they have not secured friends, the good feelings of their brethren, they are unhappy, and more so than they were 20 years ago.

. . . May the Lord bless you brethren and sisters, and may you think of these things and may we love each other, and live so to exalt ourselves as far as the Lord shall give us wisdom and ability and secure confidence with each other.[9] [See suggestion 5 on page 264.]

Suggestions for Study and Teaching

Consider these ideas as you study the chapter or as you prepare to teach. For additional help, see pages v–vii.

1. Review the story on pages 257 and 259. When have you seen that "granting one favor often leads to obtaining another"?
2. President Snow reminded us that we are all children of God (pages 259–60). How should this knowledge influence our actions toward one another? What opportunities does the Relief Society offer for women to do good to others? What opportunities does a priesthood quorum offer for men to do good to others?
3. Ponder the final paragraph on page 260. Why does our happiness increase when we help others find happiness? How can parents help their children learn this truth?
4. Why do you think we grow in wisdom when we share our knowledge with others? (For some examples, see pages 261–62.) What experiences have you had that have shown you the truth of this principle?
5. Study the section beginning on page 262. Why do you think simple acts of service have the power to bring us closer to heaven? As you ponder the messages in this chapter, think about ways you can make your home a more heavenly place.

Related Scriptures: Matthew 25:31–45; Luke 6:36–38; Mosiah 2:17; 4:14–27; D&C 81:5; 82:3

Teaching Help: "It's better to take just a few good ideas and get good discussion—and good learning—than to be frenzied, trying to teach every word in the manual. . . . An unrushed atmosphere is absolutely essential if you are to have the Spirit of the Lord present in your class" (Jeffrey R. Holland, "Teaching and Learning in the Church," *Ensign,* June 2007, 91).

Notes

1. Journal of Lorenzo Snow, 1841–47, Church History Library, 39–42.
2. *Deseret News,* Jan. 28, 1857, 371.
3. In Conference Report, Apr. 1899, 2.

4. *Salt Lake Daily Herald,* Oct. 11, 1887, 2.
5. In Eliza R. Snow Smith, *Biography and Family Record of Lorenzo Snow* (1884), 486–87.
6. In Conference Report, Apr. 1899, 2–3.
7. *Improvement Era,* July 1901, 714.
8. *Deseret News,* Mar. 11, 1857, 3; in the original source, page 3 is incorrectly labeled as page 419.
9. *Deseret News,* Mar. 11, 1857, 4.

The Prophet Joseph Smith was "a man of God, full of the spirit of his calling."

CHAPTER 23

The Prophet Joseph Smith

"I knew Joseph Smith to be an honest man, a man of truth, honor and fidelity, willing to sacrifice everything he possessed, even life itself, as a testimony to the heavens and the world that he had borne the truth to the human family."

From the Life of Lorenzo Snow

"Perhaps there are very few men now living who were so well acquainted with Joseph Smith the Prophet as I was," President Lorenzo Snow said in 1900. "I was with him oftentimes. I visited him in his family, sat at his table, associated with him under various circumstances, and had private interviews with him for counsel."[1]

In addition to these private interactions, Lorenzo Snow witnessed Joseph Smith in public—in his ministry as a friend to the Saints and as the Prophet of the Restoration. He told of a meeting Joseph Smith attended in the partially constructed Nauvoo Temple. The Prophet walked to the stand, accompanied by a minister of another faith. The minister "was intensely solemn. When anything was said that created merriment or laughter among the people, [he] remained perfectly quiet, not even showing the least change of countenance." In contrast, Joseph Smith "felt very well that morning" and made a comment that "caused some laughter among the people" before the meeting began. "After the opening of the meeting," Lorenzo recounted, "President Smith got up, and I never heard him speak with more power than on this occasion. The people were delighted, he was filled with the Spirit of God and spoke with great force and eloquence."[2]

Although President Snow was impressed by the experiences he had with Joseph Smith, his testimony of the Prophet's mission was not based on those experiences. He repeatedly declared that he had received his testimony from the Holy Ghost. He said: "As to [Joseph Smith] being a man of truth and honor I, nor any one else that knew him, have any reason to question for a moment. But then I never went forth to preach the principles of this Gospel depending entirely upon any information I received through him or any other man; but I believed on his words, coming as they did to me as the words of truth, from an inspired man of God. . . . The Spirit of God, the Holy Ghost which all men may receive and enjoy, . . . confirmed the truth of what he had told me, and it became knowledge to me of that nature which no man can give nor take away."[3] [See suggestion 1 on page 274.]

Teachings of Lorenzo Snow

When Joseph Smith received his divine calling, he was a pure, sincere, honest young man.

Joseph Smith, whom God chose to establish this work, was poor and uneducated, and belonged to no popular denomination of Christians. He was a mere boy, honest, full of integrity, unacquainted with the trickery, cunning and sophistry employed by politicians and religious hypocrites, to accomplish their ends. Like Moses of old, he felt incompetent and unqualified for the task, to stand forth as a religious reformer, in a position the most unpopular—to battle against opinions and creeds which have stood for ages, having the sanction and support of men, the most profound in theological lore; but God had called him to deliver the poor and honest-hearted of all nations from their spiritual and temporal thralldom [bondage]. And God promised him that whosoever should receive and obey his message—be baptized for the remission of sins, with honesty of purpose—might receive divine manifestations, should receive the Holy Ghost, the same Gospel blessings which were promised and obtained through the Gospel, when preached by the ancient Apostles. And this message, this promise, was to be in force wherever and to whomsoever it should be carried by the Elders, God's authorized messengers. So said Joseph Smith, the uneducated, the unsophisticated, the plain, simple, honest boy.[4]

The first time I saw the Prophet Joseph Smith I was about eighteen years of age. It was about the year 1832, in the fall of the year. It was rumored that the Prophet was going to hold a meeting in Hiram, Portage county, Ohio, about two miles from my father's home. Having heard many stories about him, my curiosity was considerably aroused and I thought I would take advantage of this opportunity to see and hear him. Accordingly, in company with some of the members of my father's family, I went to Hiram. When we reached there the people were already assembled in a small bowery; there were about one hundred and fifty or two hundred people present. The meeting had already commenced and Joseph Smith was standing in the door of [John] Johnson's house, looking into the bowery and addressing the people. I made a critical examination as to his appearance, his dress, and his manner as I heard him speak. His remarks were confined principally to his own experiences, especially the visitation of the angel, giving a strong and powerful testimony in regard to these marvelous manifestations. At first he seemed a little diffident [hesitant] and spoke in rather a low voice, but as he proceeded he became very strong and powerful, and seemed to affect the whole audience with the feeling that he was honest and sincere. It certainly influenced me in this way and made impressions upon me that remain until the present day.[5]

As I looked upon him [that first time] and listened, I thought to myself that a man bearing such a wonderful testimony as he did, and having such a countenance as he possessed, could hardly be a false prophet.[6] [See suggestion 2 on page 274.]

Throughout his life, the Prophet Joseph maintained his honesty and high moral character.

Joseph Smith, the Prophet, with whom I was intimately acquainted for years, as well as I was with my brother, I know him to have been a man of integrity, a man devoted to the interests of humanity and to the requirements of God all the days in which he was permitted to live. There never was a man that possessed a higher degree of integrity and more devotedness to the interest of mankind than the Prophet Joseph Smith.[7]

I knew Joseph Smith to be an honest man, a man of truth, honor and fidelity, willing to sacrifice everything he possessed, even life itself, as a testimony to the heavens and the world that he had borne the truth to the human family.[8]

I knew him to be a man of God, full of the spirit of his calling—a man whose integrity could not be disputed, and who was honest in all his endeavors. No one that was as intimately acquainted with him as I was could find any fault with him, so far as his moral character was concerned. . . . I bear testimony of the good character of Brother Joseph Smith, of his honesty, his fidelity, his faithfulness, his generosity, and benevolence, as a man and as a servant of God.[9] [See suggestion 2 on page 274.]

Free from hypocrisy, Joseph Smith could participate in innocent amusement as well as teach with the power of God.

I attended . . . meetings in the Temple regularly and heard the Prophet discourse upon the grandest of subjects. At times he was filled with the Holy Ghost, speaking as with the voice of an archangel and filled with the power of God, his whole person shone and his face was lightened. . . .

At times he spoke lightly, and at other times he explained the mysteries of the kingdom. The change was so noticeable that it seemed he was elevated into heaven while addressing the people who were on the earth, and then returned again to more familiar themes. . . .

Joseph Smith was always natural and extremely calm, he never became confused or irritated by persons or things around him. Many ministers called upon him and endeavored to catch him when not upon his guard, doing something with which they might find fault, but when he was not in company his actions were always the same. He never was guilty of hypocrisy. He indulged in all healthful sports, and did not think it was unbecoming to play at ball, to run a foot race or to indulge in any other outdoor sports. One minister, while at the Prophet's home, happened to look out of the window and saw the Prophet engaged in wrestling in the garden

Joseph Smith enjoyed "innocent amusement" with family members and friends.

with a friend. This, with other instances of innocent amusement convinced the minister of the Prophet's honesty and entire freedom from hypocrisy. . . .

On another occasion, Joseph Smith had indulged in playing a game of ball with some of the young men in Nauvoo. When his brother Hyrum saw it he wished to correct the Prophet and even rebuked him, saying that such conduct was not becoming in a Prophet of the Lord. The Prophet answered in a mild voice, "Brother Hyrum, my mingling with the boys in a harmless sport like this does not injure me in any way, but on the other hand it makes them happy and draws their hearts nearer to mine."[10] [See suggestion 3 on page 274.]

Strengthened by the Holy Ghost, Joseph Smith increased in spiritual power and influence.

Joseph Smith, the great prophet, was not an educated man when God chose him and made known to him his mission. The Lord bestows spiritual gifts and knowledge upon the unlearned, and the greatness of the kingdom is made known to them by the power of the Holy Ghost, and they gradually become great in the knowledge of the things of God.[11]

Toward the latter part of his life Joseph Smith became a master of strength and influence over his fellows. This fact was brought very vividly to my attention on my return from a mission to Europe. I noticed and even remarked to him that he had changed very much since I last saw him; that he had become stronger and more powerful. He admitted this and said that the Lord had endowed him with additional portions of His Spirit.

One day he called the brethren of the Twelve Apostles together and other prominent Elders of the Church to appoint them to their several labors and missions. Each sat and waited with much anxiety to hear the word of the Prophet concerning his future duties. They felt that they were in the presence of a superior being. While in Kirtland the Prophet did not seem to possess that strength and power, . . . but in later years he had become so strong in the power of the Lord that the people felt it. It was so on this occasion. The Elders realized his superior strength. "Brother Brigham," he said, "I want you to go east and attend to the affairs of the Church in the Eastern States, and Brother Kimball may accompany you." Turning to another he said, "You turn your attention to the publication of our paper," and thus appointed each one to his special mission; all accepting his word as the mind of the Lord. . . .

The Prophet had the power to impress in a remarkable manner all who approached him. There was something about him which went to their hearts. This was particularly the case with brethren when receiving from him their appointments to go forth and preach the Gospel. The inspiration that flowed from him possessed their souls and his words penetrated to the innermost recesses of their being. They loved him, and believed in him, and were ready to do whatever he directed for the furtherance of the work of God. He filled them with the power of his presence, and thrilled them with the testimony of his prophetic mission. There are many people in the world who possess an extraordinary spirit of friendship and warmth that everyone feels who meets them. I have met many such men, but never yet have I met another person in whose company I felt the peculiar and powerful influence that I felt while in the presence of the Prophet Joseph Smith. It was due to the great portion of the Spirit of God that he possessed, merely the shake of his hand would cause a person to become filled with this influence, and any sensitive nature would know that he was shaking the hand of an extraordinary person.[12] [See suggestion 4 on page 274.]

Each of us can gain a testimony that Joseph Smith was a prophet and that the gospel was restored through him.

In the integrity of my heart, with honesty of purpose to know the truth, I received [Joseph Smith's] message—I obeyed this form of doctrine, and I received, in the most tangible and satisfactory manner, a divine manifestation—the promised blessing—a knowledge of this work. Am I the only witness? How is it with the experience of thousands whom I now address? Are you also witnesses?[13]

What is the nature of our testimony? It is this: That this is the dispensation of the fulness of times; that the angel that John the Revelator saw flying through the midst of heaven having the everlasting Gospel to preach unto them that dwell on the earth, and to every nation, and kindred and tongue and people—that that angel has made his appearance and restored the Gospel to the earth, Joseph Smith being the instrument through which the restoration was effected [see Revelation 14:6].[14]

Joseph Smith affirmed that Peter, James and John visited him, and conferred on him authority to administer the holy ordinances of the Gospel through which every honest-hearted man and woman were promised the Holy Ghost, and a perfect knowledge of the doctrine.[15]

Joseph Smith was authorized to open up a channel and lay down a plan through which man could receive a knowledge of these things, so that we might not be left to depend upon the testimony of the Prophets, or the testimony of the ancient Apostles, or to the testimony of the Apostles of the present day, or to the Book of Mormon, or to anything that was done or said in the past, but that we might know for ourselves. It is an individual knowledge.[16]

I know that Joseph Smith was a true Prophet of the living God. I testify that he saw and spoke with God and with His Son Jesus Christ. The Lord gave me this living testimony and it has been burning within my soul ever since I received it. I now give it unto the whole world. I not only testify to all mankind that Joseph Smith was sent of God and that the work that was established through him is the work of God, but warn all the nations of the earth concerning the predictions made by the Prophet, and testify in the most solemn manner that I know them to be true.[17] [See suggestions 5 and 6 on page 275.]

Suggestions for Study and Teaching

Consider these ideas as you study the chapter or as you prepare to teach. For additional help, see pages v–vii.

1. In your mind, picture the event described on page 267. What does this account communicate about Joseph Smith?
2. Review President Snow's descriptions of Joseph Smith's character (pages 268–70). In what ways do you think Joseph Smith's character helped him be an instrument in the hands of the Lord?
3. What are your thoughts or feelings about the Prophet Joseph taking time for "innocent amusement"? (pages 270–71). How can we ensure that our amusements contribute to, rather than detract from, our ability to be filled with the Holy Ghost?
4. In what ways did Joseph Smith "gradually become great in the knowledge of the things of God"? (For some examples, see pages 272–73.) What can we do to follow the Prophet's example as we seek to grow spiritually?

5. Read the first full paragraph on page 273 as if President Snow is speaking directly to you. How would you answer his questions?
6. Search the section that begins on page 273. What experiences have you had in which you have needed to know for yourself that the gospel has been restored through the Prophet Joseph Smith? What advice would you give a family member or friend who wants to gain this testimony?

Related Scriptures: D&C 1:17; 5:9–10; 35:17–18; 135:3; Joseph Smith—History 1:1–26

Teaching Help: "When an individual asks a question, consider inviting others to answer it instead of answering it yourself. For example, you could say, 'That's an interesting question. What do the rest of you think?' or 'Can anyone help with this question?'" (*Teaching, No Greater Call,* 64).

Notes

1. In Conference Report, Oct. 1900, 61.
2. "Reminiscences of the Prophet Joseph Smith," *Deseret Semi-Weekly News,* Dec. 29, 1899, 1.
3. *Deseret News: Semi-Weekly,* June 27, 1882, 1.
4. *Deseret News: Semi-Weekly,* Mar. 9, 1886, 1.
5. "Reminiscences of the Prophet Joseph Smith," 1.
6. "The Grand Destiny of Man," *Deseret Evening News,* July 20, 1901, 22.
7. In Conference Report, Apr. 1898, 64.
8. *Millennial Star,* Nov. 25, 1889, 738; from a detailed paraphrase of a discourse Lorenzo Snow delivered at the October 1889 general conference.
9. *Millennial Star,* June 27, 1895, 402.
10. "Reminiscences of the Prophet Joseph Smith," 1.
11. In Journal History, Nov. 14, 1898, 4; from a detailed paraphrase of a discourse Lorenzo Snow delivered at the Box Elder Stake conference in November 1898.
12. "Reminiscences of the Prophet Joseph Smith," 1.
13. *Deseret News: Semi-Weekly,* Mar. 9, 1886, 1.
14. *Deseret News,* Nov. 22, 1882, 690.
15. *Deseret News: Semi-Weekly,* Mar. 9, 1886, 1.
16. *Deseret News,* Nov. 22, 1882, 690.
17. "Reminiscences of the Prophet Joseph Smith," 1.

"We testify to the whole world that we know, by divine revelation, even through the manifestations of the Holy Ghost, that Jesus is the Christ, the Son of the living God."

CHAPTER 24

Reflections on the Mission of Jesus Christ

"We are all dependent upon Jesus Christ, upon his coming into the world to open the way whereby we might secure peace, happiness, and exaltation."

From the Life of Lorenzo Snow

In October 1872, President Brigham Young assigned his First Counselor, President George A. Smith, to journey through portions of Europe and the Middle East. In a letter to President Smith, President Young and his Second Counselor, President Daniel H. Wells, said, "We desire that you observe closely what openings now exist, or where they may be effected, for the introduction of the Gospel into the various countries you shall visit." The journey was to conclude in the Holy Land, where President Smith would "dedicate and consecrate that land to the Lord." Presidents Young and Wells wrote, "We pray that you may be preserved to travel in peace and safety, that you may be abundantly blessed with words of wisdom and free utterance in all your conversations pertaining to the Holy Gospel, dispelling prejudice, and sowing seeds of righteousness among the people."[1] President Smith took a small group of Latter-day Saints with him, including Elder Lorenzo Snow, who was then a member of the Quorum of the Twelve Apostles. Elder Snow's sister Eliza R. Snow, who was serving as Relief Society general president at the time, was also part of the group.

As Elder Snow traveled, he frequently wrote letters describing the geography, the buildings, and the customs and conditions of the people. But when he and his companions visited sites in the Holy Land, his letters changed in tone. His thoughts turned to the Son of God, who had frequented those same places centuries earlier. For example, he wrote about his experience in February 1873 when the group approached the city of Jerusalem:

"One hour's ride . . . will bring us to Jerusalem. We move on and at length ascend an eminence [or hill], and gaze on the 'Holy City,' Jerusalem. Away to the right is Mount Zion, the city of David. Off to our left, that lofty eminence, with an aspect so barren, is the Mount of Olives, once the favorite resort of our Saviour, and the spot last pressed by His sacred feet before He ascended into the presence of His Father. These interesting historic scenes, with all their sacred associations, inspire thoughts and reflections impressive and solemn. Yes, there is Jerusalem! Where Jesus lived and taught, and was crucified, where He cried 'It is finished,' and bowed His head and died! We slowly and thoughtfully wind our way down the hill, . . . until we reach the city."[2]

After going to the River Jordan, Elder Snow wrote: "As we drank of its sweet and refreshing waters and washed in its sacred stream, our thoughts and reflections recurred to the days of childhood, when we were accustomed to peruse the Holy Scriptures describing the important events which transpired in this locality—the passage of the Israelites when the channel became dry, as the priests, bearing upon their shoulders the sacred ark, stepped into the flowing stream; the dividing of the waters by Elijah when he passed over the dry bed and was taken up into heaven from the plain on the opposite side by a whirlwind; and Elisha, as he returned, took the mantle of Elijah that fell from him, and smote the waters, saying, 'Where is the Lord God of Elijah?' thus making the third time the Jordan was divided. But another event of much deeper interest is associated with this place—the baptism of our Saviour, referred to in the following language—'John came preaching in the wilderness of Judea, and Jesus came from Galilee to Jordan to be baptized of him;' [see Matthew 3] and we were at or near the identical point where all these memorable events had taken place, standing upon the bank, looking down into the glen, and bathing in the same stream which had borne silent witness of these sublime occurrences."[3] [See suggestion 1 on page 283.]

Teachings of Lorenzo Snow

Jesus Christ came into the world to do the will of the Father and open the way for our peace, happiness, and exaltation.

This gospel has been introduced at various times into the world. It was known by the Prophets. They understood plainly and distinctly that Jesus was the lamb slain from before the foundation of the world [see Revelation 13:8; Moses 7:47], and that in due season he would manifest himself to the children of men, that he would die for their sins, and be crucified in order to complete the plan of salvation.[4]

When Jesus lay in the manger, a helpless infant, He knew not that He was the Son of God, and that formerly He created the earth. When the edict of Herod was issued, He knew nothing of it; He had not power to save Himself; and [Joseph and Mary] had to take Him and [flee] into Egypt to preserve Him from the effects of that edict. . . . He grew up to manhood, and during His progress it was revealed unto Him who He was, and for what purpose He was in the world. The glory and power He possessed before He came into the world was made known unto Him.[5]

Jesus, while traveling here on earth, fulfilling His mission, told the people He did not perform the miracles He wrought in their midst by His own power, nor by His own wisdom; but He was there in order to accomplish the will of His Father. He came not to seek the glory of men, and the honor of men; but to seek the honor and glory of His Father that sent Him. Said he, "I am come in my Father's name, and ye receive me not, if another shall come in his own name, him ye will receive." [John 5:43.]

Now, the peculiarity of His mission, and that which distinguished it from other missions, was this: He came not to seek the glory and honor of men, but to seek the honor and glory of His Father, and to accomplish the work of His Father who sent Him. Herein lay the secret of His prosperity; and herein lies the secret of the prosperity of every individual who works upon the same principle.[6]

Jesus Christ the Son of God was once placed in a condition that it required the highest effort in order to accomplish what was

In late 1872 and early 1873, Elder Lorenzo Snow and others traveled in the Holy Land.

necessary for the salvation of millions of the children of God. It required the highest effort and determination that had to be exercised before the Son of God could pass through the ordeal, the sacrifice that was necessary.[7]

Jesus, the Son of God, was sent into the world to make it possible for you and me to receive these extraordinary blessings. He had to make a great sacrifice. It required all the power that He had and all the faith that He could summon for Him to accomplish that which the Father required of Him. . . . He did not fail, though the trial was so severe that He sweat great drops of blood. . . . His feelings must have been inexpressible. He tells us Himself, as you will find recorded in section 19 of the Book of Doctrine and Covenants, that His suffering was so great that it caused even Him "to tremble because of pain, and to bleed at every pore, and to suffer both body and spirit: and would that He might not drink the bitter cup, and shrink." But He had in His heart continually to say, "Father, not my will, but Thine be done." [See D&C 19:15–19.][8]

We are all dependent upon Jesus Christ, upon his coming into the world to open the way whereby we might secure peace, happiness and exaltation. And had he not made these exertions we never could have been secured in these blessings and privileges which are guaranteed unto us in the gospel, through the mediation of Jesus Christ, for he made the necessary exertions. . . .

. . . Though he has sacrificed himself and laid the plan for the redemption of the people, yet unless the people labor to obtain that union between him and them, their salvation never will be accomplished.[9]

We understand, fully that as Jesus Christ dwelt here in a body and that He received that body and now dwells in it glorified, that we are entitled to the same blessing, the same exaltation, and the same glory.[10] [See suggestions 2 and 3 on pages 283–84.]

Jesus Christ has visited the earth in the latter days, revealing heavenly truths for our salvation.

That Being who dwelt in Heaven, who reigned there before the world was, who created the earth, and who, in the meridian of time, came down to perfect and save that which He had created, has appeared to men in this age.[11]

We testify to the whole world that we know, by divine revelation, even through the manifestations of the Holy Ghost, that Jesus is the Christ, the Son of the living God, and that he revealed himself to Joseph Smith as personally as he did to his apostles anciently, after he arose from the tomb, and that he made known unto him [the] heavenly truths by which alone mankind can be saved.[12]

There were two men in the Temple at Kirtland who saw Him. . . . The Son of God appeared to them, He who was slain by the Jews, and they said, "the veil was taken away from our mind's eye, and our understandings were opened, and we saw the Lord standing on the breastwork of the pulpit before us." . . . Under His feet was pure gold. His countenance shone above the brightness of the sun. His voice was as the sound of rushing great waters. It was the voice of Jehovah, saying, "I am the first and the last. I am He that liveth. I am He who was slain. I am your advocate with the Father. Behold, your sins are forgiven you. You are clean before me; therefore lift up your heads and rejoice. You have built this house to my name. I will accept this house, and I will pour out my Spirit upon those who keep my commandments, and I will not suffer this holy house to be polluted." [See D&C 110:1–8.] This was the voice of the same individual that the Jews rejected, and He was seen there. Now I know that these things are things that are true as God is true. But the nations of the earth are not aware of it, that Jesus, the Son of God, has come and appeared to men, and clothed them with authority to preach the Gospel and to promise the Holy Ghost to all who will believe and obey these principles, and should receive a knowledge that these principles are true.[13] [See suggestion 4 on page 284.]

The Savior will come again, and we should prepare ourselves for His coming.

We have a testimony concerning Christ, that He is coming to the earth, to reign.[14]

Jesus will come by and by, and appear in our midst, as He appeared in the day when upon the earth among the Jews, and He will eat and drink with us and talk to us, and explain the mysteries of the Kingdom, and tell us things that are not lawful to talk about now.[15]

If you are on a moving train of cars, as long as you sit still and occupy your seat that train will take you to the point you wish to go; but if you step off the cars it will be dangerous, and it may be a long time before another train will come along. It is the same with us—if we are living right, doing our work, we are going along, and if we are keeping our covenants, we are doing the work of God and accomplishing His purposes, and we will be prepared for the time when Jesus the Son of God will come in honor and glory, and will confer upon all those who prove faithful all the blessings that they anticipate, and a thousand times more. . . .

. . . I say to the Latter-day Saints, if any of you are sleepy, read the words of the Savior spoken when He was upon the earth in regard to the ten virgins, five of whom were wise, and took oil in their lamps, and when the Bridegroom came there was only one-half prepared to go out to meet Him [see Matthew 25:1–13; D&C 45:56–59]. Do not let it be so with us as Latter-day Saints. Let us try to be true to the everlasting covenants that we have made and be true to God. God bless the Latter-day Saints and pour out His Spirit upon you. May you be faithful to your God, faithful to your families,

President Snow encouraged Saints to follow the example of the five wise virgins in the Savior's parable of the ten virgins.

and conduct yourselves with prudence in all things, and labor for the interests of the kingdom of God, and that we may not be among the foolish virgins, but be found worthy to be amongst those who will be crowned as kings and queens and reign throughout eternity.[16] [See suggestions 5 and 6 on page 284.]

Suggestions for Study and Teaching

Consider these ideas as you study the chapter or as you prepare to teach. For additional help, see pages v–vii.

1. Ponder President Snow's words about the experiences he had in the Holy Land (page 278). Why do you think his thoughts and reflections became "impressive and solemn" when he was there? In what ways can we develop similar feelings about the Savior, even without visiting the Holy Land?
2. Study the section that begins on page 279, thinking about what Jesus Christ has done for you. As you ponder the Savior's

desire to "seek the honor and glory of His Father," think about what you need to do to follow God's will.

3. On page 279, President Snow shares "the secret of prosperity." How does this secret work for us?
4. Read the section that begins on page 281. How does your testimony of Jesus Christ influence your life? Ponder different ways we can do our part to share the testimony of Jesus Christ with the world. For example, what can we do to share our testimony with our families? with those we serve as home teachers or visiting teachers? with our neighbors? with people we meet from day to day?
5. In what ways can we prepare ourselves for the Second Coming of Jesus Christ? (For some examples, see pages 282–83.) How can we help others prepare?
6. In what ways have President Snow's teachings influenced your testimony of Jesus Christ? Look for ways to share your testimony with family members and others.

Related Scriptures: Luke 12:31–48; 2 Corinthians 8:9; 2 Nephi 2:7–8; 25:23, 26; Alma 7:11–13; D&C 35:2; Joseph Smith—History 1:17

Teaching Help: "Ask participants to choose one section and read it silently. Invite them to gather in groups of two or three people who chose the same section and discuss what they have learned" (page vii in this book).

Notes

1. Letter from Brigham Young and Daniel H. Wells to George A. Smith, in *Correspondence of Palestine Tourists* (1875), 1–2.
2. In *Correspondence of Palestine Tourists,* 205.
3. In *Correspondence of Palestine Tourists,* 236–37.
4. *Deseret News,* Jan. 24, 1872, 597.
5. In Conference Report, Apr. 1901, 3.
6. *Deseret News,* Dec. 8, 1869, 517.
7. In Conference Report, Oct. 1900, 2.
8. *Millennial Star,* Aug. 24, 1899, 531.
9. *Deseret News,* Mar. 11, 1857, 3; in the original source, page 3 is incorrectly labeled as page 419.
10. *Deseret News,* Nov. 22, 1882, 690.
11. In Journal History, Apr. 5, 1884, 9.
12. *Deseret News: Semi-Weekly,* Jan. 23, 1877, 1.
13. *Millennial Star,* Apr. 18, 1887, 245.
14. *Deseret News,* Apr. 11, 1888, 200; from a detailed paraphrase of a discourse Lorenzo Snow delivered in the April 1888 general conference.
15. In Conference Report, Apr. 1898, 13–14.
16. *Millennial Star,* Apr. 18, 1887, 244–46.

List of Visuals

Index

T

NOTES

NOTES

NOTES

NOTES

N O T E S

NOTES